Biblical Voices and Echoes

Biblical Voices and Echoes

The People and the Books

William Horbury

University of Chester Press

First published 2023
by University of Chester Press
Parkgate Road
Chester CH1 4BJ

Printed and bound in the UK by the
LIS Print Unit
University of Chester
Cover designed by the LIS Graphics Team
University of Chester

A catalogue record of this book is available
from the British Library

ISBN 978-1-910481-13-4

CONTENTS

v

LIST OF COLOUR PLATES

Plate 1: Virgil's Tomb, Sun breaking through (Joseph Wright of Derby, 1785) © National Museums of Northern Ireland, Ulster Museum Collection.

Plate 2: St Paul, Magdeburg Cathedral pulpit, Christoph Kapup (1595). Photograph: © Raymond Faure.

Plates 3 and 4: Cover image and title page from C.R. Conder, R.E., *Tent Work in Palestine* (2 vols., London: Richard Bentley & Son, 1879), showing work for the survey of western Palestine (1871–7).

Plate 5: St Raymond of Pennafort (*c*.1180–1275); copy of roundel from Fra Angelico, *Crucifixion with Dominican Saints*, fresco at the friary, now museum, of S. Marco, Florence.

Plate 6: King Ethelred of Mercia (reigned 675–704) finds the site for the foundation of the church of St John Baptist, Chester, window by Trena Cox, St John's, Chester.

Plate 7: Title-page of King James Bible, quarto, bound up with the Book of Common Prayer and the metrical psalms (Cambridge, 1633).

Plates 8 and 9: John Spencer (1630–93), Dean of Ely and Master of Corpus Christi College, Cambridge; details of engraving by George Vertue.

Plate 10: Narcissus Marsh (1638–1713), detail of portrait attributed to Hugh Howard (photograph © Fennell Photography, Dublin).

Plate 11: Interior of Marsh's Library, Dublin, showing window looking towards St Patrick's Cathedral (photograph by Tristan Hutchinson; © Marsh's Library, Dublin).

Plate 12: Title-page of Johann Buxtorf I & II, *De abbreviaturis hebraicis*, etc. (2nd edn, Basle, 1640, repr. Herborn, in Nassau, 1708).

Plate 13: Frontispiece and title-page of Campegius Vitringa, *De Synagoga vetere* (1696; 2nd edn, Weißenfels, 1726).

Plate 14: The house in Abbey Square, Chester, occupied by Charles Kingsley as canon of Chester.

Plates 15 and 16: Window and detail depicting St Bernard of Menthon in the cloisters of Chester Cathedral, with inscription below commemorating George Leigh Mallory and Andrew Comyn Irvine.

Plate 17: Title-page of Matthew Pole, *Synopsis criticorum*, vol. i (repr. Utrecht, 1684).

Plate 18: King Edgar (reigned 959–75), rowed up the Dee by vassal-kings who will do homage in the church of St John Baptist; west window (1887–90) by Edward Frampton, St John's, Chester.

FOREWORD

These pieces all began life in the spoken word. I was seeking to communicate with various audiences, in each case an audience broader than is usually envisaged in a university lecture. C.S. Lewis long ago found what might be almost the perfect title for a book of this kind: *They Asked for a Paper* (London, 1962). Nearly everything here was indeed 'asked for' – and yet 'paper' would not quite cover the range of the original forms. One of these pieces was a sermon, one a commemoration address; three were public lectures, two were addresses to societies, and five were Bible Talks for Chester Cathedral. In revision I have made changes – to shorten or lengthen or clarify, to remove local references where they are not needed, and occasionally to mention more recent writing.

In subject-matter the chapters follow a roughly chronological sequence. Readers move from ancient Israel and the early church (chapters 1–3) through mediaeval and early modern times (4–8) to the modern period and bird's-eye views ranging from antiquity to the present (9–12).

All these beads hang on a biblical string, and this remains true for Bar Kokhba with his biblical title 'prince of Israel', and for mediaeval piety, with its psalmody and intensely scriptural prayers. Still, biblical voices and their echoes are recalled here in different ways. The needs of particular occasions and places have interacted with my own interests and inquiries. The topics have considerable variety. Themes are often in the realm of 'the bible and …': scripture and literature, scripture and archaeology, scripture and liturgy. Times of special movement in the history of the bible are evoked through sketches of translators, interpreters, and teachers, well-known and less-known.

The subtitle 'The People and the Books' slightly modifies the familiar phrase 'The People and the Book'. 'The people' points to an overall theme: the fortune and influence of the biblical books in the life of the Jewish people and the Christian church. 'People' may

ix

also serve to indicate the individual students of scripture who come to the fore: from Paul the apostle to saints, rabbis and philosophers, archaeologists and literary scholars, novelists and poets, readers and book collectors. With 'books' in the plural I wanted to hint at the bible itself as a library or collection of books.

As visiting speakers usually do, I hope that the approaches and inquiries sketched here may be of interest and suggest something fresh. I would like to encourage appreciation of both prose and poetry, both history and legend, both scripture and tradition. At least it will be obvious that all of them matter to me.

W.H.

ACKNOWLEDGEMENTS

Grateful acknowledgement is made for permission to reproduce published material: from Cambridge University Press, for chapter 4, from *Christianity in Jewish Tradition* (Cambridge, 1999); the Prayer-book Society, for chapter 5, from an article in *Faith and Worship* 67 (2010), 24–39; the Master and Fellows of Corpus Christi College, Cambridge, for chapter 7, from *Letter of the Corpus Association* 78 (1999), 12–23; the Four Courts Press, Dublin, for chapter 8, from Muriel McCarthy and Ann Simmons (edd.), *The Making of Marsh's Library: Learning, Religion and Politics in Ireland, 1650–1750* (Dublin, 2004), 256–79; and Sage Publications, for chapter 9, from *Expository Times* 130.11 (2019), 485–95. The author would like to thank Dr Sarah Griffiths, Managing Editor of the University of Chester Press, for particularly helpful editorship, and Katharine Horbury, whose ideas, criticism and encouragement have been essential.

1
PAUL AND VIRGIL

On a spring morning, perhaps about the year 62, a ship from Alexandria was sailing north up the west coast of Italy.[1] She bore the name *The Heavenly Twins*, referring to Castor and Pollux, the sons of Zeus and Leda who became shining stars and patrons of seafarers. On board was St Paul, on his way to Rome as a prisoner. On the right or starboard could be seen the western cliffs of the isle of Capri, crowned by what had thirty years before been the villa of Tiberius, the emperor under whom Christ had been crucified. Beyond Capri the bay of Naples opened up, with the great cone of Vesuvius in the distance and beneath it towards the shore the cities of Pompeii and Herculaneum, not yet overwhelmed by the eruption which was to come in the year 79. North-west of them was Naples itself, where the bay curves back westwards towards the cape of Misenum. Within this south-facing coast of the bay, to the west of Naples, is the Gulf of Puteoli, divided from Naples by the ridge and headland of Posillipo. At the head of the gulf there would soon appear the port for which the ship was making, Puteoli itself – the name means 'Wells' (probably hot springs) – present-day Pozzuoli. The magnificent view of its waterfront and hills as seen from the sea was immortalized on what appear to be souvenir vases surviving from at least the third century.[2]

This prosperous and turbulent city was then the main Italian port for eastern trade, and a regular point of disembarkation for Rome. About two years later, in the year 64, another Jewish traveller from Judaea to Rome, the historian Josephus, would also land at Puteoli (Josephus, *Life*, 16). The apocryphal Acts of Peter (Vercelli Acts, v–vi) envisage that St Peter too landed there. Paul himself was able to spend a week with members of the church there before he began his land-journey to Rome. There had been Jews at Puteoli at least since the days of Herod the Great, as shown by Josephus (*Jewish War* ii 104, *Antiquities* xvii 328–9), and the Christian body

1

there will probably have sprung from this Jewish community and its gentile adherents.

Thus far we are informed by the narrative of Paul's passage as a captive from Malta to Puteoli – the ship put in at Syracuse and then Rhegium (now Reggio in Calabria) on the way – in Acts 28:11–15. The account in Acts bears signs of adaptation to its present context, but is clearly related by style and detail concerning the voyage to the so-called 'we-narrative' of Paul's journeyings, and is therefore of some consequence as an historical source. Yet its notice of Paul's seven days at Puteoli offers a tempting gap for speculation. Thus in modern scholarship this has been suggested as the time when the sixteenth chapter of Romans, with all its greetings, was written.[3]

Older legend, current in the thirteenth and fourteenth centuries, went further. It was imagined that Paul would have been taken on the road to Naples, which passes through the ridge of Posillipo in a tunnel constructed by Augustus's architect Cocceius, a great local sight. Just beyond the tunnel, two miles from Naples, he would have come to a still more celebrated sight, the tomb of Publius Vergilius Maro, the Latin poet Virgil (Plate 1). Here, as a mediaeval hymn relates, Paul shed a tear over Virgil, and cried aloud, 'What I would have made of you if only I had found you living, you of all poets the greatest':

Ad Maronis mausoleum
Ductus fudit super eum
      Piae rorem lacrimae;
Quem te, inquit, reddidissem
Si te vivum invenissem
      Poetarum maxime.

When to Maro's mound they brought him
Tender grief and pity wrought him
      To bedew the stone with tears;
What a saint I might have crowned thee

2

Paul and Virgil

> Had I only living found thee
>   Poet first and without peers!
>   (J.A. Symonds)[4]

The story has some verisimilitude, given the wide early fame of Virgil and his tomb. A younger contemporary of St Paul, the poet Silius Italicus, bought the site, hitherto cared for by one poor countryman, and used to visit it 'as he would visit a temple'.[5] At the same period another poet, Statius, would come to the tomb to write his own verse under the aegis of the departed master-poet.[6] Puteoli itself lies in a landscape described in Virgil's Aeneid; Aeneas meets the Sibyl at her cave nearby at the old Greek settlement of Cumae, and descends to the underworld under her guidance by the neighbouring Lake Avernus. Virgil was a local as well as an international hero.

Yet Paul's visit to his tomb is probably legend, reflecting Virgil's repute in the church as a poet who was 'not far from the truth', in the words of the early fourth-century Christian apologist Lactantius.[7] In this passage Lactantius was quoting the lines from the Aeneid where, in the abode of the blessed in the underworld, Aeneas's dead father Anchises explains to his son how one spirit sustains all things:

> Know first, that heav'n, and earth's compacted frame,
> And flowing waters, and the starry flame,
> And both the radiant lights, one common soul
> Inspires and feeds, and animates the whole
>   (*Aen*. vi 724–7, in Dryden's translation)

Virgil's lines here start with *Principio*, 'first', or 'in the beginning', an expression of much biblical resonance, in this context of universal spirit.

A comparable legend has given us an apocryphal Latin correspondence of Paul with another Roman author who seemed close to Christianity, the poet and philosopher Seneca who was Paul's contemporary. In early British tradition a similar feeling about Virgil is found in the legend of the sixth-century St Cadoc,

3

an abbot in Wales and Brittany. His beloved manuscript of Virgil was caught away by the wind and blown into the sea while his friend the historian Gildas told him that Virgil, being a pagan, was undoubtedly damned; but that night Cadoc heard in a dream a gentle voice saying 'Pray for me; I shall yet sing of the mercy of the Lord', and in the morning a fisherman brought him as a present a big salmon. Inside it Cadoc found once more his copy of Virgil.[8] The legendary apostolic pilgrimage from Puteoli to Virgil's tomb reflects the same friendly feeling as this story. It offers, nonetheless, a genuine clue to the reading of St Paul.

Virgil died in 19 BCE. Paul, born in Tarsus perhaps twenty or more years later, and brought up in Jerusalem, belonged to the Greek-speaking part of the Roman empire, and was fluent in Greek as well as Aramaic. In principle he could have known Virgil's poetry, in the original Latin if his own Latin was as extensive as that of some Greek-speakers, or through a Greek translation – the earliest known Greek translation of Virgil, or parts of his work, was made in Paul's lifetime by a freedman of the emperor Claudius, as Seneca indicates.[9] Soon after Paul the Jewish historian Josephus, who was likewise both an Aramaic- and Greek-speaker, has been thought by some to show the influence of Virgil.

Yet the importance of Virgil for the understanding of Paul does not depend on the question of Paul's personal familiarity with Virgil's books. It arises rather from the way in which Virgil was immediately and abidingly recognized. Finds of fragments on papyrus or wood show over what a vast territory parts of Virgil were already being copied and read in the first century of our era, from Masada by the Dead Sea to Vindolanda on Hadrian's Wall (to note two finds made almost simultaneously in 1973).[10] Virgil was indeed that almost forgotten phenomenon, a great poet who is hailed in all segments of society. He was close to the centre of power, being supported by Augustus's friend Maecenas, who was also the patron of another poet of genius, Virgil's close friend Horace. Yet, as countless graffiti, remnants of writing exercises, and references to dramatic presentations based on Virgil show, he belonged not just to the literary élite of Rome, but also to what Nicholas Horsfall called 'the culture of the Roman plebs'. He expressed values and concerns held in the Roman empire at a period which soon came to be thought of as outstanding, the Augustan age. As the great Victorian New Testament scholar B.F. Westcott wrote

> It may seem to be a paradox – it ought to be a truism – that the Aeneid is the Roman Gospel … Few things are more surprising in the histories of the apostolic age than that Virgil finds no place in the popular estimate of the influences at work in moulding or expressing public opinion.[11]

Virgil is indeed a mirror of movements in politics, philosophy, and religion in the early Roman empire, movements in relation to which Judaism was being interpreted by Philo, Josephus and others, and the Christianity, or Christian Judaism, of the Pauline epistles and congregations was being formed. The image of a mirror indicates, however, the problem of attempting an approach to Virgil's own views of religion and piety. A classic study by Cyril Bailey (1935) was entitled *Religion in Virgil*, not *The Religion of Virgil*. The poet reflects a wealth of lore, thought and devotion, sometimes as it seems with evident sympathy, but, unlike Paul, he is not expressly setting out his own position. Yet it was still possible in the end for Bailey to reach an estimate of what in religion was important for Virgil. On the other hand, Paul's own writing can sometimes seem outspoken and personal, but it still leaves room for debate on what is central in his religion. There are difficulties in approaching both authors, but Virgil and his works can still properly be set beside Paul and his works.

At least three aspects of Virgil then stand out. There is perhaps what can be called a 'Jewish Virgil', for aspects of his writings recall Jewish prophetic hope as mediated in Greek, he may well have had contact with Greek-speaking Jews, and Jews may have interpreted him as a witness to Judaism. This remains speculative, partly because too little remains of Jewish writing in Greek and Latin after the second century of our era. There is certainly, however, a 'Christian Virgil', as the legends just noted attest. From the seventeenth century onwards, however, the force of this Christian interpretation was tempered and set aside by strong historical focus on Virgil in his Roman setting. The poet's ancient description as 'Roman Virgil' (*Romanus Vergilius*; Petronius, *Satyricon* 118.5) was stressed, notably from the nineteenth century onwards, as in Tennyson's poem for the nineteenth centenary of Virgil's birth. Yet in the twentieth century the Christian Virgil came to the fore again, as in Kipling's poem 'The Last Ode' (both poems are reprinted in the appendix). For the last hundred years we have perhaps lived in a tension arising from awareness that the worlds of the Roman Virgil, the Jewish Virgil, and the Christian Virgil all overlap more than has been supposed. Within that overlap stand the seeming similarities between Virgil and Paul.

At Virgil's tomb his epitaph is said to have run as follows: 'Mantua bore me, the people of Calabria captured me, and now Parthenope' – Naples – 'holds me; I sang of pastures, the countryside and commanders (*cecini pascua, rura, duces*)'.[12] This refers to his three most famous works: the Eclogues or Pastoral Poems, on the life of shepherds, marked as he said himself by the boldness of youth; the Georgics, didactic poems on husbandry, written later on, when he was living at Naples; and finally his epic, the Aeneid, on the founding of Rome by a Trojan Greek hero, Aeneas, who escapes with his old father and his young son from the burning of Troy.

Virgil was a poet of landscape, and each of these works is distinguished by landscape as well as subject-matter. The pastures of the Eclogues are not green fields, but upland woods and the rocky hill-slopes beside them – 'gods too have lived in woods', says Virgil's poor shepherd Corydon (*Ecl.* ii 60). In the Georgics the poet comes down from the woods and hills to the cultivated lower ground and views the whole countryside, above all that of Italy, where the fields, the hill-top towns, the rivers gliding beneath ancient walls, and the simple life of the country people (*Georgics* ii 156–7, 173–4, 471–5, 534–8) all hint at the primaeval bliss of the Golden Age, when Saturn ruled; they represent that country life wherein the virgin Justice – the divine Astraea, who lingered on earth until human wickedness made her leave – was last able to be present.[13] In the Aeneid, by contrast, the landscape is extended and heroic, with mountains and tempestuous seas through which the hero passes from Asia Minor to Africa, Greece and the Adriatic, and wins at last to Italy.

Yet these three distinct landscapes also show something of the links between the three very different poetic works. As Aeneas at last enters Italy he encounters, together with some traces of the golden age of Saturn, the wild woods of the shepherds in the Eclogues. To find the gate of the underworld at Lake Avernus he has to seek the Golden Bough in a vast and ancient wood (*Aen.* vi 179, 186–8). As he follows the Sibyl into a cavern and ever downwards it is like a journey through dark woods by a fitful and baneful moonlight, in the underworld itself the woods prevail (*tenent media omnia silvae, Aen.* vi 131), and when he returns to the upper earth and rows his ships up the Tiber to the future site of the city of Rome, he finds again a wild and wooded landscape. The abrupt Capitoline hill, where in the future under Augustus the great temple of Jupiter, Juno and Minerva will gleam with marble and gold, still looms up bristling with trees and thickets and held in awe as the dwelling of an unknown god:

> Some god they knew, what god they could not tell,
> Did there amidst the sacred horror dwell
> (*Aen.* viii 351–2, transl. Dryden)[14]

These pervasive woods are perhaps a valid symbol of the pathos and awe and sense of the unknown – Dryden's 'horror' keeps something of the word's literal sense of the 'bristling' of the awesome woods, and also perhaps of human hairs – which in Virgil mingles with the expression of happiness and hope: 'Thou majestic in thy sadness at the doubtful doom of humankind', as Tennyson, at this point a kindred spirit, put it in his Ode to Virgil (for the full text, see the appendix).

The 'Jewish' and 'Christian' Virgil
Within this compelling imaginative world, how did early Christians discover hints at Christianity, and hints which aligned Paul with Virgil? One obvious focus of interest for Jews and Christians was Virgil's appeal to prophecy. The Fourth of his Eclogues, addressed to the poet and statesman C. Asinius Pollio when he was about to become consul (40 BCE) – it was in his consulship that the senate named Herod king of Judaea – declares that the prophecies of the Sibyl of Cumae concerning a new golden age are now to be fulfilled.

> The last age of Cumaean song has now come;
> the great order of the ages is born anew.
>
> Now the Virgin returns, the kingdom of Saturn returns,
> and a new offspring is sent down from high heaven.

The force and grandeur of the lines (*Ecl.* iv 4–7) come out in their echo by Shelley

> The world's great age begins anew,
>   The golden years return.

The beginning of this new golden age coincides with the birth of a child, addressed as 'dear offspring of the gods, great increment of Jove' – perhaps a son of Pollio, or of Mark Antony and Octavia.
    Inevitably this birth came to be linked with the nativity of Christ, but the opening declaration of the fulfilment of Sibylline prophecy was more important for Jewish and Christian approaches to Virgil. The poet seems in parallel with writers known from the Dead Sea Scrolls, with the gospels and Paul – for he declares the fulfilment of prophecy in the present. A modern interpreter of Virgil, Wilhelm Weber, entitled his 1925 book on the Fourth Eclogue: The Prophet and his God.

8

Paul and Virgil

Virgil cites the Sibyl. Her Greek poetic oracles had already
been adapted by Jews as prophecies of the rise and fall of gentile
kingdoms and the future glory of Israel, and among many Jews
the Sibyl had become a gentile prophetic figure, matching the great
gentile prophet quoted in the Old Testament, Balaam. Thus in the
early fourth century, when for the first time the Roman emperor
portrayed himself as a Christian prince, in the atmosphere shared
by Lactantius, Virgil's Fourth Eclogue had a great place in the
treatment of the Sibyl in Constantine's *Speech to the Assembly of
the Saints*.[15] Interpreters of prophecy, including Paul, can begin to
seem like prophets themselves. Virgil came to appear to Christians
almost as a prophet from the gentiles, to set beside Paul, the apostle
to the gentiles.

This Christian impression of Virgil as prophet, which has never
wholly disappeared, points to a smaller-scale but still significant
common feature of Virgil and Paul: in both, as more widely in the
ancient world, poets are considered as having a quasi-prophetic
and also quasi-philosophical character, and are cited as guides to
life. This view of course survives in the modern world, and the
argumentative force of poetry is not without defence from the
philosophical side.[16] So Paul in I Corinthians (15:32) quotes a line of
verse from Menander, 'evil communications corrupt good manners'
– possibly Paul learned this tag at school – to point his contention
that hedonism is catching, and linked with forgetfulness of the hope
of immortality.

A close poetic link with Virgil appears in Paul as depicted in
Acts, when the apostle in his speech at Athens is said to quote famous
lines from the Greek poet Aratus, who like him came from Cilicia,
on Zeus as filling and sustaining the whole world, within which we
are his offspring – the opening lines of Aratus's poem *Phenomena*;
and so Paul says to the Athenians that God 'is not far from every
one of us, for in him we live and move and have our being; as one
also of your own poets has said, We also are his offspring' (Acts
17:28). In Virgil, lines from the same passage of Aratus are quoted

in the Third Eclogue: 'From Jove is the beginning; all things are full of Jove' (*Ecl.* iii 60); and Virgil also takes from Aratus (96–136) the story of the virgin Justice mentioned in the Fourth Eclogue, 'Now the Virgin returns ...'. What is especially notable is that the Paul who predominantly quotes Hebrew scripture, and seems to expect his hearers to be familiar with it, did in fact also share the current non-Jewish education and its veneration for the poets, and the positive interest in their theology and ethics which we see abundantly in Virgil. In this respect the depiction of Paul in Acts, more developed though it is, does seem to be faithful to Paul as known through his epistles.

Then secondly, Aeneas descends to the underworld and sees the punishment of wrongdoers in Hades and the reward of the good in the Elysian fields. How close this dream-like vision seems to the tours of heaven and hell in contemporary Jewish and Christian apocalypses has been noted and debated in detail by modern scholars. It equally fascinated Virgil's early Christian readers. Among the apocalypses which circulated in the early church, they could set it especially beside the apocryphal third-century book called the Vision of Paul. This is a tour of hell and heaven, but it begins with Paul's own more abrupt and reserved account of his vision of Paradise in II Corinthians – 'I know a man in Christ ... who was caught up into Paradise and heard unutterable words, which it is not permitted to a man to speak' (II Cor. 12:2–4); compare I Cor. 2:9 'eye has not seen, nor ear heard, neither have entered into the heart of man, the things that God has prepared for those who love him'. So still for Dante, who has the apocryphal Vision of Paul in mind in the Inferno (ii 13–33), Virgil's Aeneas and Paul are *the* two who, while still 'corruptible', have entered the 'immortal' world – Dante, addressing Virgil, echoes Paul's 'this corruptible shall put on incorruption, and this mortal shall put on immortality' (I Cor. 15:53).[17] But, says Dante to Virgil who guides him, I am not Aeneas, I am not Paul; why should I enter?[18]

In this way Paul and Virgil stood together in the fourteenth century; but, even when the apocryphal Vision of Paul is set aside, they can still seem to stand together in respect of vision. The importance of vision for Paul in his apostolic venture comes out in his own writing, as just noted (I Cor. 2:9, II Cor. 12:2–4), and also in Acts, for instance in his trance in the Jerusalem temple, attributed in Acts to the time shortly after his conversion (Acts 22:17–18), or his night-time vision of Christ at Corinth, promising fruitful labours (Acts 18:9–10). This aspect of Paul recalls Virgil's Aeneas, making his foreordained way to Italy, tested by his destiny, as Anchises says to him 'son, tried by the hard fates of Troy' (*nate, Iliacis exercite fatis, Aen.* iii 182, v 725) – compare Paul's 'chastened, but not killed' (II Cor. 6:9) – tried, yet aided repeatedly by vision and oracle.[19] A realistically-described instance of oracle is Aeneas's night-time vision on board ship of the ancestral gods of Troy, who promise empire to the city which he shall found; Aeneas then comes to himself in a cold sweat, and says afterwards 'that was no slumber' (*Aen.* iii 159; 172). The Stoic belief that God prepares those who are good for himself by trials, as Seneca put it (*On Providence*, chapter 1), a belief reflected also here in Virgil, is matched in Paul on being 'chastened by the Lord' (I Cor. 11:32); he builds on scriptural passages such as Proverbs 3:11–12, and is also aware of Stoic teaching.

The 'Roman' Virgil

After the Middle Ages the 'Christian' Virgil, an interpretation which, however fanciful, points to genuine similarities between Virgil, Jewish thought and Paul, starts to give way before a more historically–focused 'Roman' Virgil. Yet in this approach too Virgil and Paul can seem to stand side by side, notably in two themes which intertwine in modern discussion of both writers: empire on the one hand, and pity or pathos on the other.

Thus the Roman empire appears as divinely ordered and guided, in Virgil and also in Rom. 13:1–7 (and perhaps in what can seem the Roman conception of the apostolic task implied by the use of names of provinces in Paul, as at Rom. 15:14–33); compare Sir William Ramsay on Paul 'as Traveller and Roman Citizen' and, more broadly, the sympathetic attitude to Greek and Roman ideals of empire attributed to Paul by the young C.H. Dodd.[20] This theme in both Virgil and Paul has during the last century caused successively fascination and pain, as experience and awareness have changed. Thus, latterly, Virgil might either be rejected as legitimizing tyranny or saved by being interpreted as having a pessimistic or negative outlook on empire or on Augustus in particular (this approach understandably began to be taken by an exile from Italy under Mussolini).[21] Paul in much the same way has been 'saved' by reinterpretation; he has been understood either as treating the Roman empire as irrelevant, so great for him is the power of divine grace through Christ, or as implicitly combating the claims of the emperor by asserting the imperial authority of Christ, requiring 'the obedience of faith' (Rom. 1:5, 15:8, 16:26) – or, in a way inspired by 'post-colonial' analysis of the reactions of subject peoples, as implicitly subverting the language of empire.

In consideration of Virgil the review of his treatment of empire is bound up with attention to the theme of pity and pathos. Virgil highlights the misery of war and exile, and the human condition more generally. Thus the Eclogues might be expected to deal with Dresden-china-like shepherds and shepherdesses, but begin with a peasant refugee driven from his piece of land by military confiscation (*Ecl.* i 3–4, 11–15, 64–78). Then in famous passages of the Aeneid, when Aeneas views a representation of the Trojan War in the temple of Juno in Carthage he says, weeping, that 'here too fame has its fitting rewards, but there are tears for events, and mortal destinies touch the heart', *sunt hic etiam sua praemia laudi, | sunt lacrimae rerum et mentem mortalia tangunt* (*Aen.* i 460–61); and when in the underworld he sees the shades pressing for their rebirth he asks sadly 'why this dread, sad longing for the light?' *quae lucis miseris tam dira cupido?* (*Aen.* vi 721).

Paul and Virgil

The intertwining of this sense of pathos with the theme of empire was well marked by early readers. Thus towards the end of the second century a tribune in the army of Septimius Severus, weary and disgusted at the losses being endured in the emperor's Parthian campaign, expressed his feelings by quoting a familiar tag from the Aeneid, from the bitter speech of Drances 'we die, a base, ignoble crowd without a name, scattered in the fields, unburied and unmourned', *nos, animae viles, inhumata infletaque turba,* | *sternamur campis* (*Aen.* xi 371–2) – and for this potentially mutinous quotation he was put to death (Cassius Dio, *History* 76.10, 2). Virgil is the poet of the defeated, the slain and the refugees as well as the victors.

In Paul too the pathos of the human condition comes to the fore, and J.W. Mackail in 1923 summed up the pathos of Virgil simply by quoting Paul: 'Virgil is felt to be the articulate voice of a whole creation groaning and travailing in pain together' (cf. Rom. 8:22).[22] In the passage which Mackail quoted Paul goes on to speak, we might say almost in Virgilian fashion, of 'tribulation, anguish, persecution, famine, nakedness, or sword' (Rom. 8:35). Yet the words which then follow in Paul ('in all these things we are more than conquerors through him that loved us'; Rom. 8:37, cf. I Cor. 3:21–3; II Cor. 2:14) have a mystical note of triumph intensified by interpretation of Christ as victor; there is no separation from divine love here or hereafter.[23] This differs from the doubtful and mournful note heard in Virgil even while he paints the after-life, as noted already; but it is not wholly alien to Virgil's depiction of the 'happy souls', *felices animae* (*Aen.* vi 669), and it recalls, although it takes further, his sense of divine presence, as when the Fauns are *praesentia numina,* 'present deities', of the country people (*Geo.* i 10), or Aeneas, conducted to the temple of Apollo at Buthrotum, feels himself *multo suspensum numine* 'tense at the strong presence of the god' (*Aen.* iii 372). On the larger scale, Paul in Romans 8 presents creation in travail yet in hope; Virgil, different as he is, to some extent anticipates the counterpoint of this presentation when he places his fullest forecast of Rome's glory, in Aeneid VI (703–892),

13

precisely in the context of cosmic origins, suffering and death, and the purification and bliss of an after-life.

Paul in the Light of Virgil: vocation and history
Tennyson's wonderful poem 'To Virgil' (see the appendix) turns away from the 'Christian Virgil' interpretation. The lines on 'the Pollio', the fourth or 'messianic' Eclogue, allow its 'chanter' no hint of Christian prophecy; the emphasis falls on

> Summers of the snakeless meadow,
>   unlaborious earth and oarless sea,

which are indeed described by Virgil, but the 'new offspring sent down from high heaven' is not touched on. Tennyson's following stanza, as noted already, picks out from Virgil's religion the notes of pathos and doubt. After the nineteenth century, however, the atmosphere changed. You can sense the difference in Kipling's poem from the 1920s (also in the appendix). This is an imaginary ode by Virgil's friend the poet Horace, Horace's 'last ode', written almost on his deathbed. Virgil here is once again a prophet who foresees a great change: the end of the old pagan order, and a new pre-eminence for the hope of immortality. As shepherd-watchers at night beneath an oak-tree hear the dawn-wind stir its branches while all is still dark,

> so Virgil died,
> Aware of change at hand, and prophesied
>
> Change upon all the Eternal Gods had made
>   And on the Gods alike –
> Fated as dawn but, as the dawn, delayed
>   Till the just hour should strike –
>
> A Star new-risen above the living and dead;
>   And the lost shades that were our loves restored
> As lovers, and for ever.

Kipling's vision of Virgil as seeing ahead to the coming of the daystar and the dawn matches his own fascination with the themes of loss and immortality, and indeed with the figure of Paul (a character in two of his short stories and the imagined speaker in another poem); but it also represents a new mood which was strong in the reading of Virgil from about 1920 to 1960. This mood could readily coalesce with the Roman imperial approaches to Paul found in Ramsay and Dodd. Part of it was a new kind of Christian interpretation of Virgil, this time of the Roman Virgil, pursued alongside some revival of the ancient positive Christian interpretation of Homer.

A distinctive instance of this new interpretation appears in the poetry of the 1930s and 1940s, when Charles Williams integrates Virgil into a remaking of the Arthurian legend. Virgil stands now for 'the City' which Aeneas and Arthur under divine guidance seek to restore, 'city' symbolizing order, civility, and mutual love in place of destruction and chaos. Arthur's poet and chief cavalry-officer Taliessin, in the battle of mount Badon when Arthur overcomes the pagan Saxons, awaits with intense patience the right moment for his troop to charge. In that waiting he has a vision of Virgil, 'standing on a trellised path by the sea … with unseeing eyes', utterly absorbed in the task of writing one of the hexameter lines of his epic:

> … the Roman sought for the word, sought for his thought,
> sought for the invention of the City by the phrase …
> Taliessin saw the flash of his style[24]
> dash at the wax; he saw the hexameter spring
> and the king's sword swing; he saw, in the long field
> the point where the pirate chaos might suddenly yield …
> The Aeneid's beaked lines swooped on Actium;
> the stooped horse charged …[25]

Thus, to quote C.S. Lewis's comment, 'as it were in a single act, Virgil writes his hexameter on his wax tablet and Taliessin writes his charge on the battle. His spear is his pen; his charge is the swooping of "the Aeneid's beaked lines"; it is, in a sense, Virgil who is winning the battle.'[26] The great line 'sought for the invention of the City by the phrase' recalls Aeneas, wandering in exile 'until he founds the City' (*Aen.* i 5 *dum conderet urbem*). It manifests, in its bearing on the battle, Williams's particular sense of the interdependence of and exchange between human beings who bear one another's burdens (Gal. 6:2), something at the heart of 'the City'; but the line also typifies a fresh public awareness of Virgil's Christian and general significance.

This recovery of Virgil was indeed a rediscovery of Virgil as an almost inexhaustible poetic guide, offering a kind of 'philosophy of life and death' (M. Bowra).[27] A landmark in it at the beginning of the 1930s, when the two-thousandth anniversary of Virgil's birth in 70 BCE was being commemorated, had been Theodor Haecker's book *Vergil. Vater des Abendlands* (Leipzig, 1931), translated as *Virgil, Father of the West* (London, 1934). The book fascinated T.S. Eliot. In England a Virgil Society was formed in 1944, with Eliot as the first president; among other authors it included the poets Cecil Day-Lewis and David Jones. Perhaps the longest survivor from this period is Hermann Broch's novel *The Death of Virgil* (1945), exploring Virgil's wish that the unfinished Aeneid be destroyed; Broch had begun his book in the mid-1930s, after reading Haecker.[28] A central text in the rediscovery of Virgil, however, was Jackson Knight's *Roman Vergil* (London, 1944), followed by a kindred shorter study in Bowra's *From Virgil to Milton* (1945), cited already (notes 19; 27). For Knight, Virgil anticipated the best in Christianity; St Augustine blamed himself for having wept for Virgil's Dido rather than his own sins, but he did not see (Knight urged) that the acceptance of the Virgil of the Aeneid which he made in his youth was like the acceptance of Christianity itself.[29]

What all this could mean in the last years of the Second World War was brought out by Hugh Stubbs, a younger colleague of Knight: '*Roman Vergil* was not only a best seller; it was a missionary tract, and just as the Oxford Movement crystallized round the tracts and sermons of a few High Church Oxford dons, so the Virgil Society crystallized round Jackson Knight's publications and lectures. T.S. Eliot, Lord Wavell, Cecil Day-Lewis and others congregated in London; here in Devon' – Stubbs was recalling

Paul and Virgil

the heavily bomb-damaged Exeter where Knight and he taught –
'retired Colonial governors, cathedral clergy, authors and poets,
met to read and discuss. Ilium was falling, Rome was arising; the
Rome of slaves was perishing and the Rome of free men was taking
its place ... there certainly was something in Vergil, as there was in
the Bible, for us all.'[30]

Within this rediscovery of Virgil from the 1920s onwards
one Virgilian theme that emerged strongly was that of personal
vocation, in connection with a broader communal history. The
divine calling of Aeneas is bound up with the founding of Rome
and Rome's own history and imperial calling. The Aeneid was read
accordingly as a pattern of Christian calling in connection with the
history of the church by two famous 'converts', Ronald Knox and
C.S. Lewis. Knox's autobiographical *A Spiritual Aeneid* (1918) was
matched and perhaps outdone by the mingled depth and sparkle
of his *jeu d'esprit Let Dons Delight* (1939), on imagined conversation
in an Oxford common-room from 1588 to 1938, with its haunting
recurrent allusion to Virgil's shepherd going into exile as a pattern
of the cost of conversion. Lewis for his part repeatedly re-read Virgil
throughout his life. In an autobiographical poem of 1931, shortly
after his return to Christianity, he described his long journey in the
terms of the Aeneid:

> At many bays and harbours I put in with joy
> Hoping that there I should have built my second Troy
> And stayed. But either stealing harpies drove me thence,
> Or the trees bled, or oracles, whose airy sense
> I could not understand, yet must obey, once more
> Sent me to sea to follow the retreating shore
> Of this land which I call at last my home ...

He came to understand the Aeneid as the great poem of the costliness
of vocation.[31]

Something different from but genuinely comparable with the
Virgilian pattern of vocation in connection with communal history
emerges in Paul's autobiographical writing. His costly apostolic

17

calling to be all things to all (I Cor. 9:19–23, 10:33–11:1) in a life of hardship and peril (I Cor. 4:9–13, 9:24–7; II Cor. 6:3–10, 11:16–12:13) and in journeys from Jerusalem to Rome and the west (Rom. 15:14–29) is bound up with the existing sacred history of Israel (Rom. 9:4–5). It has been granted to Paul to be a minister of a new covenant, in succession to that of Moses but more glorious, and to be conformed to both the dying and the living of Israel's messiah (II Cor. 3:4–4:15, Rom. 9:5), so that the liberty and deliverance for which Israel hopes are now in view (II Cor. 3:17, Gal. 4:4–5, Rom. 8:21, 11:25–6) and gentiles are one, through Christian rites, with Israel in her closest relationship with God ('All our fathers were under the cloud …', I Cor. 10:1–4). In interpretation the centrality of this theme in Paul has been brought out perhaps especially by Johannes Munck, and it is also adumbrated by N.T. Wright.[32] The theme also stands out in Acts. The ship nearing Puteoli brings to Rome a prisoner. 'Called to be an apostle' (Rom. 1:1), he is soon to be welcomed as such outside the city (Acts 28:15); but his calling has already prepared him (Acts 21:13) for the martyrdom which he narrowly escaped in Jerusalem, and which remains a possibility – 'as it is written, For thy sake we are killed all the day long' (Rom. 8:36; Ps. 44:22). In art, this aspect of Paul appears in the onward and upward glance of Christoph Kapup's alabaster figure (Plate 2); Paul's fingers grasp the sword with which he is often depicted, the symbol of his death by beheading (Acts of Paul 10.3–4).

Any too facile identification of Virgil with the particular needs and anxieties of the world of Paul is rightly suspect. Yet there can be illumination for both Paul and Virgil when the similarities between them are seriously pursued. It becomes clearer how Paul, not least as he himself embodied vocation and sacred history, could catch the imagination of gentiles in the empire for which Virgil had written.

Endnotes
[1] This chapter is based on a 2017 Chester Cathedral Bible Talk.
[2] M. Frederiksen, ed. N. Purcell, *Campania* (British School at Rome, 1984), 351, n.7.

Paul and Virgil

[3] T.W. Manson, *Studies in the Gospels and Epistles* (Manchester, 1962), 225–41 ('St. Paul's Letter to the Romans, and others').

[4] J.A. Symonds, *Renaissance in Italy: Revival of Learning* (London, 1877), 46, n.1; D. Comparetti, *Vergil in the Middle Ages* (English translation, London, 1895), 98, n.6, citing H.A. Daniel (ed.), *Thesaurus Hymnologicus* (5 vols., Leipzig & Halle, 1841–56), v, 266; J.M. Ziolkowski & M.C.J. Putnam, *The Virgilian Tradition* (New Haven, 2008), 412–14.

[5] Martial xi 48–9 (50); Pliny, *Epistles* iii 7, 8 *monimentum eius adire ut templum solebat.*

[6] Statius, *Silvae* iv 4, 51–5 *tenuis ignavo pollice chordas | pulso Maroneique sedens in margine templi | sumo animum et magni tumulis accanto magistri* (I myself, spending the summer in the bay of Naples) 'strike faintly at the strings with an idle finger – and sitting by the threshold of Maro's temple, I take heart and sing at the tomb of my great master'.

[7] Lactantius, *Divine Institutes* i 5 *nostrorum primus Maro non longe fuit a veritate*, on *Aen.* vi 724–7 *Principio caelum ac terras camposque liquentes ... spiritus intus alit …*

[8] S. Baring-Gould, *Lives of the Saints* (new edition, 16 vols., London, 1897), i, 368, under January 24, St Cadoc; Comparetti, *Vergil in the Middle Ages*, 98, n.6.

[9] Seneca, *Consolation, to Polybius*, viii 2, x 5, discussed by B. Rochette, *Le latin dans le monde grec* (Brussels, 1997), 271.

[10] A.K. Bowman, *Life and Letters on the Roman Frontier: Vindolanda and its People* (London, revised edn, 2003), 11, 88–9.

[11] B.F. Westcott, *Essays in the History of Religious Thought in the West* (London, 1891), v–vi.

[12] The *Life* attributed to Donatus, *Vita Donati* 36, in C. Hardie (ed.), *Vitae Vergilianae Antiquae* (Oxford, 1957), 10 (issued in one volume with R. Ellis (ed.), *Appendix Vergiliana* [Oxford, 1907, repr. 1957]).

[13] *Geo.* ii 173–4 *salve magna parens frugum, Saturnia tellus ...* 473–4 *extrema per illos | Iustitia excedens terris vestigia fecit:*

> Hail, sweet Saturnian soil, of fruitful grain
> Great parent …
> From hence Astraea took her flight, and here
> The prints of her departing steps appear' (Dryden)

[14] *Aen.* viii 348 *aurea nunc, olim silvestribus horrida dumis* 'golden now, but then bristling with woodland thickets'; viii 351–2 *hoc nemus, hunc, inquit, frondoso vertice collem | quis deus incertum est, habitat deus* 'this wood', he

said, 'this hill with its leaf-shadowed summit, is the abode of – which god is uncertain, but – a god'.

[15] Eusebius, *Life of Constantine, Speech to the Saints* xix–xxi, judged to be genuinely Constantinian by scholars including R. Lane Fox, *Pagans and Christians* (London & New York, 1986), 648–52.

[16] Martin Warner, *The Aesthetics of Argument* (Oxford, 2016).

[17] Dante, *Inferno* ii 13–15, 28–30, addressing Virgil:

> Tu dici, che di Silvio lo parente,
>> corruttibile ancora, ad immortale
> secolo andò, e fu sensibilmente ...
>
> Andovvi poi lo Vas d'elezione,
>> per recarne conforto a quella fede,
>> ch'è principio alla via di salvazione:

'Thou sayest that the father of Sylvius' – Aeneas – 'while still corruptible, went to the immortal world, and was there in body ... Then the Chosen Vessel' – Paul (Acts 9:15) – 'went there, to bring back strengthening for that faith which is the beginning of the way of salvation.'

[18] Dante, *Inferno* ii 31–3:

> Ma io, perchè venirvi ? o chi 'l concede ?
>> Io non Enea, io non Paolo sono;
> me degno a ciò nè io nè altri 'l crede:

'But as for me, why should I go there? or who grants it? I am not Aeneas, I am not Paul; neither I nor others believe me worthy of it.'

[19] The Stoicism of Virgil's language here was brought out by M. Bowra, *From Virgil to Milton* (London, 1945), 59–60, comparing Seneca *On Providence*, and was illustrated further from this work (chapter 2.2, the good man 'considers all adversities as trials') by N. Horsfall, *Virgil, Aeneid 3: A Commentary* (Leiden, 2006), 163, on line 182.

[20] W. Ramsay, *Paul as Traveller and Roman Citizen* (London, 1895); C. Harold Dodd, *The Meaning of Paul for To-Day* (London, 1920, repr. 1930), 24–5, 34, 41–8, 153.

[21] Francesco Sforza, 'The Problem of Virgil', *Classical Review* 49 (1935), 97–108, discussed by W.F. Jackson Knight, *Cumaean Gates* (Oxford, 1936), reprinted as Part Two of W.F. Jackson Knight, ed. J.D. Christie, *Vergil: Epic and Anthropology* (London, 1967), 273; R.J. Tarrant, 'Poetry and Power: Virgil's Poetry in Contemporary Context', in C. Martindale (ed.), *The Cambridge Companion to Virgil* (Cambridge, 1997), 169–87 (185–6).

Paul and Virgil

22 J.W. Mackail, *Virgil and his Meaning to the World of To-day* (London, n.d. [1923]), 53–4.

23 On the relation of Rom. 8:37, I Cor. 3:21–3 and II Cor. 2:14 to the theme of *Christus victor* see R. Leivestad, *Christ the Conqueror* (London, 1954), 114–15, 147–8.

24 Both the writing-stylus used with a wax tablet, and the style of Virgil's verse.

25 Charles Williams, *Taliessin through Logres* (London, 1938), third impression, reprinted in one volume with Charles Williams, *The Region of the Summer Stars* [first published London, 1944] (London, 1954), 17.

26 C.S. Lewis, *Arthurian Torso, containing the posthumous fragment of* The Figure of Arthur *by Charles Williams and a commentary on the Arthurian poems of Charles Williams by C.S. Lewis* (London, 1948), 111.

27 Bowra, *From Virgil to Milton*, 13: '... he made [the epic] contain almost a philosophy of life and death'.

28 H. Broch, *Der Tod des Vergil* (New York: Pantheon Books, 1945); English translation by Jean Starr Untermeyer, *The Death of Virgil* (New York: Pantheon Books, 1945; London: Routledge & Kegan Paul, 1946, reprinted 1977). Among later reprints of the English translation are those of London: Oxford University Press, 1983, and London: Penguin, 2000. On the process of composition and publication see Jennifer Jenkins, 'Broch's *Der Tod des Vergil*: Art and Power, Language and the Ineffable', in Graham Bartram, Sarah McGaughey & Galin Tihanov (edd.), *A Companion to the Works of Hermann Broch* (Rochester, NY: Camden House, 2019; published online by Cambridge University Press, 20 January 2023), 189–206 (190–92).

29 W.F. Jackson Knight, *Roman Vergil* (London, 1944), 309.

30 H.W. Stubbs in G. Wilson Knight, *Jackson Knight: A Biography* (Oxford, 1975), 288.

31 A.T. Reyes in *C.S. Lewis's Lost Aeneid: Arms and the Exile*, edited by A.T. Reyes (New Haven & London, 2011), 6–14. An incidental expression of Lewis's sense of the costliness of vocation is his explanation of what he means (see Lewis, *Arthurian Torso*, 199) when speaking of the 'admirable hardness' of Charles Williams's verse: 'hardness as of metals, jewels, logic, duty, vocation'.

32 J. Munck, *Paul and the Salvation of Mankind* (English translation, London, 1959); N.T. Wright, *Paul and the Faithfulness of God* (2 vols., London, 2013), ii, 495–9, 549–50.

2
HOSANNA, AN ADVENT GREETING

Blessed is he that cometh in the Name of the Lord;
Hosanna in the highest (Matthew 21:9).[1]

Hosanna: with this word we greet the advent or coming of Christ.

Hosanna may be the most familiar of all Advent texts, because of its liturgical use. In the eucharist 'Hosanna in the highest' rounds off the Sanctus – Holy, holy, holy – when the service is sung. These words are unprinted in the Prayer-book of 1662, but they take us back to the first English Prayer-book of 1549, where they are indeed to be found, translated from the missal.[2]

But when we hear Hosanna read in the Gospel we sense that we are travelling back in time far behind our own old but still relatively modern liturgy in English, back through the ages when the church in the west prayed in Latin, through the still earlier time of the early Roman empire, when the prayers were in Greek, and back to the time of the earliest Christians who still used, or were very close to, prayer in Hebrew and Aramaic. Hosanna goes together with two other words of extreme age which are Hebrew words surviving in the New Testament and Christian liturgy: Amen, and Alleluia.

In St Matthew's Gospel the multitudes cry Hosanna as our Lord comes – makes his advent – down the slope of the Mount of Olives and into the holy city. The children cry it again, with their penetrating sing-song, when he enters the temple. And the gospel itself is still not quite the beginning of this Advent cry. It was already known to the disciples and the multitudes. Hosanna is being used by them as a familiar acclamation.

Hosanna is indeed already found as a festal cry in one of the Psalms, Psalm 118 *O give thanks unto the Lord* ...:

Save us now, O Lord: O Lord, send us now prosperity.
Blessed is he that cometh in the Name of the Lord.

The English represents Hebrew which does sound like a chant in the temple, a chant of earnest petition and joy:

anna Adonai hoshi'anna, anna Adonai hatslihanna.

The words have a compelling character. Our Hosanna reflects a shorter form of the same Hebrew. Hosianna with an 'I', closer to the Hebrew in the psalm, is found in Philipp Nicolai's hymn *Wachet auf*, 'Wake, O wake, for night is flying.'

This psalm was sung at the feast of Tabernacles in the autumn, when the weather begins to change and prayer in the Holy Land is made for the urgently needed rain. At this festival, in a custom which still continues in Jewish worship, they carried green branches of myrtle and willow and cried Save us now, O Lord – Hoshi'anna, Hosanna. At this word in particular, they waved and shook their branches. The bunch of branches held itself came to be called a *Hosanna*.

This custom was adapted in the triumphal entry of Christ into Jerusalem, and is still echoed in palm processions on Palm Sunday. What was originally a petition – Save us! – had by the time of Christ taken on the overtones of an acclamation – Salvation! Compare Ps. 3:8 'Salvation belongeth unto the Lord!', and the way the petition 'God save the Queen' is also used as an acclamation.

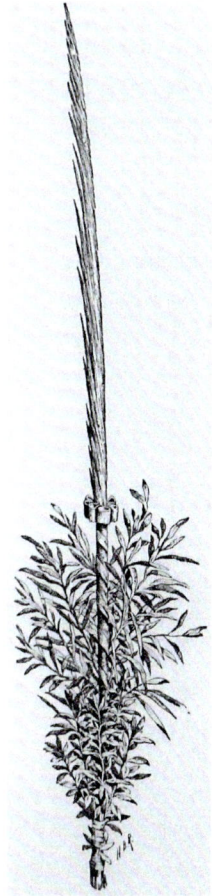

Figure 2.1: Drawing after B. Picart, of a Lulab, the branches of palm, myrtle and willow bound together and carried with a citron (Lev. 23:40) at the feast of Tabernacles (Sukkot); *Jewish Encyclopaedia* viii (New York & London: Funk & Wagnalls, 1904), p. 206.

23

Compare too the song of the multitude in heaven in the book of Revelation: 'Salvation to our God who sitteth upon the throne, and to the Lamb' (Rev. 7.10).

So my much-loved remote predecessor Charlie Wood, Rector of St Botolph's (1940–61), who was a Hebraist, suggested in an article in 1941 that one possible meaning of 'Hosanna to the son of David' was 'Salvation belongs to the son of David.'[3] The substance of this sermon may then very well have been preached from this pulpit before, but if so it was just too soon for me to hear it.

Now again the Advent season is focused in the cry Hosanna, Save us, Salvation. We greet the Advent coming with the joyful acclamatory cry of Hosanna, Salvation! But, remembering also our own need to prepare, we utter at the same time the humble petition to God: Hosanna, Save us.

Endnotes

[1] A sermon preached in St Botolph's, Cambridge on the First Sunday in Advent, 30 November 2014; the Gospel for this Sunday in the Prayer-book is Matthew 21:1–13, describing the acclamation of Christ as he enters Jerusalem and the temple.

[2] The words were dropped in the revised Prayer-book of 1552, and were not restored in queen Elizabeth's revision of 1559, but they do reappear in the Latin translation of the Prayer-book which she approved for use in colleges in 1560.

[3] C.T. Wood, 'The Word ὡσαννά in Matthew xxi.9', *Expository Times* 52 (1940–41), 357; see further R. Loewe, '"Salvation" is Not of the Jews', *Journal of Theological Studies* N.S. 32 (1981), 341–68; H. StJ. Hart, 'Hosanna in the Highest', *Scottish Journal of Theology* 45 (1992), 283–301; W.D. Davies & D.C. Allison, Jr, *The Gospel according to Saint Matthew* (International Critical Commentary; 3 vols., Edinburgh, 1988–97), iii, 124–5.

3
ARCHAEOLOGY AND BAR KOKHBA:
FROM EXPLORATION TO DOCUMENTATION

In the archaeology of ancient Judaea the Bar Kokhba war of 132–5, during the later years of Hadrian, has been of strong interest to non-Jews and Jews alike. 'Bar Kokhba' is an Aramaic nickname, 'son of the star', recalling Balaam's prophecy of a 'star from Jacob' and 'sceptre from Israel' (Num. 24:17). The rising against Rome led by Bar Kokhba took place soon after biblical times. Its history touches themes of the Hebrew bible, the books of the Maccabees, and the New Testament: independent Jewish rule, messianic hope and martyrdom. Moreover, the war is an event in Roman and Christian as well as Jewish history. Descriptions of it from all three points of view survive from the ancient world.

The rising was described by the third-century Roman historian Cassius Dio, writing in Greek without naming Bar Kokhba, as a Jewish war 'neither small-scale nor short-term', stirred up by Hadrian's action in founding his new Roman colony-city of Aelia Capitolina on the site of Jerusalem, and ended only with grievous Roman losses (Cassius Dio, *History* 69.12, 1, as preserved in an eleventh-century epitome by Xiphilinus). Then Bar Kokhba's renewal of earlier Jewish revolt, his harshness with Christians who would not join his forces, and his ultimate defeat have a prominent place in the works of the early fourth-century church historian Eusebius, a Greek writer from Palestine (he was bishop of Caesarea) who is a primary source for the history of Christianity.[1] He now names Bar Kokhba in the Greek form Bar Chochebas. His account draws on comments found in the writings of the second-century Christian philosopher Justin Martyr, who also gives this name; but he is close to rabbinic texts in what he says about the Judaean setting of events. Within Jewish literature, the rabbinic texts offer vivid glimpses of the war and its aftermath, but, even within the report that Bar Kokhba was hailed as messiah by R. Akiba, they reflect a divided and often negative opinion about him. Later on, Maimonides and other mediaeval authors show greater pride in his achievement in becoming a ruler in Judaea.

Bar Kokhba's war figures accordingly in histories of the Roman empire, from before the time of Gibbon and down to the present. Then the passages on the war in Eusebius and Dio have regularly been discussed, together with rabbinic and mediaeval Jewish accounts, in Christian study of scripture and of the history of ancient Israel and the early church. The war is commonly treated in modern histories and atlases of Israel in biblical times, church histories, and histories of the Jews. The ancient and mediaeval Jewish accounts have had broad influence in Jewish thought and education, notably during revival of national feeling from the nineteenth century onwards, and in connection with the establishment of the state of Israel. In all, it is not surprising that Bar Kokhba's war has attracted attention in Holy Land archaeology.

Moreover, the Greek and rabbinic literary sources have characteristics which might particularly strike an archaeologist; they give indications which archaeology and associated finds could illuminate. An example is the Roman siege of Bar Kokhba's forces at a place named in the Greek of Eusebius (*Ecclesiastical History*, iv 6, 3) as Beththera or Bitthera, and in Rufinus's Latin translation of Eusebius as Bethera or Bethara. These Greek and Latin forms of the name, with the ending -a, reflect Aramaic and recall Hebrew Bether (Song of Sol. 2:17, probably a place-name). The similar Hebrew forms Beth-ther and Bethar are found in rabbinic texts which likewise present traditions of a siege here. Eusebius calls Beththera 'a very strong citadel, not far from Jerusalem'. The description invites identification and investigation of the place. Another literary indication which seems to demand archaeological commentary appears when both Cassius Dio (*History*, 69.12, 3) and rabbinic texts mention underground passages and secret strongholds and caves in Judaea, occupied by the rebels and the population.

Archaeology and Bar Kokhba

Whatever the causes, non-Jewish as well as Jewish interest, gaining impetus in the early nineteenth century through fresh historical treatment, has been strong enough to make the Bar Kokhba war a topic which runs like a thread through the long development of archaeology in the Holy Land.[2] As I was reading in connection with study of the Jewish risings under Trajan and his successor, Hadrian, it seemed to me that the topic of Bar Kokhba gives you an impression of the principal phases in this archaeology, viewed together with the topographical inquiry which can be called the handmaid, or sometimes better the aunt or even the mother, of archaeology. For the present purpose four phases may be distinguished.

The first phase would begin with the preliminary survey of parts of Palestine including Jerusalem by the Royal Engineers in 1840–41, following the part played by the Royal Navy in the ending of Ibrahim Pasha's rule and the restoration of Palestine to the Ottoman empire. Also in 1841 the American scholar Edward Robinson published the report of his pioneering 1838 topographical journeys in Palestine, undertaken mainly for the identification of biblical sites, but also including a careful survey of the 'Tombs of the Kings' in Jerusalem, to the east of the Nablus road.[3] The following years saw the foundation of the Palestine Exploration Fund (1865), much further topographical work, and the establishment of the Holy Land as a regular tourist destination for European visitors.

In this phase we are still in the period when emphasis lies on exploration rather than archaeology. The making of trustworthy maps is the prime consideration. C.W. (later Sir Charles) Wilson completed the ordnance survey of Jerusalem in 1865. Yet in the mid-nineteenth century archaeological excavation develops. In Jerusalem Félicien de Saulcy, famous for his expeditions to the Dead Sea, studied once more and then excavated the 'Tombs of the Kings' – the tombs of the royal house of Adiabene (1850–51, 1863–4).[4] Captain (later Sir Charles) Warren conducted an investigation of the walls of the temple area by means of shafts and tunnels, carried

27

out (1867–71) under the auspices of the Palestine Exploration Fund by Royal Engineers.[5] The first phase ends with the Engineers' great survey of western Palestine in 1872–4 and 1877, connected especially with the names of Lieut. C.R. Conder (in command) and Lieut. H.H. Kitchener (later Lord Kitchener). The survey was published from 1880 to 1884.

A second phase begins with this survey and runs over the next sixty years, roughly until the last decade of the British Mandate in Palestine (1938–48). At the end of the 1880s Conder could already write with pride that, for history and the historical interpretation of the bible, 'we no longer depend on literature alone. We have actual monuments before our eyes. We have inscriptions, coins, seals, statues, chased metal-work, and pottery; we have collected measurements of tombs, walls, synagogues, and reliable photographs of every famous place.'[6] This summary is incidentally a reminder that the survey of western Palestine was also an epoch in study of the ancient monumental synagogues of Galilee. 'Lieut. Kitchener paid special attention to them', wrote R.A.S. Macalister, 'and determined the plan on which they were built'.[7] Then sixty years after Conder, looking back at the end of this period over a long succession of excavations and investigations, the American scholar W.F. Albright wrote in his 1949 handbook *The Archaeology of Palestine* 'The Palestine Exploration Fund … has done the lion's share of all work in Palestine … German and French expeditions are generally supplied with government funds.' Albright went on to note discreetly the important part played by American benefactors and institutions.[8]

Then a third, initially overlapping, phase is marked by ever-increasing archaeological commitment on the part of Jewish residents first of mandatary Palestine and then of the state of Israel. Their interest was heralded from 1913 onwards by the internationally supported work of the Jewish Palestine Exploration Society, but the definite beginning of this phase can perhaps best be set in 1942, when a Department of Archaeology, led by L.A. Mayer and E.L. Sukenik, was established in the Faculty of Humanities at the Hebrew University of Jerusalem, and annual archaeological conferences began to be held there.[9] Special emphasis naturally lay on the archaeology of Palestine, which by 1949 figured as a separate subject taught within the Institute of Jewish Studies by Sukenik, assisted by N. Avigad, J. Licht, and, for Talmudic Archaeology, Y. Brand; B. Maisler (later Mazar) was the lecturer responsible for another separate subject, the Historical Geography of Palestine.[10]

This commitment by Jewish residents and institutions gradually became the mainspring of archaeological work, although non-Jewish involvement by no means ceased. That continues to be the position, but with regard to Bar Kokhba a fourth phase can be dated from 1967, when archaeologists from the state of Israel gained access to the West Bank territory, now occupied, and so to further areas of ancient Judaea which were of importance in the Bar Kokhba war.

Phase I
The first phase of archaeological history was marked in our topic by what seems to be the first clear scholarly identification of the site of the Bether, Beththera or Bethar defended by Bar Kokhba as Bittir, 10 km south-west of Jerusalem (see Map 3.1, overleaf). This is in George Williams's topographical and antiquarian work *The Holy City*, modestly presented as a companion to the Royal Engineers' 1841 survey of Jerusalem. Williams was a Fellow of King's College, Cambridge. Edward Robinson in his fundamental *Biblical Researches in Palestine* (1841), the source of so many identifications of ancient sites through attention to their modern Arabic names as well as ancient sources, had given an account of Bar Kokhba's revolt; but when he mentioned the siege of 'Bether', he accepted that its site was unknown, and in the account of his journeys he mentioned Wadi Bittir without discussing the place-name Bittir.[11] Williams, however, visiting the site in 1843, now drew attention to the continuity between the Arabic Bittir or Beitir and the ancient

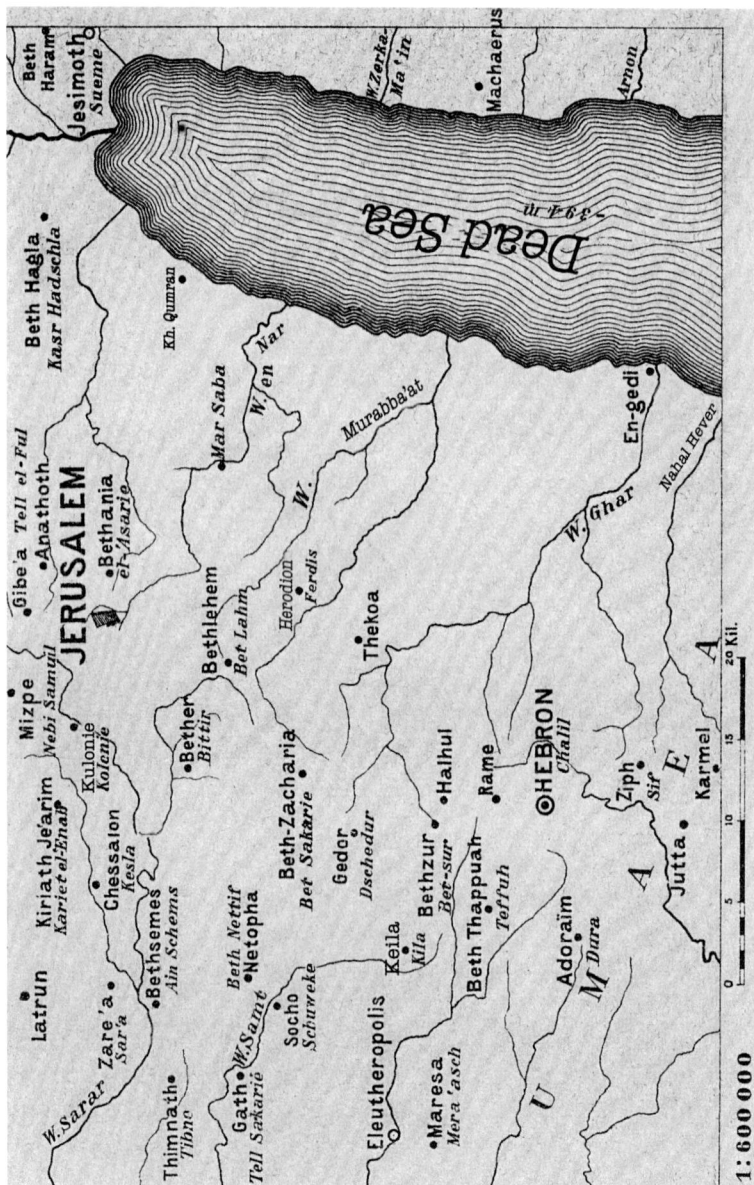

Map 3.1: Judaea and the Dead Sea (1891, adapted), showing Bether/Bittir, Khirbet Qumran, Herodium (Herodion) and Wadi Murabba'at, and Ziph and Nahal Hever.

Aramaic and Hebrew toponyms Beththera (known from Eusebius) and Beththter – and also to traces of a siege on the spot.

Williams's account of his visit on 28 April 1843, guided along the valley from Jerusalem by an inhabitant of the Palestinian village of Ain Karim, remains one of the clearest descriptions of the site.[12] To quote a little of what he says, 'the first feature that attracted my attention, as I approached the spot, was a lofty hill projecting into the valley, which surrounds it on three sides, attached to the modern village by a rocky isthmus. On this hill my guide pointed out *Khirbet el-Yehûd* …'. He adds 'the valley makes an elbow, in which stands the hill …, on a kind of promontory. The valley then continues its course in the same direction as before …'. He goes on 'Following a track down which a copious stream of water was flowing, I came to a fountain which rises above the village, having a passage cut through the solid rock to the source'… 'I ascended [to the hill], passing on the way some large caverns in its rocky sides'. On top of the hill he found remains of towers and walls. The spring from which he started his ascent is the famous spring of Bittir, the secret of the continuance and prosperity of a community here over the centuries and a feature of importance in the time of Hadrian, as later discoveries would show.

The valley followed by Williams runs with many turns westwards from the vale of Rephaim (II Sam. 5:18) at a point near Malha (el-Maliha), south-west of Jerusalem, down towards Beth Shemesh and the coastal plain.[13] The village of Bittir is on the left or south side of the valley, and the dominant hill of Khirbet el-Yehud, 'ruin of the Jews', the site of the small city defended by Bar Kokhba, projects here from the south side. Its strength as a citadel, emphasized in Eusebius, derives in the first instance from its situation with ravines on three sides and a saddle (Williams's 'isthmus') on the fourth. The Roman road from Jerusalem to Eleutheropolis/Beth Gubrin, dated by milestone inscriptions to 130, shortly before the war, runs along the valley past Bittir, leaving the valley shortly afterwards to bear south-west. The eighth Roman milestone from

Jerusalem was found *c.*1893–4 below the hill of Khirbet el-Yehud on the north-eastern side.[14] The railway line from Jerusalem to Beth Shemesh and Lod (Lydda) winds, likewise with the valley, round the northern slope of the hill.

Eventually it was recognized that the site is already mentioned as Baither or Bether in the book of Joshua, in a list of eleven places including Bethlehem and Manach/Manahath, identified with Malha. The list was lost from the Hebrew text, but survives in the Septuagint Greek rendering (Josh. 15:59a), from the late BCE period. It is translated as part of Josh. 15:59 in the New English Bible (1970) and the Revised English Bible (1989).

The phase of archaeology to which Williams's identification of Beththera belongs brought further contributions towards the topography of areas which later discoveries would show to have been important in the Bar Kokhba war. De Saulcy's journey around the Dead Sea in 1850–51 included the area of the Wadi Murabba'at and En-gedi, and ultimately also, on the coast further north, Ain Feshka and Khirbet Qumran, later to be famous for the discovery of the Dead Sea Scrolls. Inland and higher up, he also explored Herodium (Herodion), between Tekoa and Bethlehem (see Map 3.1 on p. 30), and on returning in 1863 had a detailed plan of the site prepared.

Just after de Saulcy, in 1852–3, the land was visited by A.P. Stanley, later Dean of Westminster. He became the author of a repeatedly reprinted book, *Sinai and Palestine* (1856), which brilliantly expressed the growing current sense of the importance of the geography and the remains of ancient Judaea for an understanding of biblical history. Particularly notable in our context is his singling out of the historical importance of one geological feature. Like all limestone formations, he says,

> the hills of Palestine abound in caves … In these innumerable rents, and cavities, and holes we see the origins of the sepulchres which, partly natural and partly artificial, perforate the rocky walls of the Judaean valleys … We see in them the shelter of the people of the

land, as when Lot went up out of Zoar to the mountain, and dwelt in a cave ... We see in them, also, the hiding-places which served for the defence of robbers and insurgents and for the refuge of those "of whom the world was not worthy" (Heb. 11:38) ... The stream of [Israelite] national existence ... from time to time disappears from the light of day, and runs underground in these subterraneous recesses, to burst forth again when the appointed moment arrives; a striking type, as it is a remarkable instance, of the spiritual life of the Chosen People, "burning, but not consumed," "chastened, but not killed." (Exod. 3:2, II Cor. 6:9)[15]

Stanley's verdict can now seem to foreshadow the future Bar Kokhba cave discoveries and the continuing life, as well as the disasters, which they betoken.

In the history of archaeology, more broadly, his book stands for the very wide support which was growing at this stage for every aspect of 'Palestine exploration'. This support was concurrent with the growth of European tourism. Thus in 1858 Anthony Trollope, sent on official business to Egypt by the Post Office, also visited the Holy Land and began his novel *The Bertrams*, with its chapters on a group of English visitors in Jerusalem. Their expedition on donkeys to see the biblical sites of Aceldama and the Kidron valley includes a generously-provided picnic, spread out with some incongruity by the ancient tombs near the Kidron – the Tomb of St James offering shelter when needed.[16]

Phase II
The second phase begins with perhaps the most famous instance of Palestine exploration, the survey (see Plates 3 and 4) of western Palestine led by Conder from 1871 onwards. He described its rigours and adventures in his book *Tent Work in Palestine* (1878). The cover is stamped with a gilt impression of the work of the survey; one officer stands bent over his instrument under a sun-shade, another sits on the ground holding a map or plan. They covered of course the wilderness west of the Dead Sea, and made their way down a route which will also have been important in the Bar Kokhba war,

from Tekoa down to En-gedi; the difficulties which such journeys present even for mules are underlined when they arrive at the top of the cliffs above En-gedi and for safety's sake have to unload their mules before they send them down precipitous paths to drink at the spring below.[17]

George Adam Smith later reports that the way from En-gedi up to Tekoa is more practicable than a steeper route from En-gedi to Herodium; this is on the basis of journeys undertaken in 1880 and later.[18] He recalled that in II Chronicles 20 Jehoshaphat goes to meet the invading Ammonites and Moabites in the wilderness of Tekoa, and suggests that the invaders could have come up this way from En-gedi. As we know now, some at least of Bar Kokhba's supplies passed this way up from En-gedi, on donkeys.

The profit which archaeology and epigraphy soon made from the enhanced topographical knowledge to be extended further by the Survey is illustrated by Charles Clermont-Ganneau. This brilliant young pupil of Ernest Renan burst upon the scene in Jaffa and Jerusalem in 1869, when he was just twenty-one, and was appointed chancellor at the French consulate. He is described as he appeared in these years in a novel by Miriam, the daughter of the antiquities dealer Moses Shapira whom he attacked as a forger: a young man on a horse in Christian Street in the Old City of Jerusalem, extremely handsome, extremely serious, wearing on his head a fluttering Bedouin head-dress.[19] In 1873–4 he undertook researches on behalf of the Palestine Exploration Fund, including a rapid visit to Bittir. In 1870, he says, a woman from the village told him that an ossuary with carvings and an inscription had once been found there; he also heard of an inscription surviving on the spot at Bittir, and on 9 August 1874 he went to look for it.[20]

The drawing which he published of the road to the spring, at the isthmus joining the village to the hill of Khirbet el-Yehud, shows the hill rising up on the right. The Roman inscription by the spring became famous through Clermont-Ganneau; it records in Latin the presence of forces from two legions, V Macedonica and XI Claudia.

The case for a connection with the period of the siege, as Clermont-Ganneau thought likely, was strengthened by discovery of an Aelia Capitolina foundation coin representing a legionary standard with the legend 'LE. V' – once again, V Macedonica.[21]

The mainstream of Holy Land archaeology was at this point turning to the excavation of some of the series of Tells, the mounds formed by the accumulated debris of successive settlements, which had been disclosed by the Survey of Palestine. By the same token, interest turned towards very early as well as later periods of settlement. In March 1890 Flinders Petrie began digging at Tell el-Hesi, west of Hebron, work noted by Kathleen Kenyon as 'the first beginnings of stratigraphic excavation in Palestine'.[22] Nevertheless, the recorded traces of a siege of Khirbet el-Yehud at Bittir also accumulated. They appear to include the two sorts of stones, 'some sent by hand, some by engines', which Cassius Dio notes were used (by the defenders) during the siege of Jerusalem by Titus (*Hist.* 66.4, 3). Thus near the foot of the hill, higher up than the find-spot of the milestone, there was found a large stone ball of a weight (41 kg) judged to be nearly that of the 'stones of a talent's weight' hurled by the artillery of the Tenth Legion in 70, according to Josephus; perhaps at Bittir too it was a relic of the attack.[23] Again, when three Bittir families were clearing their land on top of the hill in 1907 they turned up many broken spears and stone balls, perhaps sling-stones such as have been found in numbers there more recently; the defenders evidently still had a considerable supply when the final Roman attack came. An 'extraordinary number' of coins were also found, including many from this revolt (examples showing a rosette or star above the temple-façade are noted).[24] Lastly, in the 1920s during further investigations at Bittir by the German Archaeological Institute in Jerusalem, remains of the Roman siege circumvallation were identified.[25] This was a final confirmation, if more were needed, that Bittir is indeed the ancient Beththter, Beththera, or Bethar defended by Bar Kokhba.

The caves noticed by Williams in the hill of Khirbet el-Yehud were viewed again in these reinvestigations. More broadly, the inquiries needed into the subject of artificially made or improved caves were noted by R.A.S. Macalister in the early twentieth century, on caves inspected *c*.1900 at Tell Zakariya (Azekah) and elsewhere in the Eleutheropolis area, and in 1926 by E. Brandenburg – in a monograph on rock-architecture published under the auspices of the Jewish Palestine Exploration Society – on the area north of Jerusalem.[26] The subject was not studied, however, with special reference to the Bar Kokhba war.

Phase III
The third phase of archaeological work, from the early 1940s onwards to 1967, was marked by the famous wave of discoveries by Bedouin and then by archaeologists in the Judaean wilderness. These discoveries spanned the troubled years around the ending of the British mandate in 1948, and then continued into the 1960s. The best-known finds were the Dead Sea Scrolls, writings found in a series of caves at and near Khirbet Qumran. At this northern end of the western Dead Sea coast (see Map 3.1 on p. 30) it emerged that Khirbet Qumran and nearby Ain Feshka had both been under Bar Kokhba's control, as finds of coins attested.

Outstanding finds further south in the wilderness, however, were the Bar Kokhba letters in Hebrew, Aramaic and Greek, with other documents dated by his era, and further written material. Letters and documents disclosed the original form of his name, Simeon bar Kosiba. Now archaeology related to Bar Kokhba had become documentation in the most basic sense.

The main discoveries were made in caves in the deep gorges of two wadis running east, down to the Dead Sea (see Map 3.1). The northernmost, Wadi Murabba'at, reaches the Sea north of En-gedi. It continues ravines which begin near Herodium and Tekoa, south of Bethlehem. The second, Nahal Hever (Wadi Habra), emerging south of En-gedi, continues ravines which begin in the district of

Ziph, south of Hebron. Insurgents and local inhabitants took refuge in caves in these wadis during repression of the rising.

The 1949 border between the West Bank to the north and Israel to the south crosses the wilderness, running west-south-west from the Dead Sea coast just north of En-gedi to the Judaean hill-country, which it rounds south of Hebron to turn north-east towards Jerusalem. Wadi Murabba'at is north of this border, Nahal Hever south of it. On both sides of the border finds were made by Bedouin, who crossed it as they searched the caves. The archaeologists who followed worked separately north and south of the border, under the aegis of Jordan and Israel, respectively.

The letters first published, in Hebrew and Aramaic, were found in Wadi Murabba'at. They were addressed to Jeshua ben Galgula, 'head of camp', probably based in Herodium (three letters, with fragments of three others which were probably in his hands, and further small fragments probably from letters). A Greek remarriage contract of the year 124 (Mur 115) executed in Bethbasi (I Macc. 9:62), between Herodium and Bethlehem, for Salome daughter of John Galgula, perhaps Jeshua's sister, suggests that his family were from Bethbasi.[27]

One letter (Mur 42) is addressed jointly 'to Jeshua ben Galgula and to the men of Ha-baruk'. This place is probably the village known as Caphar Bericha, in the south of Judaea, east and a little south of Hebron on a commanding eminence overlooking the descent to the Dead Sea – here Abraham (Gen. 18:16–22) was thought to have taken leave of his angel-visitors when they went down towards Sodom. Caphar Bericha, present-day Bani Na'im, was on the way south from Herodium and Tekoa down to Ziph and Aristobulias, which lie on the edge of the wilderness south-east of Hebron. The dense Jewish population of this southern region was involved in the revolt. A surviving Greek marriage contract of the year 130 from Aristobulias was probably found south of the Israel-West Bank border, in a cave used for refuge in the upper part of Nahal Hever (Wadi Habra), near Aristobulias.[28]

A second group of letters, found south of the border in the Cave of Letters further down Nahal Hever, were addressed to Jonathan (son of Ba'ya or Ba'yan, Beianus in Greek) or jointly to this Jonathan and Masbala (twelve letters, Hebrew and Aramaic but including the two in Greek, from a find of fifteen, all of which may have been in Jonathan's hands). Jonathan was the brother of Miriam, a previous or other wife of Eleazar; Eleazar was the second husband of Babatha, who owned a large body of documents found in the Cave of Letters.[29] One letter, from Simeon bar Kosiba 'to the men of En-gedi, to Masbala and to Jonathan', mentions 'fruits to be unloaded from the boat that is with you', and indicates Bar Kokhba's control of En-gedi and its Dead Sea port.[30]

The Cave of Letters, high up in the cliff on the north side of the wadi, is almost unreachable. The similarly inaccessible Cave of Horror (so named from the number of skulls and skeletal remains within it), visible from the Cave of Letters, is on the southern side. 'Here ..., as in the other cave-refuges, remnants of rope were found.'[31] The perilous exploration of these and other caves during the search for documents in the years 1950–60 under the leadership of Y. Aharoni and Y. Yadin, has been vividly described.[32] Investigation in 1955 involved long rope-ladders; in a recent fresh search under the auspices of the Israel Antiquities Authority, the investigators were 'rappelling down to caves located between heaven and earth'.[33] Lastly, a fragmentary Hebrew letter addressed 'to Simeon ben Kosiba prince of Israel' by Simeon ben Mattaniah was among papyri brought to the Palestine Archaeological Museum in 1952, and was found by Bedouin possibly also in a cave in Nahal Hever.[34]

The 'rediscovery' of Bar Kokhba in the 1960s, above all through these letters, brought a new outburst of enthusiasm for the history and legend of his rising. This was exemplified in the field of imaginative writing in the historical novel by the Liverpool author Merton Finch, *Simon bar Cochba: Rebellion in Judea* (London, 1969). His immediate inspiration came from archaeology; he had read an *Observer Magazine* article on the discovery of Bar Kokhba letters and other items in Nahal Hever.[35] The novel also shows the impact on the author of news of the Six-day War in June 1967, and his remembrance of cousins killed serving in the 1948 war of Israel's independence. Recollections of this kind inevitably surrounded much of the archaeological work on Bar Kokhba and on the interpretation of the letters and the other finds deriving from those who took refuge in the caves.

Equally important were the discoveries of deeds dated by the era of Bar Kokhba, a method of dating already known from coins. One of these deeds, bought from Bedouin in the 1950s, prepared for publication by 1958, and finally printed in 1961, gave the new information that a 'camp' of the adherents of Bar Kokhba was settled at Herodium. The document consists of a number of copies of the record of a leasehold agreement: 'I of my own free will have leased from you some of the soil which is in Ir Nahash, in the leased land which you have leased from Simeon prince of Israel'; but the important part in the present context consists of the first four lines giving the date and place of this agreement: 'on 20th Shebat in the second year of the redemption of Israel at the hand of Simeon ben Kosiba prince of Israel, in the camp settled in *Herodes*' – a transliteration of the Greek name Herodes, applied to the place Herodium.[36] This deed, in conjunction with the letters and with other finds left in caves from officers and refugees, identified the importance in Bar Kokhba's realm of Herodium as well as En-gedi and Bethther, and of course showed the continuity of administration and agriculture under his rule.

These finds shed light from within on Bar Kokhba and his realm and governance. For the first time it was possible to see the full personal name of Bar Kokhba in Hebrew, 'Simeon ben Kosiba'. One can note how readily this could be adapted not only into the laudatory Kokhba 'star', but also into the opprobrious nickname 'Koziba', 'liar', commonly used in rabbinic texts; thus, in a bitter tradition in Midrash Lamentations Rabbah, ii 4, on Lam. 2:2 'The Lord has swallowed up all the habitations of Jacob', the early third-century R. Johanan says that his teacher R. Judah ha-Nasi 'used to explain "There shall come forth a star [Hebrew *kokhabh*] out of Jacob" (Num. 24:17) in this way: read not *kokhabh* but *kazabh* [lie].'

His title 'prince' (Hebrew *nasi'*) was also known from coins. It suggests political rule over Israel; compare the title in the form 'prince *over* [Hebrew *'al*] Israel' found in an Aramaic letter from Simeon ben Kosiba (P. Yadin 54, line 1; written on wood).[37] The title *'nasi'* was applied in later strata of the biblical books to the king of Israel (as at Ezek. 21:25, Zedekiah; I Kings 11:34, Solomon – here probably through an adapted vocalization of the Hebrew text) and the tribal princes (Num. 7:2). In Qumran rule literature, similarly, the 'prince of the congregation' is the royal figure who co-operates with the high-priestly ruler; each receives a special blessing in the collection of Blessings which follows the Community Rule and the Messianic Rule in the copy from Cave 1 (1Q28b). The name 'Eleazar the priest' on some coins of the Bar Kokhba rising suggests that, as in Qumranic and biblical thought (Num. 27:15–21, Zech. 4:14), Bar Kokhba the 'prince' governs, at least notionally, with the high-priest in a joint rule. In rabbinic texts, comparably, at the end of the second century and in the years following R. Judah ha-Nasi and his successors in Judaea have this title, and exercise governance, as confirmed by the early third-century statement of the Christian teacher Origen that the Jewish 'ethnarch' in Judaea exercises power almost as a king (Origen, *Letter to Africanus*, 14).[38] The 'camp', Hebrew *mahaneh*, comparably, is a group of Israelites in a particular place, as with the four 'camps' of Judah, Reuben, Ephraim and Dan in Numbers 2, and corresponding use of *mahaneh* in Qumran texts.

As has appeared, the interpretation of these documents converged with fresh study of the coins of the revolt. Throughout the twentieth century these coins had been increasingly found and studied; but until at least the 1930s the name Simeon was not always thought to apply to Bar Kokhba, although this had long been suggested in the light of rabbinic reference to 'Kozbian' coins (Tosefta, Maaser Sheni i 6, probably reflecting early third-century teaching). Now the connection became clear, and the coins dated by years of his era could be correlated with the documents dated in the same way. It became possible for a distinguished numismatist to write a study of Bar Kokhba coins which amounted also to a history of the revolt.[39]

Soon after the publication of the deed executed in Herodium, excavation began in the fortress of Herodium (1962–7), carried out by the Franciscans of the Studium Biblicum Franciscanum in Jerusalem, under the direction of Virgilio Corbo. Here too Bar Kokhba coins were found, further attesting occupation by his adherents. One or two of the small finds, while not necessarily from the years of the revolt itself, illustrate the conditions of the time. Thus an ostracon, a sherd used for writing, gives a Hebrew alphabet in script of the same kind as is attested in the Murabba'at documents, which also include a number of alphabets.[40] Abecedaries of this sort can be associated with scribal training, which may of course include attempts to learn a new script; to understand and speak Aramaic or Hebrew, as might be true of some whose first language was Greek, need not necessarily imply writing ability. This ostracon may then recall the situation of bilingualism – or only partial bilingualism – illustrated in a famous Greek letter from Soumaios to the officers Jonathes (Jonathan) son of Beianus and Masbala. The letter (P. Yadin 52) commands delivery of wands and citrons 'to the camp of the Jews' (for the feast of Tabernacles); here the sender excuses himself for having had the letter written in Greek (*hellenesti*), because it was impossible to write *hebraesti* – in Aramaic or Hebrew, or in the script used by Jews for these languages.[41] This apology is part of the letter-text written by the sender's secretary, for the closing formula 'Soumaios. Farewell.' is written in a different hand. The sender was perhaps not Simeon ben Kosiba, but in any case at the time when he had to send the letter, no doubt in haste, he could not find a writer, Jewish or gentile, who could use the 'Hebrew' script; and he knew that the recipients, although they might not understand the Greek script, would have at hand someone who did. The importance attached to the message is underlined by another letter, now in Aramaic, from a Simeon (it is disputed whether the writer is Bar Kokhba and whether he is identical with the Soumaios of the Greek letter) to Judah son of Manasseh in Kiriath Arbaia, noting that 'I have sent you two asses' for the transport of palms and citrons, which will be provided by Jonathan and Masbala, 'to the camp'.[42]

In this third phase, then, sensational finds of letters and documents began to illuminate both the extent and the operation of the realm of Bar Kokhba. It clearly included, at least, a good part of the hill-country of Judaea, from Beth-ther in the north-west south-eastwards in the region of Bethlehem to Herodium on the heights above the Dead Sea, nearby Tekoa, and En-gedi further south on the Dead Sea coast, and also territory inland to the east and south of Hebron, including Cephar Bericha, Ziph, and Aristobulias. Bar Kokhba will have controlled much of the realm assigned to David in Israelite tradition when he was king of Judah in Hebron (II Sam. 2:1–11). The glimpses of his administration in detail which the documents permit are consistent with Cassius Dio's statement that the rising had been prepared well in advance (*History* 69.12, 2–3). The publication and discussion of the letters and documents and other finds has of course extended far into the fourth phase of archaeology, beginning in 1967.

Phase IV
One immediate result of the new situation after the war of 1967 was an archaeological survey of the area of ancient Judah, by M. Kochavi, and the Judaean wilderness, by P. Bar-Adon, under the aegis of the Association for the Archaeological Survey of Israel. Particular initiatives included the preparation of Herodium as a tourist site (1968–9), supervised by Gideon Foerster. Foerster also uncovered tunnels and cisterns which eventually proved, as shown in new excavations conducted by Ehud Netzer, to form a system mainly dating from the time of the Bar Kokhba war.[43]

Khirbet el-Yehud at Bittir was also the subject of renewed investigation, undertaken by D. Ussishkin.[44] The site lies outside and immediately south of the 1949 border of Israel, which runs towards Jerusalem along the main valley here. Ussishkin found among other things yet further slingstones, and adaptations of the walls, bastions and towers on top of the hill were now dated to the period of the war.

Y. Hirschfeld later studied the site of En-gedi, and it became possible to put together his archaeological findings with inferences drawn from the cave discoveries.[45] Roman recapture of En-gedi will probably have been imminent when caves accessible from the town were occupied. These included the Cave of Letters in Nahal Hever (Wadi Habra) and the Cave of Horror, on the southern side of the same wadi, where the occupants perished.[46] These caves had been subject to a siege, as shown by Roman camp-sites on top of the cliffs above them. In Nahal David, nearer to En-gedi, the occupants of the Cave of the Pool appear to have survived, but in two other caves occupants left traces behind, in one case (the Har Yishai cave) a purse containing money and two Greek documents, the record of a property transaction or loan and what may be a private letter; it seems likely that the owner was killed or enslaved.[47] En-gedi itself appears to have been largely abandoned after the rising.[48] Eventually, however, the scene changed again. Although En-gedi had suffered in the repression, it was by Eusebius's time 'a very large village of Jews', as he puts it.[49]

Two further aspects of documentation, now in an extended sense, stand out in this phase. The first is the study of refuge caves, the archaeological response eventually made to the challenge presented by their importance in Cassius Dio and rabbinic texts. Their familiarity in the second century was indeed clear from these texts, for the word *mahabo*, 'hiding-place', used for David's refuges in the wilderness ravines near Ziph in I Sam. 23:23, recurs from the second century onwards, in the Mishnah and elsewhere, in discussion of the plight of women who are sheltering in hiding-places. Thus R. Meir notes that, for a woman in a hiding-place, menstruation may be delayed by fear (Mishnah, Niddah iv 7). The rabbinic narrative of the siege of Bethar comparably envisages entry being made from outside through an underground passage (Aramaic *biba*, 'duct', in Talmud Yerushalmi, Taanith iv 8, 68d, foot). Refuges of the kind mentioned by Dio, made with warfare as well as shelter in view, have been amply attested archaeologically during this post-1967 phase, commonly but not always underneath settlements, as in the excavated village of Ethri (Kh. Umm es-Suweid), perhaps the Caphethra (Caphar Ethra) of Josephus (*Jewish War* ii 552), in the Shephelah north-east of Beth Gubrin.[50] A hundred and twenty-five such sites in Judaea had been counted by the beginning of the twenty-first century.[51] They can now be associated with Dio's reference to the final Roman capture not only of 'fifty forts' (*phrouria*) but also of 'nine-hundred and eighty-five villages' (Cassius Dio, *History* 69.14, 1). Yet they may also help to document the extent of Bar Kokhba's realm or influence.

A second aspect of documentation is the witness offered by finds in the refuge caves to the daily life of those who used them during the war. One important category is formed by written texts. Letters and documents have been noted already. There are also, however, copies of biblical texts. Thus among the finds in the Wadi Murabba'at caves were Hebrew fragments of Genesis, Exodus, Numbers (possibly all from a single Torah scroll), Deuteronomy, and Isaiah. Extensive remains of a Hebrew scroll of the twelve Minor Prophets were in a small cave near the four principal caves investigated. The scroll had perhaps been deliberately laid near a burial.[52]

Particularly important has been a fragmented Greek scroll of the Minor Prophets found by Bedouin. This scroll was received by the Palestine Archaeological (Rockefeller) Museum in August 1952, in the same lot as the Hebrew letter to Simeon ben Kosiba mentioned already.[53] The archaeological recovery of further fragments of the same scroll from the Cave of Horror in Nahal Hever in 1961 showed that the scroll came from this cave.[54] After a fresh search there by archaeologists the discovery of still further fragments of the scroll, from the books of Nahum and Zechariah, was announced in March 2021.[55]

The Greek Minor Prophets scroll from the Cave of Horror has received intensive consideration ever since 1963, when D. Barthélemy, who had been working on it since it entered the Rockefeller Museum, published a full discussion of the significance of the translation, together with a provisional edition of the text.[56] The text was fully edited in 1990, and was tentatively assigned on the basis of the handwriting to the later first century BCE.[57] Like some Jewish Greek biblical manuscripts from early Roman Egypt, it gives the divine name YHWH in palaeo-Hebrew characters. The Greek version in the scroll represents not the widely attested Septuagint or Old Greek translation, going back to the third or second century BCE, but a revision, an attempt to give a close rendition of the Hebrew biblical text known to the translator. Barthélemy viewed it as a hitherto unknown precursor of the probably second-century Jewish Greek translation of Aquila, famous for its particularly close representation of Hebrew. The Cave of Horror scroll can be compared not only with Aquila and other probably second-century Jewish Greek biblical translations, those known as Theodotion and Symmachus, but also with some translations corrected towards a Hebrew text which have entered the textual tradition of the Septuagint, having replaced the Old Greek in the passages or books concerned. This find gave a new attestation of the revision by Jews of their Greek translations of the bible in the pre-Christian period, and the currency of such revised texts in Judaea. It is a document of the history of the bible, as well as a document of Jewish life in En-gedi and its neighbourhood in the early second century.

At the end of the archaeological journey from exploration to documentation one may remember one humbler graffito from Herodium: the drawing of a donkey (see Figure 3.2 overleaf), the beast of burden needed in Bar Kokhba's time, and without whose help the nineteenth- and early twentieth-century exploration could still hardly have taken place.[58] This graffito may or may not date from

Figure 3.2: Graffito of mule and plant, Herodium: drawing by E. Testa, *Herodion* IV, I *graffiti e gli ostraca* (Pubblicazioni dello Studium Biblicum Franciscanum, 20; Jerusalem, 1972), fig. 24b (reproduced by permission of Studium Biblicum Franciscanum Photographic Archive).

the precise period of the war, but it illustrates the means of transport in war or peace in the Judaean realm of Bar Kokhba. Two donkeys carried palm-branches and citrons for Bar Kokhba's followers. Later on, de Saulcy needed the mules of whom, describing a moment when his journey south along the Dead Sea coast reached the brink of the Wadi Murabba'at, he wrote bitterly 'these intelligent animals generally select the most dangerous and impracticable paths'.[59] The donkey stands likewise for the continuity of life after the war, despite devastation.

Within the context of the development of archaeology, the donkey's long-term presence is a reminder of other things too. One central strand in Holy Land archaeology has always been its correlation with the bible and ancient literature in interpretation of historical events. That is inevitably manifest when the Bar Kokhba war is used as a thread to trace the phases of archaeology, but the discoveries considered have been important in other concerns of archaeological work. One is the study of early settlement. That was noted in passing in connection with the first excavations of Tells, but of course caves too are classical loci for discovery of remains of prehistoric culture. Thus the Nahal Hever caves became famous, at the same time as the spectacular Bar Kokhba discoveries, for shedding new light on something quite different – the ancient culture termed Ghassulian, after the site near Jericho where pottery, household goods and weapons belonging to it were first discovered.[60] An allied archaeological concern represented by the donkey is a general interest not simply or even primarily in the discovery of documents and inscriptions, but in the whole material culture to which they belong and which the investigation is disclosing. Even so momentous an event as the war of Bar Kokhba is situated, by excavation, within a continuum of material conditions. In this way, as well as by the great finds of texts and inscriptions, archaeology educates an approach to the biblical books and the history of Jews and Christians.

Endnotes

[1] Eusebius, *Chronicle*, Olympiads 227–8, Hadrian years 16–18, corresponding to 132–6 CE; *Ecclesiastical History* iv 6, 1–4; iv 8, 1 (here quoting Justin Martyr). A selection of rabbinic texts, and the accounts by Dio and Eusebius, with extracts also from Jerome and Epiphanius, are presented in translation in Y. Yadin, *Bar Kokhba* (London, 1971), 255–9.

[2] Pioneering work by the Danish church historian Friedrich Münter, *Der jüdische Krieg unter den Kaisern Trajan und Hadrian* (Altona & Leipzig, 1821) was taken up in Germany in the histories of the Jews by I.M. Jost (1820–28) and Heinrich Graetz (1853 onwards), and in England in the history of the Jews by H.H. Milman (1830 onwards), who drew on Jost. Early nineteenth-century interest in movements for national independence favoured the topic of the Bar Kokhba war.

[3] Edward Robinson, *Biblical Researches in Palestine* (3 vols., London, 1841), i, 528–38.

[4] F. de Saulcy, *Narrative of a Journey round the Dead Sea and in the Bible Lands* (English translation, 2 vols., London, 1854), ii, 111–22.

[5] C. Warren, *Underground Jerusalem: An Account of some of the Principal Difficulties encountered in its Exploration, and the Results obtained* (London, 1876); J. Simons, *Jerusalem in the Old Testament* (Leiden, 1952), 29–30.

[6] C.R. Conder, *Palestine* (London, 1889, repr. 1891), 240.

[7] R.A.S. Macalister, *A Century of Excavation in Palestine* (2nd edn, London, 1930), 66–7, 311–13.

[8] W.F. Albright, *The Archaeology of Palestine* (1949, revised reprint Harmondsworth, 1960), 9–10.

[9] A. Mazar, 'Israeli Archaeology: Achievements and the Current State of Research', *Strata: Bulletin of the Anglo-Israel Archaeological Society* 29 (2011), 9–22.

[10] 'Academic Staff of the Hebrew University', in *The Hebrew University of Jerusalem 1925–1950* (Jerusalem, 1950), 187–8.

[11] Robinson, *Biblical Researches in Palestine*, ii, 4; 6–7, citing Münter; 13.

[12] G. Williams, *The Holy City: Historical, Topographical and Antiquarian Notices of Jerusalem* ([1845]; 2nd edn, 2 vols., London & Cambridge, 1849), ii, 205–14.

[13] G. Dalman, *Sacred Sites and Ways* (English translation by P.P. Levertoff; London, 1935), 18.

[14] J. Germer-Durand, 'Épigraphie Palestinienne', *Revue Biblique* 3 (1894), 613–14.

[15] A.P. Stanley, *Sinai and Palestine* (repr. London, 1910), 120–21.

[16] A. Trollope, *Autobiography* ([1883] repr. London, 1923), 106–17 (from chapters vi–vii), and *The Bertrams* (1859; repr. Gloucester, 1986), chapter ix 'Miss Todd's Picnic'.

[17] C.R. Conder, *Tent Work in Palestine* (2 vols., London, 1879), ii, 124–37.

[18] G.A. Smith, *Historical Geography of the Holy Land* (4th edn, 1896, repr. London, 1910), 271.

[19] Myriam Harry, *La petite fille de Jérusalem* (Paris, 1914), 140.

[20] C. Clermont-Ganneau, *Archaeological Researches in Palestine* (2 vols., London, 1896–9), i, 463–9.

[21] E.M. Smallwood, *The Jews under Roman Rule* (corrected reprint, Leiden, 1981), 447–8, n.73; L. Kadman, *The Coins of Aelia Capitolina* (Jerusalem, 1956), 21; 81, no.1.

[22] Kathleen M. Kenyon, *Archaeology in the Holy Land* (4th edn, London, 1979), 330.

[23] Germer-Durand, 'Épigraphie Palestinienne', 614, citing Josephus, *Jewish War* v 269–70.

[24] T.E. Dowling, 'Interesting Coins of Pella and Bittir', *Palestinian Exploration Fund Quarterly Statements* 1907, 295–7.

[25] M. Noth, *The History of Israel* (revised English translation; London, 1960), 453.

[26] Macalister, *A Century of Excavation in Palestine*, 56–60; E. Brandenburg, *Die Felsarchitektur bei Jerusalem* (Kirchhain, 1926), 73–4 (on an artificial cave of uncertain purpose).

[27] J.T. Milik in P. Benoit, J.T. Milik & R. de Vaux, *Les grottes de Murabba'at* (Discoveries in the Judaean Desert 2, 2 vols., Oxford, 1961), i, 156.

[28] Milik in Benoit, Milik & de Vaux, *Les grottes de Murabba'at*, i, 160; Hannah M. Cotton & Ada Yardeni, *Aramaic, Hebrew and Greek Documentary Texts from Nahal Hever and Other Sites* (Discoveries in the Judaean Desert 27, Oxford, 1997), 5, 253–4; Jerome, *Letter* 108.11, on Abraham taking leave of his visitors.

[29] Y. Yadin, J.C. Greenfield, A. Yardeni & B.A. Levine, *The Documents from the Bar Kokhba Period in the Cave of Letters: Hebrew, Aramaic and Nabataean-*

Aramaic Papyri (Judean Desert Studies 3, Jerusalem, 2002), 237–348; 351–66 (H.M. Cotton, 'Greek Letters').

[30] P. Yadin 49, in Yadin, Greenfield, Yardeni & Levine, *The Documents from the Bar Kokhba Period in the Cave of Letters: Hebrew, Aramaic and Nabataean-Aramaic Papyri*, 279–86.

[31] Y. Aharoni, 'Expedition B – The Cave of Horror', *Israel Exploration Journal* 12 (1962), 186–99 (187).

[32] Y. Yadin in N. Avigad, Y. Aharoni, P. Bar-Adon & Y. Yadin, *Judaean Desert Caves* (reprinted from *Israel Exploration Journal* 11–12 [1961–2], 2 vols., Jerusalem, 1961–2), i, 36–52, and ii, 227–34; Yadin, *Bar Kokhba*, 28–171; S. Dar, 'The Search for Scrolls in the Judaean Desert Caves in the Years 1950–60 – an Archaeological Memoir', *Strata* 28 (2010), 141–57.

[33] Aharoni, 'Expedition B – The Cave of Horror', 187; statement by Israel Hasson, director of the Israel Antiquities Authority, as reported in the London *Daily Telegraph*, 17 March 2021, 17.

[34] Cotton & Yardeni, *Aramaic, Hebrew and Greek Documentary Texts from Nahal Hever and Other Sites*, 1–2 (R. de Vaux on 30 September 1952 announces the arrival of texts including a Hebrew letter addressed to Bar Kokhba), 103–104.

[35] Obituary of Merton Fink (192/1–2015) by his daughter, Judith Field, in the *Jewish Chronicle*, 24 July 2015; he used 'Finch' as a nom de plume.

[36] Papyrus denoted Mur. 24, edited with translation and commentary by J.T. Milik in Benoit, Milik & de Vaux, *Les grottes de Murabba'at*, i, 122–34.

[37] Yadin, Greenfield, Yardeni & Levine, *The Documents from the Bar Kokhba Period in the Cave of Letters: Hebrew, Aramaic and Nabataean-Aramaic Papyri*, 308–309.

[38] N. de Lange, *Origen and the Jews* (Cambridge, 1976), 33–4; for fuller discussion of the argument on Bar Kokhba's title, see W. Horbury, *Jewish War under Trajan and Hadrian* (Cambridge, 2014), 355–62.

[39] L. Mildenberg, *The Coinage of the Bar Kokhba War* (Aarau, 1984).

[40] Benoit, Milik & de Vaux, *Les grottes de Murabba'at*, i, nos. 10–11 (skin), 73, 78–80 (ostraca).

[41] H.M. Cotton, 'Greek Letters', in Yadin, Greenfield, Yardeni & Levine (edd.), *Hebrew, Aramaic and Nabatean-Aramaic Papyri*, 351–66.

[42] Yadin, *Bar Kokhba*, 128–32; P. Yadin 57, in Yadin, Greenfield, Yardeni & Levine, *The Documents from the Bar Kokhba Period in the Cave of Letters: Hebrew, Aramaic and Nabataean-Aramaic Papyri*, 322–8.

[43] For these excavations in the setting of Netzer's work as a whole see D.M. Jacobson, 'E. Netzer and Herodian Archaeology', *Strata* 30 (2012), 9–36; on the tunnels, with plans, D. Raviv, 'Hiding Complexes in Fortified Sites of the Bar Kokhba War', *Journal of Jewish Studies* 74 (2023), 273–302 (290–92).

[44] D. Ussishkin, 'Archaeological Soundings at Betar, Bar Kochba's Last Stronghold', *Tel Aviv* 20 (1993), 66–97.

[45] Y. Hirschfeld, with contributions by R. Amir and others, *The En-Gedi Excavations II: Final Report (1996–2002)* (Jerusalem, 2007).

[46] Yadin, *Bar-Kokhba*, 31, 46–8.

[47] N. Avigad, 'Expedition A – Nahal David', *Israel Exploration Journal* 12 (1962), 169–83 (181); R. Porat, H. Eshel & A. Frumkin, 'Finds from the Bar Kokhba Revolt from Two Caves at En Gedi', *Palestine Exploration Quarterly* 139 (2007), 35–54.

[48] Hirschfeld, *The En-Gedi Excavations II*, 643.

[49] R.S. Notley & Z. Safrai, *Eusebius, Onomasticon* (Boston & Leiden, 2005), 84, no. 428.

[50] B. Zissu & A. Ganor, 'Horvath 'Ethri – a Jewish Village from the Second Temple Period and the Bar Kokhba Revolt in the Judean Foothills', *Journal of Jewish Studies* 60 (2009), 90–136.

[51] A. Kloner & B. Zissu, 'Hiding Complexes in Judaea: An Archaeological and Geographical Update on the Area of the Bar Kokhba Revolt', in P. Schäfer (ed.), *The Bar Kokhba War Reconsidered* (Tübingen, 2003), 181–216.

[52] Benoit, Milik & de Vaux, *Les grottes de Murabba'at*, i, nos. 1–3, 88, and 50; ii, Plates 19–21, 56–73.

[53] See n.29, above.

[54] Aharoni, 'Expedition B – The Cave of Horror', 197–8 and Plate 32B.

[55] *Daily Telegraph* report cited in n.33, above.

[56] D. Barthélemy, *Les devanciers d'Aquila* (Leiden, 1963).

[57] E. Tov, *The Greek Minor Prophets Scroll from Nahal Hever (8HevXIIgr)* (Discoveries in the Judaean Desert, 8; Oxford, 1990).

[58] E. Testa, *Herodion IV: I graffiti e gli ostraca* (Jerusalem, 1972), 39, no. 24; 41, fig. 24b; 111. Donkeys figure in ancient anti-Christian polemic, but it seems debatable whether the drawing is indeed an anti-Christian sketch, as Testa suggested in connection with Bar Kokhba's harsh treatment of Christians.

[59] de Saulcy, *Narrative of a Journey round the Dead Sea and in the Bible Lands*, i, 170.

[60] Kenyon, *Archaeology in the Holy Land*, 51–64.

4
CHRISTIANITY IN ANCIENT JEWISH TRADITION

Non-Jews had asked what Jewish tradition has to say about Christianity at least since the second century, when the pagan Celsus rebutted Christian claims with information from a Jewish source.[1] Still, gentile inquiry into Christianity in Jewish tradition entered a new phase among Christians in thirteenth-century western Europe. Intensive Christian Hebrew study in the twelfth century had already meant that Christian recourse to Jewish knowledge and teaching went on side-by-side with attempts to show that Jews were unreasonable in adhering to their own ancestral tradition. The thirteenth century then developed Christian exploration of Jewish writings, now in the context of large-scale efforts to commend the faith of Christ to those who dwelt among Christians but were reckoned as unbelievers or heretics. Thus the conversion or segregation of Muslims and Jews were promoted, and Jews began to wear the badge decreed at the Fourth Lateran Council of 1215; but repressive measures which would end with expulsions of communities were matched by literary research.

This research could mix the ludicrous with the oppressive and the tragic; but it was largely through its preoccupation with Jewish tradition on Christianity that it laid the foundation – so I would argue – for later study of ancient Judaism and early Christianity in general, on the basis of a wide range of Jewish literature in Hebrew, Aramaic and Greek. This broader approach was encouraged in the thirteenth century, as concern with remarks on Christianity in Jewish literature became entwined with interest in the topic of 'Christianity in Jewish tradition' understood in a different sense: Christianity as, at least in the eyes of the Christian beholder, somehow implicit in ancient Jewish tradition.

The atmosphere of thirteenth-century research is evoked by the development of the town of Cambridge in the years before Jews were exiled from it. The swift expansion of the new university of Cambridge under Henry III and Edward I coincided with the last sixty years of mediaeval Jewish residence in Cambridge.[2] The Cambridge Jews were obliged to leave for Huntingdon in 1275, being one of four communities banished at the request of the queen-mother, Eleanor of Provence, from her four dower-towns. These local expulsions anticipated by fifteen years the exile of the Jews from the whole realm, ordered by Edward I in 1290. All Saints' Passage, at the corner of which the Selwyn Divinity School now stands facing St John's College, was known in the Middle Ages as Jews' Lane, Vicus Iudaeorum. It runs roughly east to west (see Map 4.1, opposite), from the present-day Bridge Street and Sidney Street across to St John's Street. All Saints' Church, then standing in the old churchyard divided from the Divinity School by a branch of All Saints' Passage, was known as All Saints Jewry, All Saints in Iudaismo. The streets around the Divinity School will accordingly have formed a focus of Jewish–Christian intermingling. Thus the Jewish scholar-magnate Benjamin of Cambridge, at the beginning of the century, has been judged a likely participant in the lively controversial exchanges between individual Jews and Christians which figure in mediaeval Jewish apologetic writings, and which show how Christian interest in Jewish tradition was matched by Jewish knowledge of the New Testament and Christian literature and legend.[3] In 1266, gentile awareness of the Jewish community here is indicated by the insertion of a record of their suffering in the Barons' War into a local source, the Old Book of the Archdeacon of Ely: a contemporary note in the calendar of the book, among one or two entries relating to the Barons' War, reads '12th August: Slaying of Jews at Cambridge' (*Interfectio Iudeorum apud Cant'*).[4] To turn to less sorrowful matters, Cambridge Jews will have been among those sought out as teachers of Hebrew by Christians; as Roger Bacon wrote in Oxford, later in the thirteenth century, it's no trouble to

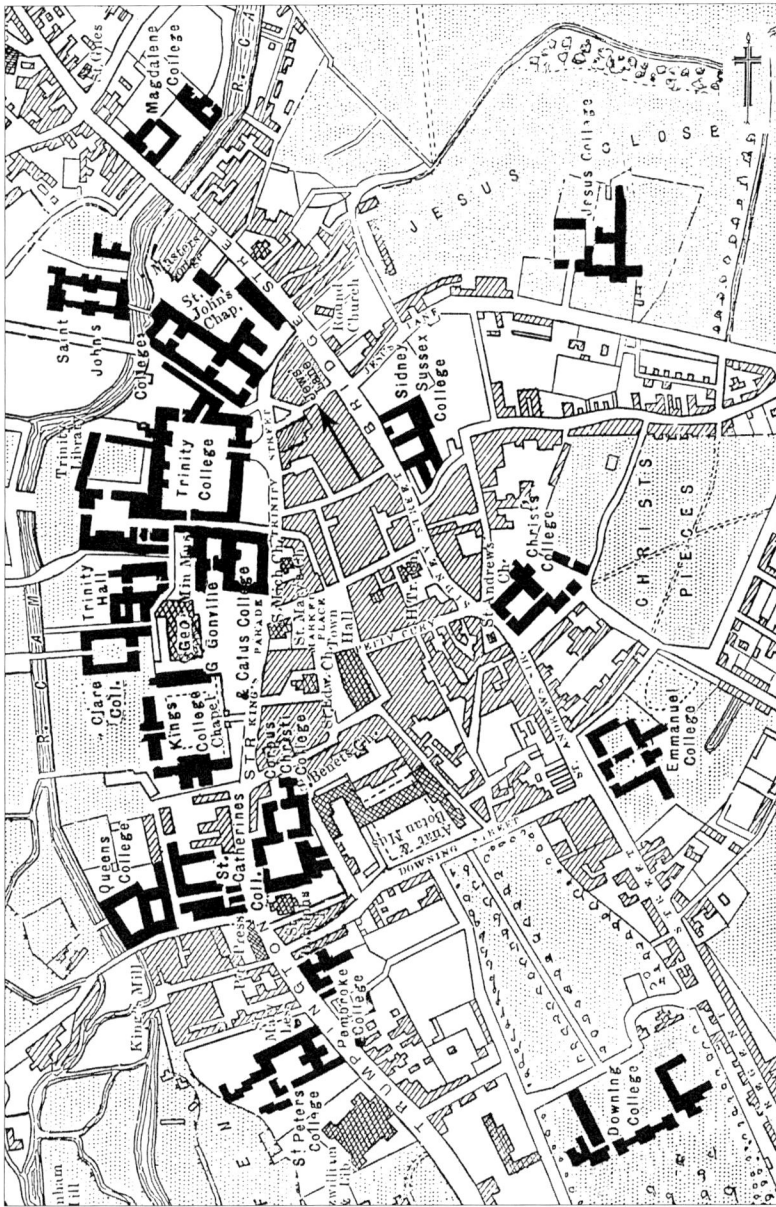

Map 4.1: Cambridge (1840 map adapted); the mediaeval Jews' Lane (Vicus Iudaeorum), later All Saints' Passage, is shown by the arrow above Bridge Street.

learn Hebrew, because everywhere you can find Jews to teach you (*Compendium Studii Philosophiae*, vi; ed. J.S. Brewer, 1859, p. 434).[5] Yet although intermingling clearly persisted, it had to contend with an increasingly unfavourable atmosphere. This gradual change was symbolized in Cambridge by the establishment of a new Christian institution at either end of Jews' Lane.

The impact of this development upon the Jews has been shown especially with respect to St John's Hospital, the predecessor of St John's College, founded about 1200 opposite the west end of Jews' Lane.[6] More important when literary inquiry is in view, however, was development a little later near the other end of Jews' Lane. This arose indirectly from the arrival of the mendicant friars in England in the 1220s. When the Friars Minor, the Franciscans or Greyfriars, came to Cambridge in 1224 they settled in a Crown property let to the bailiffs, on or near the present Guildhall site, some way south of Jews' Lane. This house had once belonged to the Jew Benjamin, probably the scholar just mentioned, and in it there was said to have been a synagogue – perhaps an indication of more widely dispersed Jewish residence in Cambridge, although this has been disputed. Later on, however, the Greyfriars built a new house and a spacious church on the site now occupied by Sidney Sussex College. The west front of their church faced Bridge Street at the corner of Jesus Lane, to use present-day names, and was therefore nearly opposite the east end of Jews' Lane – All Saints' Passage. In 1267 a Christian fugitive from the sheriff's officers, being spotted in Jews' Lane, fled for refuge 'right into the church of the Friars Minor'.[7]

By 1267, therefore, Jews' Lane led from St John's Hospital at one end to the Greyfriars at the other, and the focus of Jewish residence was in a sense being squeezed between the two. Cambridge Greyfriars who took part in action or writing *adversus Iudaeos* in the thirteenth century included the theologian Roger Marston, and, later on, Duns Scotus, who threw his weight behind aspirations for large-scale Jewish baptisms in the near future. A Jewish view on the Greyfriars as neighbours can then perhaps be inferred from an incident which took place in 1277, probably in Northampton, where the Jew Samson was detained by the sheriff as having allegedly donned a Franciscan habit and preached a mimic and subversive sermon.[8] Cambridge Jews may accordingly have echoed a thirteenth-century northern French Jewish comment on Deut. 32:21 'I will move them to jealousy with those that are not a people – these are the Cordeliers [Greyfriars] and Jacobins [Blackfriars] who oppress Israel.'[9]

It was in an age when coexistence persisted despite tension, therefore, that thirteenth-century Christian knowledge of Jewish literature was gained – from books, from gentile teaching, and sometimes from converse with Jews. Now in the ancient world Jews and Christians had commonly shared both the Greek language and the venerable Greek biblical version known as the Septuagint (not to speak of the Aramaic common to Jews and Christians in Syria and Mesopotamia). In the mediaeval west, by contrast, Greek was unfamiliar, and the Latin of biblical reading and exposition in the church stood over against the Hebrew of Jewish biblical reading and rabbinic tradition, despite the importance for both Jews and Christians of vernaculars like French.

Nevertheless, the ancient Jewish writings discussed by thirteenth-century Christians were not simply those which in Latin translation had become part of western Christian tradition, such as the Old Testament apocrypha and related works, the New Testament itself, which can largely be classified as Jewish literature, or the writings of Philo and Josephus. These were known together with some of the references to Jews in the classical authors, thanks not least to the mediaeval relish for Roman satire and epigram. Beyond the limits of these more or less familiar writings, material preserved only in Greek was being explored again, and systematic notice was now also being taken of works which had been handed down in the Jewish community in Hebrew and Aramaic, the encyclopaedic Babylonian Talmud above all. This vast composition, edited in the eastern diaspora perhaps mainly in the sixth century, is later as a whole than the shorter and less authoritative Palestinian Talmud compiled in Galilee. It comprises a great body of traditional learning in the halakhah or 'walking', the study of how to walk in all the circumstances of life according to Torah, and the haggadah or 'telling', the refreshing garden of pomegranates which opens up vistas into narratives of moral and theological teaching and legendary lore. Moreover, Christians gained some familiarity with later Jewish authors who interpreted biblical and rabbinic writings, especially Rashi the great eleventh-century commentator and Maimonides the twelfth-century philosophical systematizer of law. Thirteenth-century examples include commentaries ascribed to William Milton, a Greyfriar who taught in Cambridge, which use Rashi and other Jewish comment;[10] and the argument of William of Auvergne, of Paris, which took up the defence of the reasonableness of the laws of sacrifice set out in the *Guide to the Perplexed* of Maimonides.

To stand back from their studies for a moment, one line which they followed is visibly continued in modern biblical and theological inquiry. It embraces the learning of Greek and Hebrew, and Aramaic and Arabic too, for the sake of access both to the original texts of the bible – awareness of defects in Latin biblical translations is exemplified in Hebrew–Latin copies of biblical texts from thirteenth-century England – and to the great scholars who had written in Greek and the Semitic languages. To quote Roger Bacon again:

> Many books of the sacred text are not translated: two books of the Maccabees which I know to be extant in Greek [probably 3–4 Maccabees], and many other books of many prophets cited in the books of Kings and Chronicles [perhaps an allusion to the Greek Lives of the Prophets] … The Latins are lacking innumerable books of Hebrew and Greek expositors, like Origen … and other most noble doctors both in Hebrew and in Greek; and the church is asleep, for she does nothing in this area … (*Compendium Studii Philosophiae*, viii; ed. Brewer, p. 474)

This line of thought led to the remarkable series of windows planned for the library of St Albans Abbey in the fifteenth century, in which, alongside the great doctors in other fields of learning, both Rashi and Maimonides were depicted in stained glass.[11] In another line of thought, however, Hebrew and Arabic are learned especially for the sake of missionary work, and their study becomes bound up with 'the politics of conversion', to adopt a phrase applied to mission in a later period by Christopher Clark.[12] This motive intertwines with the other, and both together led in 1312 to the decree of the council of Vienne prescribing university study of Hebrew, Greek, Aramaic and Arabic – a decree which then had long-term benefits as an authority which could be appealed to whenever Hebrew and Greek study were revived.

At the heart of thirteenth-century study, given these intertwining motives, were the Jewish–Christian disputations held by royal command at Paris in 1240 and Barcelona in 1263. The differing Christian arguments presented on these two occasions roughly correspond to the two alternative interpretations of the title of this lecture. In 1240 the Talmud and associated writings were condemned, partly because they were held to give a misleading or blasphemous account of Christian origins; here Christianity as explicitly mentioned in Jewish tradition was a main concern. In 1263, on the other hand, it was urged that these same Jewish writings, if properly understood, support a Christian interpretation of the Hebrew scriptures; here it was being suggested that Christianity is somehow implicit in Jewish tradition.

This thirteenth-century development of scholarship and apologetic has often been described. Here I should simply like to draw attention to the range of writings brought together in this setting for inquiry into Christianity in ancient Jewish tradition, in both the senses outlined above. In this connection England has sometimes been considered separately from continental Europe, and Greek separately from Hebrew, but here I am treating relevant work, English or continental, on Jewish writings in Greek or

Hebrew, as part of the attestation of one single western European movement of inquiry. A short list of five newly considered books then emerges; the giant among them, the Talmud, will be noticed twice.

The public examination of the Talmud in the university of Paris was initiated in June 1239, the date of letters from pope Gregory IX addressed to the kings and archbishops of France, England, Spain and Portugal. A covering letter to William of Auvergne, bishop of Paris, mentioned already as a reader of Maimonides' *Guide to the Perplexed*, shows that these letters were sent in the first instance to him, by the hand of Nicholas Donin.[13] Nicholas was a Jew of La Rochelle who had accepted baptism and took part in the instigation of these proceedings, but appears to have been influenced well before his baptism by inner-Jewish criticisms of the seeming irrationality of parts of the Talmud – criticisms possibly stimulated by Maimonides, but in any case reflecting the contemporary emphasis on reason. It is tempting to suspect some convergence between Nicholas' views and the Maimonidean outlook of William of Auvergne, who prized the literal sense of scripture and its concord with reason, and seems to have eschewed spiritual interpretation of the sacrifices as types of the Christian dispensation.[14] An understanding of rabbinic teaching as issuing in part from Mosaic tradition which foreshadowed the gospel, on the lines followed later at Barcelona, would hardly have fitted easily into these interpretative options.

The possible contribution of a rationalizing trend in biblical exegesis to negative criticism of the Talmud should not be overrated, yet the letters to the kings and archbishops sketch a view which well suits contemporary reaffirmation of the reasonableness of the Pentateuchal law in its literal sense. The letters state first of all that (as it is asserted) Jews are not content with the divine law published through Moses in writing, but wholly pass it over because they consider the Talmud as another law delivered to Moses orally and preserved unwritten (as they falsely affirm) until the time of those whom they call wise men and scribes [cf. Matt. 23:34]; these reduced it to a written form which vastly exceeds the bible in length, and includes shameful invective. Since the Talmud is said to be the main cause of the Jews' persistence in unbelief (the letters continue), all their books are to be seized on the first sabbath day of the coming Lent.

This command seems to have been honoured only in France. The proceedings which ensued in Paris from 1240 onwards included examination of the books by regent doctors of Paris; a debate before the queen-mother Blanche, related in a lively Hebrew narrative; the public burning of the Talmud and other books; and a confirmation of the fittingness of burning in a letter of Innocent IV in 1244, which identifies the Talmud with 'traditions of the elders' of the kind condemned in the gospel for frustrating the law of Moses (Matt. 15:1-9), and describes it as a large book containing blasphemies and fables. The case was reopened at Jewish request in 1247, on the ground that the Talmud might be considered indispensable for Jewish observance of the biblical law (the relevant letter of Innocent IV acknowledged a divinely-ordained duty of tolerating the Jews in their ancestral law); but the sentence of burning was reaffirmed in 1248 by the papal legate (the Paris chancellor Odo of Châteauroux), on the advice of the university and the bishop of Paris. The aftermath included a continuing series of confiscations of Jewish books in various places.

In the present context the most significant outcome of these proceedings was the composition of a lengthy Latin work called *Extracts from the Talmud*.[15] It was probably not the first collection of its kind, for something similar is likely to have fuelled the twelfth-century attack on the Talmud by Peter the Venerable; and it can broadly be compared with contemporary Latin translations of the Qur'an made for the purposes of Christian apologetic. It includes an introduction to the Talmud and much closely translated material from the Babylonian Talmud, Rashi, and other sources, and was widely copied; but the very numerous extracts are passages thought open to censure, and they are brought together, not without reason but still to baneful effect, with opprobrious mediaeval Jewish terms for Christian institutions. This collection therefore ominously foreshadows the many later collections of ostensibly blameworthy Talmudic passages which have been issued in order to injure the Jewish community.

Nevertheless, it also presents material which has been central in serious consideration of Christianity as mentioned in Jewish tradition. Thus the *Extracts* quote passages (Sanh. 67a, Gittin 57b) on Jesus as the son of Pandera – an allegation known independently through the second-century Celsus, cited by Origen – and on his punishment in Gehenna – a passage where he is treated as one of the great enemies of Israel. Other and perhaps more important passages were also translated, notably those on the condemnation of Jesus for sorcery and false prophecy (Sanh. 43a), and on his erring from the right path after he had been harshly treated by his teacher (Sanh. 107b). The Jewish spokesman, Jehiel of Paris, argued that another Jesus was intended, given the widespread attestation of the name among Jews in antiquity. In the Hebrew narrative of debate, mentioned already, he is said to have urged his case by what was a bold argument to use in the presence of the queen-mother: not all children called Louis are the same, and not all of them are kings of France. Although the case for mistaken identity is strong in one or two instances, a general application of it is made unlikely by correspondence between some of these passages and early pagan and Jewish comments on Christianity preserved in Greek sources.

To move to a second item in the list of books, the Paris examiners also took note of a Hebrew text of Toledoth Jeshu. This legend-like Jewish account of the life of Christ and the rise of Christianity was current in a proliferation of mediaeval forms, but is essentially from the ancient world. The text which they saw in the 1240s had an opening precisely corresponding to that found in a copy in a surviving Hebrew manuscript of later date.

Echoes of these proceedings seem discernible in England. One possible but uncertain link between the Paris debate and Cambridge is the Franciscan scholar William Milton or Middleton, mentioned already. He came to the Cambridge Greyfriars to teach perhaps in the 1250s. With fair probability, he has been conjecturally identified with the Franciscan 'brother William of Meliton', one of the Paris masters in theology named as advisers in the 1248 legatine sentence on the Talmud.[16] The work of William, the Paris master, included editorial responsibility for the *Summa* of Alexander of Hales (died 1245); here Maimonides is cited, but the Talmud is regarded as a book containing blasphemies.

An echo of the 1240 proceedings is connected with a Franciscan Paris teacher of a later generation, John Peckham, who became archbishop of Canterbury in 1279; he appears to have begun his first period of residence in the university of Paris (where later on he was the teacher of Roger Marston) in his youth in the 1240s.[17] His knowledge of the Talmud trials then seems not unlikely to have played a part in the issue of a papal letter of 1286, from Honorius IV to the archbishops of Canterbury and York, on the Talmud and Jewish prayers.[18] The letter repeats arguments current in the 1240s from the papal letters of 1230 and 1244; the Talmud was composed with mischievous fraud, it contains abominations and falsehoods, the published law of Moses is postponed to it, and by it Jews are driven from the way of truth. The names of John Peckham and perhaps also William Milton thus suggest that the Paris proceedings left traces in England. These traces would correspond to indications from other countries of the widespread impact of the Paris trial, which will have strengthened the impetus not only of propaganda against Jews, but also of existing inquiry into Jewish literature.

In England this inquiry had of course embraced the Hebrew biblical text, as the bilingual biblical manuscripts noted already testify; but Josephus and the tenth-century Hebrew book of Josippon (based indirectly on Josephus) figure in an English episode which seems to presage the Paris trial, half absurdly yet not without a touch of menace. The little that Josephus himself seems to have written on Christianity gave his Christian reader Origen, in the third century, the impression that the Jewish historian did not accept the messiahship of Jesus; but then Eusebius of Caesarea, at the beginning of the fourth century, quotes in his *Ecclesiastical History* (i 11, 7) a laudatory paragraph on Christ from Josephus' *Antiquities* (xviii 63–4), in the treatment of Pilate's governorship. This largely or wholly inauthentic 'testimony' of Josephus to Christ was well-known in Latin in the mediaeval west, through Jerome and through the Christian compilation from Josephus current under the name of Hegesippus (ii 12). It was quoted accordingly by twelfth-century authors in apologetic writing, including that directed against Jews.

Now Gerald of Wales, having himself just quoted the testimony, goes on to say that Jews unjustifiably claim that it was never found in their Hebrew books.[19] Yet (he adds) Robert of Cricklade, prior of the canons of St Frideswide's at Oxford in the second part of the twelfth century, was regarded with some favour by Jews because he was not ignorant of Hebrew; they therefore acceded to his request when he wrote to all the English cities and towns with Jewish communities in order to ask for copies of Josephus in Hebrew. In two of these copies, according to Gerald, the testimony was found entire, but it appeared to have been just recently erased; in the others it seemed never to have been there. Robert evidently saw Hebrew books. They will have been copies not of Josephus, but of Josippon. In much of the textual tradition of Josippon there is no mention of the founder of Christianity, but in a possibly interpolated passage in one form of the text Jesus figures as the principal flatterer of the emperor Caligula, with echoes also of a form of Toledoth Jeshu. This adventurous narrative thereby likens the Christ-cult to the imperial cult, and may ultimately derive from the Jews of late antiquity.[20] In another branch of the text there is a much shorter summary passage, again recalling Toledoth Jeshu, on the wonders worked by Christ until the Pharisees overcame him. A passage on Christianity in either of these forms would in any case have been judiciously erased within the Jewish community from the two copies in which it occurred, before they were submitted to Robert. The end of Gerald's

story is that Robert summoned the Jews of Oxford, who lived of
course on his doorstep in what is now St Aldate's, and on the basis
of these erasures convicted them of malice and uncharitableness
towards the faith of Christ.

After this story has been seasoned with salt, it still seems likely
that Robert knew some Hebrew and obtained Jewish copies of
Josippon; it is not even impossible that he should have summoned
Jews to a public reproof. The method and outcome of his inquiry into
Jewish transmission of Josephus would then have foreshadowed the
Paris Talmud trial. Yet he also made a real if ludicrous attempt at the
problem of Josephus on Christianity, which still engages students
of Christian origins; moreover, his story is an early indication of the
currency of a form of Josippon including a narrative of Christ. The
Greek Josephus and the Hebrew Josippon therefore together form
the third item in the list of books. All three so far have figured in
connection with Christianity as mentioned in Jewish tradition.

With a fourth item, the Testaments of the Twelve Patriarchs,
Christianity as possibly implicit in Jewish tradition comes to the
fore. Robert Grosseteste, bishop of Lincoln from 1235 to his death
in 1253, was an austere upholder of the segregation policy, but also
a creative scholar devoted to Greek learning and concerned with
Hebrew. Thus he sponsored a Hebrew–Latin psalter with a literal
rendering of the Hebrew as an aid to study.[21] From Greek literature
he made available in Latin translation a series of texts, by authors
ranging from Aristotle to St John of Damascus. Among these were
the Testaments of the Twelve Patriarchs, a Jewish work of the second
century BCE transmitted in Greek with some Christian additions.[22] A
copy (now Cambridge University Library, MS. Ff.i.24) was obtained
for Grosseteste by John of Basingstoke, archdeacon of Leicester
and formerly resident in the Latin Duchy of Athens. About 1242
Grosseteste translated it into Latin, with the help of Nicholas the
Greek, later canon of Lincoln; and it immediately enjoyed a great
vogue, above all for its messianic prophecies – which supplement
and elaborate those ascribed in Genesis to Jacob, the father of the

Twelve. Grosseteste himself quoted the Testament of Judah (xxi 2–4) to Henry III in order to clarify the relationship of royal and ecclesiastical authority; for this Testament, in line with the tendency of the Second-Temple period, of course unequivocally sets the king beneath the High Priest: 'God gave me the kingdom', says Judah, 'and him [Levi] the priesthood, and subjected the kingdom to the priesthood.'[23]

The purpose of the translation perceived by contemporaries was not so much, however, the instruction of kings as the confutation of the Jews. The atmosphere in which the translation was made can be further sensed from literary work undertaken at the same period – still the period of the Paris Talmud trial – by another member of Grosseteste's household, William of Arundel, archdeacon of Huntingdon. A royal letter to the sheriff of Huntingdon, dated 18 June 1240, notes that the archdeacon has written 'a treatise concerning the conversion of the Jews, for the translation (*interpretatio*) of which he needs to call on the advice and help of a good Jewish translator (*interpres*)', and he is given permission accordingly to have a Jew to lodge with him.[24] Translation, in the context quoted, probably signifies translation into Hebrew. William of Arundel's treatise, as far as I know, has not been identified among extant works of this kind; but the knowledge that it was written or planned sets a question mark against the view which is sometimes urged that Grosseteste, in connection with the Testaments of the Twelve Patriarchs, was concerned simply with the confutation of the Jews, not with their conversion. It may be supposed that William's apologetic undertaking and the contemporary work on translating the Testaments could both have been discussed in Grosseteste's circle.

The royal letter is also important as suggesting that written commendation of Christianity in Hebrew was envisaged in England relatively early in the thirteenth century. Hebrew-based Christian apologetic writing is best known from Spain, towards the end of the century and later still. Perhaps the closest surviving parallel to the work planned by William of Arundel is the early fourteenth-century Hebrew apologetic and polemic of a former member of the Castilian Jewish community, Alphonsus of Valladolid, called until his baptism Abner of Burgos. Already in 1240, however, the archdeacon of Huntingdon attests the outlook associated especially though not exclusively with the Friars Preachers in Spain, above all with St Raymond of Pennafort, who not long before this time provided for Moors and Jews to be approached by friars who had learned Arabic and Hebrew (see Plate 5). Raymond's views on Hebrew were probably known in Grosseteste's household, a valued member of which was the Dominican John of St Giles, archdeacon of Oxford (and Grosseteste, writing to Raymond at the papal court to ask for his good offices over a paper on the diocese of Lincoln, says [letter 137, ed. Luard, p. 128] that he knows him well by report); but these views also probably converged in the bishop's circle with an existing zeal for languages, perhaps including the view met in Gerald of Wales that some knowledge of Hebrew eases relations with Jews.

This combination of work on the Greek Testaments of the Twelve Patriarchs and on Hebrew apologetic in the household of the bishop of Lincoln between 1240 and 1242 therefore coincides with the Paris proceedings in time, but also recalls contemporary Hebrew study in a missionary context in Spain. The Testaments of the Twelve Patriarchs, the last new item in the short list of ancient Jewish texts freshly studied in these years, lead in this connection to a second mention of the Talmud – now as a work considered, like the Testaments, to show that Christianity is not only spoken of, but also implicit, in Jewish tradition.

In later development of Spanish Hebrew study, the Barcelona Disputation of 1263, at which rabbinic literature was invoked by the Friars Preachers to support a Christian interpretation of messianic prophecy, was the forerunner not only of renewed public debate in Paris, now on these different lines,[25] but also of the Dominican Raymund Martini's great book *Pugio Fidei*, 'Dagger of Faith', composed about the year 1278. His new statement of this Christian argument was a treasure-house of Hebrew and Aramaic quotations from Talmud and midrash, and in this respect formed a vast counterpart to the Paris *Extracts from the Talmud*; but Raymund's preference for quoting the original as well as a translation corresponded to an outlook very different from that encountered in the Paris examination. Thus, Raymund was ready to take seriously the rabbinic view that Talmudic literature forms the written deposit of oral law which Moses received from Sinai. The papal letters of 1239, 1244 and 1286 had echoed and would echo the dismissal of this view as incredible; but Raymund says expressly that although doubt on this score is often justified, it is not unreasonable to hold that a number of Talmudic texts – those of course which seem consonant with Christian biblical interpretation – do indeed derive from God-given oral tradition (3=6–7; 45=360).[26] A not dissimilar opinion seems to be implied by a contemporary Friar Preacher who studied and taught in Paris, St Thomas Aquinas. In his *lectura* on 1 Timothy he identifies the 'fables' against which Timothy is warned (1:4) as 'the law given orally, that is the Talmud; not the things which Moses handed down orally, but the things which others added, such as foolish fables'. This careful formulation associates the Talmud mainly with fables, as in Aquinas's comments on 1 Tim. 4:7 and Tit. 1:14, but seems also to allow for a genuine oral tradition from Moses, such as is centrally important for Raymund Martini. Neither of the contrasting views of the Talmud associated with the *Extracts* and the *Pugio Fidei*, respectively, was without antecedent in Christianity; but in Raymund's case the more positive view is bound up with and strengthens his option for Hebrew as a Friar Preacher. Thus the strong Hebraism of his book also corresponds to the conviction already mentioned, that Jews must be approached with an essentially Hebrew-based argument, showing that the Jewish Hebrew-language exposition of the Hebrew Bible supports Christian biblical interpretation.

Hence, although ostensible errors of rabbinic literature are freely blamed in the *Pugio Fidei*, the Talmud and midrash are regularly understood to be at least pointing to the way of truth. Moreover, rabbinic passages which seem to mention Jesus are treated with a serenity which contrasts with their utter condemnation at Paris in the 1240s, and is of course rhetorically far more effective. It is shown that, perhaps surprisingly, they accord with Christian documents. For example, it is suggested that the term 'son of Pantera' refers to the tradition in St John of Damascus that the Blessed Virgin's grandfather and great-grandfather bore this name (361–5=289–92; more probably, this Christian tradition is an attempt to domesticate a disturbing Jewish assertion). Again it is urged that the note on Jesus as 'near to the kingdom' in the Talmudic passage on the hanging of Jesus on Passover eve reflects the New Testament tradition of his Davidic descent (416=332). Alternatively, it can be urged that these traditions in fact support Christianity; so a long passage of Toledoth Jeshu is translated as part of an argument that the Jews know and admit Christ's miracles (361–3=289–91). Thus explicit references to Christianity in Jewish tradition, adverse though they are, are used to show that Christianity is indeed implicit in Jewish tradition, even in its post-biblical and apparently hostile forms. Whatever force this argument may or may not possess, it permitted a free, and occasionally appreciative, approach to post-biblical Jewish literature.

A great step is therefore represented by the modest list of books brought freshly under review: Talmud, Toledoth Jeshu, Josephus and Josippon, the Testaments of the Twelve Patriarchs. The topic of Christianity in ancient Jewish tradition, in both the senses distinguished above, could for the first time at least in principle be approached on the basis of a synoptic view of the Jewish literature handed down in the church, now with an eye to the Greek as well as the Latin tradition, together with the writings handed down in the Jewish community. This viewpoint was won through inquiries pursued with marked unity amid diversity throughout western

Europe, from Barcelona to the diocese of Lincoln. From now on the Jewish writings from the ancient world handed down among the Jews could be viewed together with those preserved among eastern as well as western Christians, and the foundation of all later study of ancient Judaism and early Christianity had been laid.

Such is the hole of the pit in university and ecclesiastical life whence these studies are digged. The depths of the hole indeed expose missionary aims which, though not ignoble, can be far from contemporary sympathies, methods which arouse indignation, and the mingling of Christianity with antisemitism; but one can perhaps still say, in the words of the First World War cartoon, 'If you knows of a better 'ole, go to it', or in the words of the rabbinic adage, 'Let everyone study in the law even if not for the sake of the law; for out of that which is not for its sake may come that which is for its sake' (Rab, in Babylonian Talmud, Nazir 23b).

So in this hole in fact was found that searching attention to a range of original texts, external as well as domestic, Hebrew and Aramaic and Greek as well as Latin, which forms the foundation of the subject. For the study of ancient Judaism and early Christianity in general, the importance of the range attained in that thirteenth-century book list is suggested by continuing tendencies towards pulling the list apart for concentration on one portion only, roughly speaking that which came down in ecclesiastical or Jewish tradition, respectively. For the study of the topic proposed in the title of this lecture, the little list itself suggests how Christianity as mentioned in Jewish tradition can, and perhaps should, be studied against the background of Christianity as implicitly present in Jewish tradition.

Without losing sight of these two contentions, I should now like rapidly to link the thirteenth-century inquiries with those of the present. I therefore pass over, as Cicero might have said, a great deal which supports my case, in order to mention four later developments which particularly affected the study of Christianity in ancient Jewish tradition.

Christianity in Ancient Jewish Tradition

First, the little list of books which gained fresh thirteenth-century attention makes no special reference to Jewish mystical traditions, although the dream-visions in the Testaments of the Twelve Patriarchs form a reminder of early Jewish mysticism, and the Babylonian Talmud includes traditions on rabbinic mystics. The long Aramaic text which became dominant among later mystical writings, the Zohar, was itself still being compiled in the thirteenth century. Presenting itself as the work of the second-century Simeon ben Yohai, it was taken up by Christians, and until the nineteenth century played a big part in the argument that ancient Judaism was indeed very close to Christianity. Dr Pusey in the 1870s still maintained the traditional second-century date of the Zohar, despite general recognition of its later origins, and it is easy to smile at this characteristic piece of his conservatism; but Pusey can be imagined smiling gently in return, for although the Zohar is late, the researches of Gershom Scholem and others since Pusey's time have shown how important Jewish mysticism already was in the Second-Temple and rabbinic period, the age of apocalypses and of speculation on cosmogony, the divine stature, the angelic powers and the throne-chariot of the cherubim. These aspects of ancient Jewish literature and speculation were equally prominent in early Christianity.

Then, secondly, the thirteenth-century list could not include ancient writings known only through discoveries made in modern times. A prominent example is formed by some of the rules, expositions and hymns from the Dead Sea Scrolls, found in the Qumran caves in the middle of the twentieth century – although part of this literature, notably copies of the Damascus Document, survived in mediaeval Jewish transmission; moreover, the Testaments of the Twelve Patriarchs puts the mediaeval west in touch with the priestly as well as royal messianic hope which is also met in writings found at Qumran. Documents of ancient Jewish life have also been recovered on a large scale, however, in the form of inscriptions (sometimes associated with decoration

69

and representative art) as well as non-literary manuscripts such as leases, receipts and marriage contracts.

At first sight one might say, not without a measure of truth, that this newly recovered material makes the likeness between ancient Judaism and ancient Christianity more obvious. Thus the Qumran rules underline the importance of the Jewish ascetic movements already reflected in Philo, Josephus and rabbinic texts. Again, among non-literary discoveries, the inscribed ossuaries of Jerusalem from the time of Christian origins attest the importance of the Greek and Aramaic which would later be common to Jews and Christians; and the synagogue art of the later Roman empire is contemporary with early Christian art, and suggests antecedents for it. Yet the material made known through modern discoveries, like the literature transmitted in the church and the Jewish community, resists any one-sided emphasis on features which seem to anticipate Christianity. Thus Jewish inscriptions in Ptolemaic and early Roman Egypt sometimes recall the apocalypses in their concern with mortality and after-life, but they also reflect communal organization focused on the 'prayer-house' (*proseuche*). Similarly, the Qumran rule literature represents not only the asceticism characteristic of the Greek and later of the Christian world, but also a halakhic concentration on the Torah like that which is central in later Jewish tradition. Moreover, among Jewish literary finds from Judaea and Egypt, perhaps the largest single element is formed by early Hebrew, Aramaic and Greek copies of known texts from the books of the Old Testament – the Pentateuch above all – and the associated writings. Hence, although the steady flow of fresh discovery invites continuing reassessment, new finds often pose the same question on Christianity and Jewish tradition that arises from literature which is already known.

Thirdly, the seventeenth century took up the work of the thirteenth, not only through the first printings of the *Pugio Fidei*, Grosseteste's Greek manuscript of the Testaments of the Twelve Patriarchs, and the Greek text of Origen against Celsus, but also through prodigious labours in post-biblical Hebrew literature. Old and New Testament work impinged on the question of Christianity in ancient Judaism in two different ways, both exemplified in Cambridge. John Spencer of Corpus Christi College, in his great book on the ritual laws of the Hebrews (1683 onwards), proposed a more radical development of those views of Maimonides on the sacrifices as a concession to idolatry which had been adapted by William of Auvergne. The biblical rites, Spencer urged, were usually drawn from the rites of non-Jews, especially the Egyptians. If a new defence of the reasonableness of the ritual laws was thereby suggested, it also became harder (as seems also to have occurred in the case of William of Auvergne) to envisage them as prefiguring the Christian dispensation. On the other hand, John Lightfoot of St Catharine's College became the effective founder (1658 onwards) of the tradition of commentary on the New Testament from rabbinic texts. This tradition led, through its important extension by J.C. Schoettgen of Dresden (1733 onwards), to the famous commentary on the New Testament from the Talmud and midrash which was initiated by H.L. Strack, but is mainly the monumental work of Paul Billerbeck (1921 onwards). The special significance of this tradition for the present argument lies in its cumulative demonstration that there is affinity between rabbinic sources preserved in Hebrew and Aramaic and early Christian sources preserved in Greek, despite those differences in language, outlook and date which Billerbeck repeatedly underlines. The importance of rabbinic texts for New Testament interpretation, even though rabbinic literature was compiled after the New Testament books, has been indirectly confirmed by the Dead Sea Scrolls; if some New Testament passages require rabbinic material for their interpretation, how much more is that true of the rather earlier Dead Sea Scrolls.

Lastly, the mighty works of the nineteenth-century Jewish scholars who integrated rabbinical learning with philological science in the *Wissenschaft des Judentums* were accompanied by more popular apologetic, which helped to change approaches to the topic

of Christianity in Jewish tradition. What may be called the romantic
defence of the Talmud arose. In an atmosphere symbolized and
governed by the wizardry of Sir Walter Scott, the fanciful narratives
of the haggadah, which had evoked anxiety and satire from
rationally minded Jews and Christians, could now be admired like
the correspondingly criticized legends of mediaeval Christendom.
Both together were put into English verse by Sabine Baring-Gould,
better known as the author of 'Onward Christian Soldiers'.[27] So in
1851 the *Hebrew Melodies* of Heinrich Heine, written on his sickbed,
include a classic commendation of the Babylonian Talmud as at once
a military training school – the halakhah; and a garden of delight
– the haggadah. It is a dream-like garden, best compared with
the fabulous hanging gardens which like the Talmud itself grew
up in Babylonia long ago; palm-trees, cypresses, orange trees and
fountains are held up by colossal pillars and interlinked by hanging
bridges which look like climbing plants, and which shelter not a
parliament of rooks but a kind of seminar of birds, the rabbinical
teachers of all kinds and moods:

> Solemn birds, large, many-coloured,
>   All deep thinkers, never singing,
> While around them finches flutter
>   Keeping up a merry twitter –
>
> *Grosse bunte ernste Vögel*
>   *Tiefe Denker, die nicht singen*
> *Während sie umflattert kleines*
>   *Zeisigvolk, das lustig trillert.*

After this and kindred manifestations of the romantic defence of
the Talmud, never again was it quite so easy to be shocked by the
features condemned in Paris in 1240. So in 1867 Emanuel Deutsch,
skilfully appealing to contemporary taste in a celebrated article in
the *Quarterly Review*, compared those put off by seemingly uncouth
aspects of the Talmud to ignorant beholders of a Gothic church, who
mistake the gargoyles outside for the saints within. The way was
clear which led, via a modest but notable clutch of studies of Christ

in the Talmud by Robert Sinker, W.H. Lowe and A.W. Streane, in 1902 to Samuel Krauss's edition of Toledoth Jeshu, and in 1910 to H.L. Strack's sober collection of passages on Christianity from the Talmud and the Toledoth Jeshu together with the relevant Greek passages from Celsus and St John of Damascus.

These two books formed the basis of twentieth-century study of Christianity in ancient Jewish tradition, in the sense of Christianity as mentioned in Jewish tradition, and they return us, in conclusion, to the question of how the topic in both senses can now be addressed. The allusions to Christianity studied by Krauss and Strack belong, as has already been emphasized, to a Jewish tradition which itself repeatedly recalls Christian tradition. The period from the Septuagint to the Talmud includes a considerable time during which such resemblance can be put down wholly or partly to the influence of Christianity; a consideration underlined by a series of scholars, but drawn to my own notice especially by Professor C.F.D. Moule. Yet this consideration is not offered as an explanation of the whole phenomenon. Resemblances are already there in the pre-Christian period, for instance in the Septuagint, in Philo and in some of the apocalypses and newly discovered material mentioned already; and the ancestry of these likenesses can be glimpsed in the Hebrew Bible. Moreover, some of the Talmudic and midrashic passages which resemble Christian traditions arose in settings where Greek was known, and where the internal influence of the Septuagint, its revisions and its interpretations may have been more important than the external influence of Christianity.

At the beginning of the twentieth century, in reaction against the importance which Wilhelm Bousset attached to apocalypses in his vivid description of ancient Jewish religion, there were those who wished to exclude them as witnesses in favour of rabbinic texts; but this view, resisted by some rabbinic scholars at the time, has become still more difficult to hold since the researches of Gershom Scholem mentioned above. It is better to retain the range of witnesses, as the thirteenth century did. Whatever Raymund

Martini did not prove, he showed, I believe, that there is real continuity and overlap between ancient Judaism, both before and after the time of Christ, and the derivative and concurrent early Christianity. Israel Abrahams, Reader in Talmudic and Rabbinic Literature in Cambridge from 1902 to 1925, went so far as to call it, speaking generally, 'continuity in which stress varies, rather than actual content'.[28]

Acknowledgement of this continuity would not involve a claim that Judaism is the prophecy and Christianity the fulfilment, and it would not imply a forced reading of the Old Testament as a Christian document. On the contrary, it would depend on the observation that precisely when Old Testament documents are studied with attention to the times in which they were composed, edited and collected, they seem to present features which show continuity with the later Christianity as well as the later Judaism. This continuity will then be one important factor in the origins of some of those rabbinic teachings which Raymund Martini was inclined to affirm as genuine remnants of an ancient and inspired tradition.

Against the background of this continuity float the adverse Jewish anecdotes and legends of the rise of Christianity known mainly from Celsus, the Talmud and the Toledoth Jeshu, and current from the second century onwards. Here I shall restrict myself to the Talmud. To begin with two general comments on approach, the opposition to Christianity which is often apparent in the Talmudic passages can be recognized, against the background of continuity just noted, as opposition towards a movement which may seem in some ways like the real thing, yet is judged in the end to be false. The attitude is comparable with inner-Christian opposition to movements identified as heresies. Yet, secondly, the background of continuity is perhaps also reflected in the very nature of the references or possible references to Christianity. The Talmudic and midrashic material, viewed globally, remains close to themes which are important in Christianity, or in the range of rabbinic discussion which sometimes recalls Christianity: the parentage, disciples, miracles, teaching,

Christianity in Ancient Jewish Tradition

resurrection and divinity of Jesus, the liberty or licence of Christian morals, and the discussion of angelic powers in heaven – a subject which has sometimes been classified as Gnostic, but which, as can be seen from Origen and his predecessors, was a focus of Christian Christological thought. It also seems that characteristic points of Christian interest were regarded as less foreign to Jewish concern than might perhaps be expected, for they were not left without notice or response.

These general comments may be accompanied by just two observations of a more detailed kind. First, although the Tosefta and the Palestinian Talmud offer some important material on Christianity – for example a probably early narrative of an encounter with a Christian in Sepphoris which has been much in the limelight because of excavations there – the weight of the traditions on Christianity is in the larger but later Babylonian Talmud. They are part of the mass of probably Palestinian haggadic material which has been incorporated, with editorial development, in this Talmud. Within that material, they might in general be compared with a series of traditions concerning Hasmonaean and Herodian rule, often somehow related to Josephus. The passages on Christianity may likewise sometimes be related to written sources, perhaps from the New Testament or the New Testament Apocrypha.

Secondly, I have argued elsewhere that one important passage of this kind (Babylonian Talmud, Sanh. 43a) has a second-century core including the words 'he was hanged on Passover Eve, because he used witchcraft and enticed and drew away Israel'. The three charges echo legislation in Deuteronomy, on sorcery and on the false prophecy which draws individuals or communities into idolatry, which is taken up in the Mishnah. They also have clear points of contact with charges mentioned in the Gospels and the apocryphal Acts of Pilate: he casts out devils by the prince of the devils; he leads the multitudes astray; he is a sorcerer. Here, however, I only want to stress that this estimate of the works and teaching which led to the emergence of Christianity, thoroughly negative as it is, is also deeply thought out and serious. Groups as well as individuals among the people, it implies, were drawn away through attending to seeming prophecy, which was commended by works which seemed to be signs and wonders, but must have been in fact from below rather than above. In this judgment, which follows a line envisaged in Deuteronomy, there is something of the depth and gravitas of rabbinic thought.

Here at the same time, you may well say, is an argument against the belief that Christianity is somehow close to Jewish tradition, or implicit in it. Yes – and perhaps also No: for it remains striking that Christian origins can be summed up negatively indeed, but also so readily, in the terms of the Mishnah. Debate will go on, but enough has been said if I have shown not only that there may still be ways to approach this material on Christianity in ancient Jewish tradition, in both the senses considered here, but, more important, that it is intrinsically worth approaching. And whatever your own views on the continuity or discontinuity of Christian and Jewish tradition, I hope you may agree that the scattered explicit references to Christianity in Jewish tradition ought not to be studied apart from the wider searching of that tradition which became so prominent in the thirteenth century.

In the hole of the pit from which we are digged, they laboured impartially over a great range of Jewish and Christian and pagan texts, and they freely blamed much of what they read; but they were also prepared to be impressed. As one of them said at the beginning of the fourteenth century – it was Dante hearing himself speak to Virgil – May long study avail me, and the great love which has made me search your volume: *Vagliami il lungo studio, e il grande amore.* As was said in the ancient world concerning the law itself (Aboth v 22), 'Turn it about and turn it about, for all is in it.' It is no use our studying the literature of ancient Jews and early Christians, unless we are prepared now and then to be stirred, with and through steady critical attention, to affection and admiration.

Endnotes

[1] This chapter is reproduced with revision from W. Horbury, *Christianity in Jewish Tradition* (Cambridge, 1999), based on a public lecture in the Selwyn Divinity School building mentioned below. On Celsus's book, known through quotation by Origen in the third century, see H. Chadwick, *Origen: Contra Celsum, translated with an Introduction and Notes* (corrected edn, Cambridge, 1965); J. Carleton Paget & S. Gathercole (edd.), *Celsus in his World* (Cambridge, 2021).

[2] See R.B. Dobson, 'The Jews of Medieval Cambridge', *Transactions of the Jewish Historical Society of England* 32 (1990–92), 1–24.

[3] C. Roth, *The Intellectual Activities of Medieval English Jewry* (The British Academy Supplemental Papers, 8, London, 1949), 29–32.

[4] C.H. Feltoe & E.H. Minns (edd.), *Vetus Liber Archidiaconi Eliensis* (Cambridge, 1917), 158.

[5] See further Judith Olszowy-Schlanger, *Learning Hebrew in Medieval England* (Toronto: Pontifical Institute of Mediaeval Studies, 2023).

[6] Miri Rubin, *Charity and Community in Medieval Cambridge* (Cambridge, 1987), 108–109, 205–206.

[7] J.W. Clark (ed.), *Liber Memorandorum Ecclesie de Bernewelle* (Cambridge, 1907), 126.

[8] H. Jenkinson, *Calendar of the Plea Rolls of the Exchequer of the Jews*, iii (London, 1929), 311–12, with C. Roth, *The Jews of Medieval Oxford* (Oxford, 1951), 44–5.

[9] J. Rosenthal (ed.), *Sepher Joseph Hamekane* (Jerusalem, 1970), 62–3, n.3.

[10] B. Smalley and R. Loewe in B. Smalley, 'Some Thirteenth-Century Commentaries on the Sapiential Books', reprinted from *Dominican Studies* 2 (1949), 318–55, 3 (1950), 41–77, 236–74, in B. Smalley, *Medieval Exegesis of Wisdom Literature*, ed. R.E. Murphy (Atlanta, 1986), 1–115 (57–9).

[11] M.R. James, 'On the Glass in the Windows of the Library at St Albans Abbey', *Proceedings of the Cambridge Antiquarian Society* 35 (1894), 213–20.

[12] C.M. Clark, *The Politics of Conversion: Missionary Protestantism and the Jews in Prussia, 1728–1941* (Oxford, 1995).

[13] S. Grayzel, *The Church and the Jews in the Thirteenth Century* (2 vols., New York, 1966–89), i, 238–42, nos. 95–8; 250–53, no. 104.

[14] B. Smalley, 'William of Auvergne, John of La Rochelle and St Thomas Aquinas on the Old Law', reprinted in B. Smalley, *Studies in Medieval Thought and Learning from Abelard to Wyclif* (London, 1981), 121–82 (135–56);

Biblical Voices and Echoes

Lesley Smith, 'William of Auvergne and the Jews', in Diana Wood (ed.), *Christianity and Judaism* (Studies in Church History 29, Oxford, 1992), 107–17.
[15] Text with English introduction in U. Cecini, O. de la Cruz Palma, et al. (edd.), *Extractiones de Talmud* (2 vols., Turnhout, 2018, 2021).
[16] H. Denifle & E. Chatelain, *Chartularium Universitatis Parisiensis*, i (Paris, 1889), 210 (this name among names of those responsible for the sentence); Smalley, 'William of Auvergne', 126n; D.L. d'Avray, 'Milton [Meliton, Middleton, Mildditone, Milton], William of', *Oxford Dictionary of National Biography* 38 (2004), 349–50.
[17] D.L. Douie, *Archbishop Pecham* (Oxford, 1952), 5.
[18] Grayzel, *The Church and the Jews in the Thirteenth Century*, ii (ed. K.R. Stow), 157–62, no. 50.
[19] Giraldus Cambrensis, *De Principis Instructione*, i, ed. G.F. Warner in J.S. Brewer et al. (edd.), *Giraldi Cambrensis Opera* (Rolls Series, 8 vols.), viii (London, 1891), 65–6.
[20] E. Bammel, 'Jesus as a Political Agent in a Version of the Josippon', in E. Bammel & C.F.D. Moule (edd.), *Jesus and the Politics of His Day* (Cambridge, 1984), 197–209.
[21] R. Loewe, 'The Medieval Christian Hebraists of England: The *Superscriptio Lincolniensis*', *Hebrew Union College Annual* 28 (1957), 205–52.
[22] R.W. Southern, *Robert Grosseteste: The Growth of an English Mind in Medieval Europe* (2nd edn, Oxford, 1992), 8–9, 181–6, 269, 283n.; M. de Jonge, 'Robert Grosseteste and the Testaments of the Twelve Patriarchs', *Journal of Theological Studies* N.S. 42 (1991), 115–25.
[23] Letter 124 in H.R. Luard (ed.), *Roberti Episcopi quondam Lincolniensis Epistolae* (Rolls Series, London, 1861), 351.
[24] *Close Rolls of the Reign of Henry III, 1237–42* (London, 1911), 238 (m.10d), discussed by J.C. Russell, 'The Preferments and "Adiutores" of Robert Grosseteste', *Harvard Theological Review* 26 (1933), 160–72 (168–71).
[25] J. Shatzmiller, *La deuxième controverse de Paris* (Paris & Louvain, 1994).
[26] The page-numbers in brackets refer first to the edition of Leipzig, 1687 (reprinted Farnborough, 1967), then to that of Paris, 1651.
[27] S. Baring-Gould, *The Silver Store: Collected from Mediaeval Christian and Jewish Mines* (London, 1868 and reprints).
[28] I. Abrahams, 'Rabbinic Aids to Exegesis', in H.B. Swete (ed.), *Essays on Some Biblical Questions of the Day, by Members of the University of Cambridge* (Cambridge, 1909), 161–92 (183).

78

5
PRE-REFORMATION PIETY IN THE PRAYER-BOOK

Reappropriation of aspects of mediaeval liturgy and devotion took place widely in the Church of England during the first half of the twentieth century.[1] It was effected mainly through the medium of the Book of Common Prayer (1549, revised 1552, in use mainly as revised in 1662). It appealed to the affection for the mediaeval Christian inheritance, including but not restricted to church foundation and rebuilding (Plate 6), which had been a force since the early nineteenth century. It built on the consequent renewal of study of mediaeval biblical interpretation, mediaeval church architecture and, towards the end of the century, the mediaeval mystics; but it also took up the accompanying sense for both national tradition and social awareness in ecclesiastical life and in arts and crafts. It had links with John Ruskin and William Morris as well as John Mason Neale and Sir Walter Scott.

One influential publication was Percy Dearmer's *Parson's Handbook* (1899; revised editions, 1903, 1907), illustrating the aptness of the Prayer-book to the mediaeval usages and church furnishings familiar when it was compiled, and crusading against the dire social and aesthetic effects of 'industrialism'; 'a modern preacher often stands in a sweated pulpit, wearing a sweated surplice over a cassock that was not produced under fair conditions and, holding a sweated book in one hand, with the other he points to the machine-made cross at the jerry-built altar, and appeals to the sacred principles of mutual sacrifice and love'.[2] A second influential book was the *English Hymnal* (1906 and revisions), which enlarged the fund of mediaeval hymns already to hand in *Hymns Ancient and Modern*, and added liturgical matter, including the scriptural mediaeval Propers said or sung each Sunday. A large-scale counterpart to these books was F.E. Brightman's *The English Rite* (1915), placing the Sarum rite – the

Salisbury liturgical use which had special importance in sixteenth-century England side-by-side with the Prayer-book, and showing their similarity.

In the first half of the twentieth century the movement encouraged by publications like these gained in definition in the Church of England. Its best-known symbol was the so-called 'English altar', with riddel-posts, often surmounted by carved angels, between which curtains were suspended on the east, south and north.[3] There was a long-term struggle between adherents of this movement and those who, pointing to its seeming insularity and antiquarianism, and often themselves in tune with early twentieth-century admiration for baroque architecture and seventeenth-century literature, favoured adoption of continental usage and furnishings, and aimed at integration with international western Christian tradition. Yet this struggle in the parishes was superseded from the 1960s onwards by preoccupation with fundamental liturgical revision, in a cultural and political atmosphere which had changed again. Revision was often reacting, to affirm the part played by the congregation, against the sense of gradation and mystery conveyed by mediaeval prayers and custom. These successive developments in the liturgical field may have overshadowed the renewed piety, social awareness and apprehension of scripture which accompanied the affirmation of mediaeval aspects of the Prayer-book.

At any rate, the atmosphere has now inevitably changed once more. There is some renewed sympathy for mediaeval insights in liturgy, thought and devotion, manifest side-by-side with our inheritance from the late twentieth century of rewritten liturgies, and non-liturgical types of worship and devotion which look back to the push for liberties as well as new order in the Reformation itself. The continued use of the Prayer-book can to some extent be associated with this further change of atmosphere. Against this background I should like to note again some of the pre-Reformation aspects of the

Prayer-book. They impart what I take to be refreshing streams of a piety bound up with liturgical interpretation of scripture.[4]

The Prayer-book and its Mediaeval Inheritance
The Prayer-book is indeed a document of the Reformation – and to emphasize this point has been one trend in study. So Diarmaid MacCulloch called Cranmer's 1549 book 'the public, ceremonial face of Protestant Reformation', and draws attention to the possibly Lutheran context of what may seem the conservative modifications made to it in 1559, after Elizabeth's accession; he suggests that it was the use of the Prayer-book rather than the intentions of compilers and revisers, specifically its liturgical interpretation in cathedrals and in the context of the threefold ministry during Elizabeth's reign, which helped, by the time of Richard Hooker (*c.*1554–1600) and Lancelot Andrewes (1555–1626), to create a perception of the continuity of the reformed English church with mediaeval and early Christian usage. This perception may not have been wholly absent from the mind of Cranmer and others when the Prayer-book was first compiled and revised. Moreover, archbishop Matthew Parker (1504–75) presented the Elizabethan settlement as a revival of customs of the old English church before the Norman Conquest. MacCulloch would stress, however, that any such perceptions should not disguise the zeal for reform which was a chief motive of Cranmer's work.[5]

Yet there is still something in those similarities, which seemed so striking to a scholar like F.E. Brightman in the early twentieth century, between the Prayer-book and the Sarum rite, and also the late-mediaeval primers of private prayer. Laying emphasis on these similarities, which appear immediately even if you simply compare the communion service with the mass, and thinking perhaps too of the appeal to the church fathers in Cranmer's preface to the Prayer-book and the discourse Of Ceremonies, C.S. Lewis wrote that the compilers 'wished their book to be praised not for original genius but for catholicity and antiquity, and it is in fact the ripe fruit of centuries of worship'.[6]

Here I am interested not so much in the intentions of the makers and revisers of the Prayer-book, important though it is to try to grasp them, as in the texts that they did give us and the use that was made of them from Tudor times onwards – texts and usage which indeed often emphasized the continuity of the Prayer-book with the centuries of worship which preceded it. Again, I am interested not so much in the undoubted fact that the Prayer-book contains pre-Reformation elements, as in the value of the mainly mediaeval and more neglected portion of these elements, as I take it to be, for the enrichment of contemporary piety and religious sentiment.

Prayer Addressed to Christ
A first instance is provided by the phenomenon of public prayer and praise addressed to Christ. C.S. Lewis rightly emphasized that the Prayer-book has the character of public rather than private prayer, and suggested that this is one but not the only reason for its sobriety and its withdrawal (despite its ardour and depth) from many of those more obviously emotional appeals which you find in the Primers of private prayer. Yet these emotional moments do occur sometimes also in the old tradition of public prayer. Thus when Cranmer was translating the collects, he was also, as Lewis shows, at the same time occasionally restraining their expression of emotion, for example in the Good Friday collect 'Almighty God, we beseech thee graciously to behold this thy family, for which our Lord Jesus Christ was contented to be betrayed, and given up into the hands of wicked men, and to suffer death upon the cross ...'. Here the original 'to undergo the torment of the cross', *crucis subire tormentum*, has become simply 'to suffer death upon the cross'. In such places, Lewis suggested, the graver, more deliberative temper of Cranmer and the early Tudor age comes into view.[7]

Yet, illuminating though this observation is, there are also texts in the Prayer-book in which revising or new writing does

82

nevertheless appeal more plainly to the emotions, taking up the strand of freer expression from mediaeval piety. A group of these passages is focused on the address of prayer and praise directly to Christ. Address to Christ has always been controversial as regards liturgy and hymnody. Like the less-often found address to the Holy Ghost, it is typical of hymnody and individual devotion rather than public prayer.

It plays a part of course in the Prayer-book in hymnody inherited from the early church, such as the Te Deum in Mattins ('Thou art the king of glory, O Christ … we therefore pray thee, help thy servants …') and Gloria in excelsis in the communion service ('O Lord, the only begotten Son, Jesu Christ, O Lord God, Lamb of God, Son of the Father … have mercy upon us'). Within the early church, however, such prayer and praise was eventually not taken as the norm in public prayer, despite its clear antiquity and its New Testament antecedents; we may think of the Christians questioned by Pliny in the early second century who said that they sang hymns to Christ as to a god (Pliny, *Letters*, 10.96, 7), and of New Testament passages including the acclamations to Christ as he entered Jerusalem, and St Stephen's prayer 'Lord Jesus, receive my spirit' (Acts 7:59). In the third century, however, Origen urges prayer to the Father through the Son (*On Prayer*, xv), and the Third Council of Carthage in 397 prescribes that at the altar prayer shall be directed only to the Father (canon 23). This usage is reflected in the collects for Sundays and holy days translated from old Latin originals in the Prayer-book, although, as we shall see, new Prayer-book collects could depart from it.

Yet perhaps the greatest instance of extended prayer to Christ in the Prayer-book is the English Litany, compiled by archbishop Cranmer and originally issued in 1544. With the Litany we are somewhere between private and public prayer, but historically litanies entered the beginning of the eucharist (the Kyrie eleison of the old mass is a reflection of this), and a litany in the form that Cranmer adapted was in use in the Middle Ages at ordinations and as an independent service used in procession in Lent or on the Rogation Days. Litanies therefore entered service-books like Pontificals, presenting the orders of service needed by bishops, and Processionals, setting out the responses, psalmody and prayers used in the processions, ending with an English bidding prayer, which took place just before mass on Sundays and holy days; but litanies also had an important place in Primers of private prayer, which might be used by individuals and small groups.[8] The 1544 Litany was itself issued with an exhortation to prayer 'to be read to the people afore processions', as the title says; the litany itself is entitled 'a Litany with suffrages to be said or sung in the time of the said processions'.[9] It was a major change in public worship when the processions were abolished by royal injunction in 1547. Instead, this litany, already used during processions, was now to be said or sung by clergy and choir not in procession, but kneeling in the midst of the church.

Cranmer's Litany, incorporated in the 1549 Prayer-book, was thus a definitely public form. In 1544 it began with an appeal to the Holy Trinity, followed by invocations of 'Saint Mary, mother of God, our Saviour Jesu Christ', the angels and blessed spirits, and finally all saints: 'All holy patriarchs, and prophets, apostles, martyrs, confessors and virgins, and all the blessed company of heaven, pray for us.' These three invocations introduced a central section of deprecations addressed to Christ, with the response 'Good Lord, deliver us' (*libera nos, Domine*), followed by obsecrations addressed to Christ, with the response 'We beseech thee to hear us' (*Te rogamus, audi nos*), and concluded with appeals to Christ as Son of God and Lamb of God. In all this the mediaeval structure of a litany was being followed.

In 1549 Cranmer omitted the three invocations of saints and angels, but followed his earlier litany very closely in other respects, from 'Remember not, Lord, our offences … spare thy people, whom thou hast redeemed with thy most precious blood …', through the series of deprecations including the famous 'By the mystery of thy holy incarnation …', all with the response 'Good Lord, deliver us', to the series of obsecrations beginning 'We sinners do beseech thee to hear us, O Lord God' (here 'Lord God' is addressed to Christ, as in the Gloria in excelsis), down to 'Son of God, we beseech thee to hear us', and 'O Lamb of God …'.[10]

This extended address to Christ has received a good deal of attention, being emphasized in the nineteenth century from sharply differing points of view by H.P. Liddon, who notes it in his demonstration of the orthodoxy of Prayer-book formulae in his treatise on *The Divinity of our Lord*, and on the other hand by Charles Merivale, Dean of Ely, well-known as a Roman historian, who notes how much the Litany addressed to Christ recalls the ancient Roman custom of addressing in litany-like prayer not Jupiter but those deities who were thought to be nearest and most accessible.[11]

For our present purpose I would like to highlight the contribution of the Litany – Tudor, yet also mediaeval – in bringing to devotion to Christ, which will always be a central strand in piety, an almost Roman combination of dignity and tenderness – 'by thine agony and bloody sweat, by thy cross and passion, by thy precious death and burial' (a close translation of mediaeval Latin wording) – 'that it may please thee to preserve all that travel by land or air or water' – I quote here the English version as updated in 1928 – 'all women labouring of child, all sick persons and young children; and to shew thy pity upon all prisoners and captives …' (seemingly a combination of various sources).

Cranmer brought this same Christocentric devotion of deep but disciplined feeling into the series of collects themselves, on occasions when particularly heartfelt petition might seem appropriate.[12] One of these is the First Sunday in Lent, where Cranmer continued the theme of abstinence from the old collect, but boldly rewrote it as a prayer to Christ himself:

> O Lord, who for our sake didst fast forty days and forty nights, give us grace to use such abstinence …

Biblical Voices and Echoes

Here again we have the clear but restrained emphasis on Christ's sufferings which was continued from old formulae in the Litany (compare 'by thy baptism, fasting and temptation').

Somewhat comparably, just after Christmas, the old Collect for St Stephen, asking that we may learn to love our enemies, because we are keeping the Nativity of him who prayed even for persecutors, becomes a prayer to the Christ to whom Stephen's prayer was directed (Acts 7:59–60): 'Grant us, Lord, to love our enemies by the example of thy martyr Saint Stephen, who prayed to thee for his persecutors' – a notably neat and apt rewording which is kept but expanded in the 1662 Prayer-book.

Yet, lest one should make too much of this, the collect for Innocents' Day, which in its old form beginning 'God, whose praise this day the martyred Innocents confessed ...' was understood as a prayer to Christ, as its ending shows, became in Cranmer's hands a prayer to God the Father; and for the Sunday after Ascension he comparably moulded an old antiphon addressed to Christ into a regular Collect directed to the Father, as the old Collect for this Sunday had been. Lastly, however, the revisers for the 1662 book added a new collect addressed to Christ at the Third Sunday in Advent: 'O Lord Jesu Christ, who at thy first coming didst send thy messenger to prepare thy way before thee ...', perhaps a specially earnest supplication with the custom of Advent ordinations in view.

In all, then, the Prayer-book Collects second the Litany in boldly placing petition to Christ in public prayer; they keep the old norm of liturgical address to the Father, but they take up a thread in ancient and mediaeval public prayer which was present although not the norm, and which recalls some of the prayers of the New Testament. The Litany and these Collects together tend to accept the forceful devotion which will always spring up in this connection, but to encourage its expression in words of free and deep yet still disciplined feeling. This Prayer-book development of mediaeval piety suggests how, within the tradition of prayer to the Father, the

86

instinct to address Christ himself can be affirmed, but expressed with depth and dignity.

Marian Devotion

As a pendant to these words on the cult of Christ one may note briefly the place of our Lady in the piety of the Prayer-book. The pruning of invocation of saints, just noticed in the case of the Litany, can be sensed too when the Prayer-book instructions to godparents are silent on the prayer of salutation to the Virgin, Ave Maria. Marian devotion is then focused above all in the three great feasts of Christmas, Candlemas and Lady Day.[13]

The Collect and proper preface for Christmas remember Mary with the words (in the Collect) 'as at this time to be born of a pure Virgin' – a newly created phrase not in the old collects; and (in a newly created Preface)

> because thou didst give Jesus Christ thine only Son to be born as at this time for us; who by the operation of the Holy Ghost was made very man of the substance of the Virgin Mary his mother, and that without spot of sin, to make us clean from all sin.

The two feasts of Candlemas and Lady Day, which follow on 2 February and 25 March, respectively, are red-letter days in the Prayer-book, and their Prayer-book titles emphasize their connection with Mary. To quote the 1662 forms, Candlemas is headed in the series of Collects, Epistles and Gospels 'The Presentation of Christ in the Temple, commonly called the Purification of Saint Mary the Virgin', but in the Kalendar is simply called 'The Purification of Mary the Blessed Virgin'; both the earlier Prayer-books, like their mediaeval source, had used this title (the Purification, without mention of the Presentation) in the series of Collects as well. The 1662 Prayer-book restored the old Epistle from Malachi 3, on the Lord coming to his temple, and (an incidental outcome of adoption of the 1611 Authorized Version of the bible for the liturgical Epistles and Gospels in the 1662 revision) the mention of 'her' purification at the beginning of the Gospel (Luke 2:22).[14] The Gospel was then extended, by comparison with the Sarum and earlier Prayer-book provisions, to bring in Simeon's address to Mary, Anna's thanksgiving, the return to Nazareth and the growth of the Child (Luke 2:40).

Lady Day in the 1662 series of Collects, Epistles and Gospels is 'The Annunciation of the Blessed Virgin Mary', following both earlier Prayer-books and their mediaeval source. In the 1662 Kalendar it is 'The Annunciation of the Virgin'; here, however, the Sarum Kalendar had 'The Annunciation of the Lord', *Annunciatio dominica*, and the two earlier Prayer-books simply 'The Annunciation'. By 1662, then, we see the Kalendar entry for the Annunciation being conformed to the Collects, and perhaps too a movement towards what was obviously common usage connecting the day with the Virgin, as in the Table of Proper Lessons from Queen Elizabeth (1559) onwards, where it is 'The Annunciation of our Lady'; compare the popular title 'Lady Day'. The Epistle from Isaiah 7 and the Gospel from Luke 1, both continued from the old service, both continue to speak of both the Virgin and her Son.

The Christocentric Lady Day Collect in the Prayer-book is that which had formed the mediaeval Postcommunion collect for the day:

> We beseech thee, O Lord, pour thy grace into our hearts, that as we have known the incarnation of thy Son Jesus Christ by the message of an angel, so by his cross and passion we may be brought unto the glory of his resurrection …

In the fifteenth and sixteenth centuries this was also becoming the climactic prayer of the Angelus – a devotion which was still in its early stages when the Prayer-book was first compiled, but, in this respect to some extent like the Prayer-book, retained the impress of the double emphasis of the Lady-day provisions, an emphasis on Christ as well as Mary.

Reformation critique of 'Purification and other fond feasts of our Lady', to quote the 1560 *Book of Discipline* of John Knox and his fellow-reformers, had an echo in Roman Catholic liturgical revisions of the 1960s and 1970s.[15] Now both Candlemas and Lady Day became simply feasts of our Lord (compare the Sarum Kalendar for 25 March). This move was followed largely but not completely in the lists of holy days in the Alternative Service Book (1980) and then in Common Worship (2000); both give 'The Presentation of Christ in the Temple' (followed in Common Worship by 'Candlemas' in brackets) and 'The Annunciation of our Lord to the Blessed Virgin Mary', dismissing the Purification but leaving a foothold for the Marian associations of Lady Day. The change underlined the importance of Christ himself in these commemorations, but it had the possibly unintended side effect of shifting the liturgical focus of Marian devotion away from scenes described in the gospels of St Matthew and St Luke to scenes in the apocryphal narratives of Mary's Conception, Nativity and Assumption, narratives remembered in the background of the corresponding festivals. These feasts, apart from the Assumption, are there in the 1662 Prayer-book, but simply as black-letter days.

Hence, broadly speaking, the cult of our Lady in the Prayer-book preserves a mediaeval form, rooted in three red-letter days – Christmas, Candlemas and Lady Day – and focused on the gospels common to the whole church. The aureole of apocryphal narratives evoked in the black-letter feasts is left in the background. The liturgical developments of the 1960s reinforce devotion to Christ, but have paradoxically helped to shift Marian devotion in the west away from Christmas, Candlemas and Lady Day, with their gospel roots, and towards the commemorations which are linked with apocryphal writings. Aspects of the mediaeval and Prayer-book pattern which seem of abiding value include concentration on gospel texts which are the common property of all Christians, and the emphasis laid thereby on the intertwining of devotion to Mary with devotion to her Son. This emerges especially in the new Christmas collect:

Almighty God, who hast given us thy only-begotten Son to take our nature upon him, and as at this time to be born of a pure Virgin; grant that we being regenerate and made thy children by adoption and grace, may daily be renewed by thy holy Spirit.

The Creed, the Lord's Prayer, and the Ten Commandments
Having noted much which pertains to feeling and religious sentiment, I should like now to mention what may be called a rational element in Prayer-book piety, once again inherited from the Middle Ages: its emphasis on the teaching and learning of the Creed, the Lord's Prayer and the Ten Commandments. This comes out most obviously in the address to the godparents at the end of Baptism on the forms which the child shall learn, taken over from the Sarum address; the Creed and Lord's Prayer are common to both, but the Prayer-book drops Ave Maria and adds the Decalogue.[16] Emphasis on the Decalogue as well as the Creed and the Paternoster is nonetheless itself mediaeval, figuring in injunctions to parish clergy to instruct their people in these things, especially in Lent; so for example the teaching of the Decalogue is the first item to be mentioned in the thirteenth-century statutes for clergy in the diocese of Ely – typical of many sets of diocesan statutes and based on archbishop Peckham's *Constitution* of 1281; and they go on to mention explanation of the creeds as well, separately from the simple learning by heart of the Creed, Paternoster and Ave Maria which is required of children.[17]

In the Prayer-book itself the Creed, the Lord's Prayer and the Ten Commandments are of course the staple of the Catechism and preparation for Confirmation, and the Catechism too, although it is a Reformation composition, is close to mediaeval practice, as the injunctions already mentioned show. The individual application of this general and official practice is seen in a popular mediaeval work of devotion like the early thirteenth-century Mirror of St Edmund of Abingdon, which circulated in English as well as Latin.[18] Here the exposition of the Ten Commandments and the Lord's Prayer, with other forms for moral guidance like the lists of the Seven Virtues and the Seven Sins, comes together with personal prayer addressed to Jesus – in a manner uniting what I have called the rational element in piety with an individualized form of that heartfelt devotion to Christ considered at the beginning. The Prayer-book carried on this healthy combination of heart and head.

The Holy Spirit

Lastly, this sketch of some streams running from mediaeval devotion into the Prayer-book would be misleading if it did not note the abundance of piety connected with the Spirit. In the Prayer-book as in the wider liturgical tradition, direct appeal to the Spirit is (as already noted) rare, heartfelt and hymnodic, attested in the opening Trinitarian petitions of the Litany and in the *Veni Creator* in the Ordinal. Yet an emphasis on the Spirit is deep and pervasive.

As might be expected, the Prayer-book continuation of ancient and mediaeval emphasis on the Spirit comes to the fore in Baptism and Confirmation. Thus the bishop's prayer before the laying-on of hands at Confirmation, simply translated from the Latin of the Sarum rite, affirms the gift of the Spirit in the candidates' Baptism ('Almighty and everliving God, who hast vouchsafed to regenerate these thy servants by water and the Holy Ghost'), and asks now for the sevenfold gifts of the Spirit promised to the offspring of the stem of Jesse in Isa. 11:2 – 'the spirit of wisdom and understanding, the spirit of counsel and ghostly strength, the spirit of knowledge and true godliness', ending 'and fill them, O Lord, with the spirit of thy holy fear'.[19]

For the laying-on of hands itself, no longer accompanied by anointing, Cranmer in 1552 introduced the memorable formula 'Defend O Lord this thy child with thy heavenly grace, that (s)he may continue thine for ever, and daily increase in thy Holy Spirit, more and more, until (s)he come unto thy everlasting kingdom'. The prayer for the candidates after their Confirmation likewise asks 'let thy Holy Spirit ever be with them'. These petitions transferred into new prayers the emphasis on the gift of the Spirit from the old versicles, responses and collect after the anointing.[20]

Similarly, the Prayer-book Baptism service retains in a new form the prominence given in the old rite to the gift of the Spirit, for which the congregation now prays corporately ('give thy Holy Spirit to this infant, that (s)he may be born again'). It also includes a thanksgiving that the child is 'regenerate and grafted into the body of Christ's church'. This thanksgiving is initiated by the Lord's Prayer, which is used at Baptism and Confirmation, as in the Communion Service, at the point in the rite when one can be considered as having been brought near to God – just after reception of baptism, confirmation, or holy communion.

Prayer-book continuation of an old emphasis on the gift of the Spirit in baptism and confirmation emerges also elsewhere in the liturgy. Instances appear in varying uses made of the Miserere, Psalm 51, in adoption of old usage. Thus this psalm provides the closing versicle and response, taken over from Prime, at Mattins and Evensong: 'O God make clean our hearts within us, And take not thy Holy Spirit from us'; compare Ps. 51:10–12

> Make me a clean heart, O God: and renew a right spirit within me.
> Cast me not away from thy presence: and take not thy holy Spirit from me.
> O give me the comfort of thy help again: and stablish me with thy free Spirit.

As a versicle and response in the office the quotations from verses 10–11 become a kind of daily reminder of baptism and confirmation. Coverdale's version of verse 12 recalls the New Testament with its renderings 'comfort' (compare 'the comfort of the Holy Ghost', Acts 9:31, and the 'Comforter' of John 14:16, etc., and the Te Deum); and 'free Spirit' (compare 'where the Spirit of the Lord is, there is liberty', II Cor. 3:17).

At the beginning of Lent the Miserere with these verses comes in again, said 'by the Priest and Clerks kneeling', in the Ash

Wednesday prayers which form the second part of the Commination Service and were simply taken over from the Sarum rite.[21]

Other parts of the network of Prayer-book allusions to the Spirit appear in the collects. A group of great collects, nearly all simply translated from the Sarum rite, take up in various ways the Pauline affirmation that 'the love of God is poured into our hearts by the Holy Ghost which is given to us' (Rom. 5:5). This is paraphrased, in combination with the prayer of Ps. 51:10 (the versicle 'O God, make clean our hearts within us'), in the Collect for Purity at the start of the communion service:

> Cleanse the thoughts of our hearts by the inspiration of thy Holy Spirit, that we may perfectly love thee …

Rom. 5:5 is paraphrased again in the petition 'Send thy Holy Ghost …' in Cranmer's new Collect for Quinquagesima, just before Lent, now in connection with I Corinthians 13, the Epistle for the day:

> O Lord, who hast taught us that all our doings without charity are nothing worth: Send thy Holy Ghost, and pour into our hearts that most excellent gift of charity, the very bond of peace and of all virtues, without which whosoever liveth is counted dead before thee.

Elsewhere allusion to Rom. 5:5 brings the Spirit to mind implicitly, as in the Sarum and Prayer-book Collect for Trinity VI:

> O God, who hast prepared for them that love thee such good things as pass man's understanding: Pour into our hearts such love towards thee, that we, loving thee above all things, may obtain thy promises, which exceed all that we can desire.

Here Rom. 5:5 ('Pour into our hearts …') is combined with I Cor. 2:9–10 'Eye hath not seen, nor ear heard, neither have entered into the heart of man, the things which God hath prepared for them that love him. But God hath revealed them unto us by his Spirit …'. The Epistle for Trinity VI which follows (Rom. 6:3–11) is on Baptism.

A similar allusion to Rom. 5:5 opens the Lady Day collect mentioned already: 'We beseech thee, O Lord, pour thy grace into

Biblical Voices and Echoes

our hearts …'. Rom. 5:5 is likewise at the heart of the Sarum and Prayer-book Collect for Trinity VII:

> Lord of all power and might, who art the author and giver of all good things, graft in our hearts the love of thy Name, increase in us true religion, nourish us with all goodness, and of thy great mercy keep us in the same.

This Collect begins with allusions to James 1:17; 21 'every good gift and every perfect gift is from above … receive with meekness the engrafted word'; but it goes on to Rom. 5:5 ('in our hearts the love of thy Name'), and then recalls the gifts of godliness and holy fear ('true religion', 'goodness') from the sevenfold gifts of the Spirit in Isa. 11:2, mentioned in the Bishop's prayer before confirmation.

All these apart from the Quinquagesima collect are translations of old collects. Cranmer followed their line of allusion to the gift of the Spirit not only at Quinquagesima but also in the echo of baptism and confirmation in his new collect for Christmas, asking, as already noted,

> that we, being regenerate and made thy children by adoption and grace, may daily be renewed by thy Holy Spirit.

Here the final phrase on renewal by the Spirit joins II Cor. 4:16 on daily renewal ('the inward man is renewed day by day') with Ps. 104:30 on the Spirit:

> When thou lettest thy breath go forth they shall be made: and thou shalt renew the face of the earth' (Authorized Version 'Thou sendest forth thy spirit, they are created …)

These words formed a versicle and response praying for the candidates in the Sarum rite of confirmation cited above ('Send forth thy Spirit and they shall be made, And thou shalt renew the face of the earth'). They were used too in the Sarum preparatory prayers for clergy and assistants at the eucharist.

Finally, the Prayer-book provisions for the Feast of Pentecost itself extend this Spirit-centred devotion. The new Collect for the

94

previous Sunday, adapting an old antiphon as noted already, dramatically turns the Sunday after Ascension and the succeeding days before Pentecost into a time of apostolic waiting (Luke 24:49, Acts 1:4) and prayer for the gift of the Spirit, expressed in the terms of Christ's promise of the Comforter to the disciples, noted already from the Fourth Gospel:

> O God the King of glory, who hast exalted thine only Son Jesus Christ with great triumph unto thy kingdom in heaven, we beseech thee, leave us not comfortless [compare John 14:16–18]; but send to us thine Holy Ghost to comfort us, and exalt us unto the same place whither our Saviour Christ is gone before.

Preparation for Whitsun is now focused on prayer for the gift of the Spirit, recalling the corporate prayer for the Spirit highlighted in Cranmer's baptism service.

Then the proper psalms for Whitsun, taken over from the Sarum rite, interpret the work of the Spirit. *Exsurgat Deus*, Psalm 68, is appointed for Whitsun in the 1662 Prayer-book following mediaeval usage, although in 1549 it had been allotted to the Ascension. With the Epistle to the Ephesians (4:7–11) this psalm was taken to allude to the Ascension – 'Magnify him that rideth upon the heavens' (Ps. 68:4); 'Thou art gone up on high, thou hast led captivity captive …' (Ps. 68:18) – and also to the ensuing Pentecostal gift of the Holy Ghost, and the apostolic preaching:

> Thou, O God, sentest a gracious rain upon thine inheritance: and refreshedst it when it was weary.
> Thy congregation shall dwell therein: for thou, O God, hast of thy goodness prepared for the poor.
> The Lord gave the word: great was the company of the preachers
> (Ps. 68:9–11)

This association with Ascensiontide and Pentecost, given by the Epistle to the Ephesians, was further encouraged by aspects of the pre-Christian Septuagint Greek translation, rendered into

Latin in Jerome's 'Gallican Psalter' which was used in mediaeval liturgy. Thus Ps. 68:4, where these versions have 'him who ascends above the sunset', could readily be linked with the Ascension. Comparably, the day of Pentecost can be recalled by verses 24–7, the glowing description of 'how thou, my God and King, goest in the sanctuary', mentioning the singers, the minstrels, the damsels playing with the timbrels, Benjamin and the princes of Judah, Zabulon and Nephthali. In these versions it is indeed a scene of Pentecostal mystic enthusiasm, felt in particular by Benjamin: 'There is the young Benjamin in a trance' (verse 27).

The Prayer-book version from the Great Bible follows what became the usual Jewish reading tradition of the Hebrew text here, with 'There is little Benjamin their ruler' (Ps. 68:27); but it still keeps the Pentecostal atmosphere, for it has rendered the previous verse (Ps. 68:26)

> Give thanks, O Israel, unto God the Lord in the congregations: from the ground of the heart.

For the last words the Authorized Version has 'from the fountain of Israel', but the Great Bible took 'Israel' as a vocative and 'fountain' in the transferred sense of 'source' or 'origin'. Here 'ground' seems almost like the language of Meister Eckhart or other mediaeval mystics, in which 'ground' can refer to the inward abyss of the soul, the depth of our being.[22]

Another of the Pentecostal Proper Psalms is Ps. 104, already quoted for the use of verse 30 'When thou lettest thy breath go forth they shall be made: and thou shalt renew the face of the earth' as a versicle and response in the mediaeval rite of confirmation, and for the allusion to it in the prayer for renewal by the Spirit in Cranmer's new Christmas collect. The use of Ps. 104 as a Proper Psalm replaces this verse on creation and renewal by the Spirit in the context of the whole psalm on the making and maintenance of the world. This magnificent context in turn explicates the work of the Spirit as 'giver of life' and *Creator Spiritus* – two traditional descriptions which themselves look back, through such passages as John 6:63, II Cor. 3:6 and Gen. 1:2, 2:7, to Ps. 104:30.

The Spirit-centred continuation of mediaeval devotion in the Prayer-book, now sketched in part, gives an attention to the individual which is rooted in each person's share in baptism and confirmation and explores, in collects and in psalmody, the depths of the individual heart. The passing approximation to mystical language in Ps. 68:26, where Israel is to give thanks 'from the ground of the heart', suits this broader context, notably the reminiscences in the Collects of the love of God 'poured into our hearts by the Holy Ghost which is given to us' (Rom. 5:5). The heart's thanksgiving is then the effluence of the love imparted by the Spirit.

At the same time there is also a recognition of the corporate dimension of devotion to the Spirit; we partake of the Spirit by incorporation into the church. The versicle and response from Psalm 51, the Miserere, and the Ash Wednesday use of the Miserere itself, and the Collects which evoke the thought of the purification of the individual heart through infusion of the Spirit – all these are communal: a common prayer in the case of the Miserere, a prayer expressed in the first person plural in the case of the versicle and Collects. Correspondingly, at Baptism we give thanks, in a new prayer, that the candidate is regenerate, adopted as God's own child – and incorporated into his holy church. After receiving Holy Communion we give thanks, again in a new prayer, for the assurance that we are 'very members incorporate in the mystical body of [God's] Son, which is the blessed company of all faithful people'.

These new developments take up an existing traditional emphasis on the gift of the Spirit in the church, but, following the New Testament, express church membership in the typical Pauline terms of incorporation in Christ. The Collects and the petitions from the Miserere, all focused on the gift of the Spirit, are earnestly seeking holiness; but the church in view in the further prayers just mentioned is not a restricted group of the holy, but a universal church praying to be inspired continually with the spirit of truth, unity and concord. This conjunction avoids some potential Pentecostal perils, perhaps at the expense of tolerating laxity. Yet a deep Spirit-centred desire for holiness is an unmistakable part of the Prayer-book's mediaeval inheritance, a part which was welcomed and developed by its compilers and revisers.

The work of the Spirit in creation is recognized, but it appears most characteristically when the continuity of the Spirit's creation and re-creation in nature with new creation in humanity is affirmed, as in the use made of Ps. 104:30 'renew the face of the earth' in the Christmas Collect asking for our 'daily renewal'. Overall, the Prayer-book development of the mediaeval piety of the Spirit brings to the fore the individual heart, the gift of divine love, and renewal within the community, rather than the work of the Spirit in creation and nature, although that is certainly not forgotten. In this proportion and emphasis, however, the piety of the Prayer-book is perhaps not far from that of the New Testament itself, where language specifically connected with the Holy Spirit is concerned. New Testament emphasis too falls mainly on the Spirit 'among Christians and as the agent of the "new creation" – the bringing persons to new life in Christ'.[23]

In all, then, I should like to highlight the value of the Prayer-book's continuation and development of mediaeval devotion. Some instances of this have now been noted in regard to Christ and our Lady, the intellectual and moral foundations of Christian faith, and the Holy Spirit. The prayers concerned combine and give fresh life to verses from the psalms, the gospels and the epistles. Their ethos is deeply felt but unsentimental, thought out and scriptural but touched with warmth and ardour, speaking to the individual heart but surrounded by awareness of the blessed company of all faithful people. Recourse to them and renewed contact with their outlook can perhaps play a part in contemporary piety.

Endnotes

[1] Reproduced with revision from a lecture published under the same title in *Faith and Worship* 67 (2010), 24–39.

[2] P. Dearmer, *The Parson's Handbook* (11th edn, London, 1909), 5, quoted in discussion of Dearmer's influence by P.F. Anson, *Fashions in Church Furnishing, 1840–1960* (London, 1960), 305–15.

[3] This extensively revived arrangement was typical of the later Middle Ages, especially in northern Europe; 'there is nothing peculiarly English or insular about it', writes C.E. Pocknee, *The Christian Altar* (London, 1963), 58.

[4] I have used the word 'piety' in the title and occasionally throughout because it suggests practice more plainly than 'spirituality' does.

[5] D. MacCulloch, *Reformation* (London, 2005), 133; 257; 291.

[6] C.S. Lewis, *Poetry and Prose in the Sixteenth Century* (Oxford, 1954, repr. 1990), 215. Lewis had been a younger colleague of Brightman among the Fellows of Magdalen College, Oxford.

[7] Lewis, *Poetry and Prose in the Sixteenth Century*, 220–21.

[8] H.B. Swete, *Church Services and Service-books before the Reformation* (London, 1896), 172–91.

[9] 1544 text, reprinted in W.K. Clay, *Private Prayers put forth by Authority during the Reign of Queen Elizabeth* (Parker Society; Cambridge, 1851), 563–76 (Appendix). I have modernized the spelling.

[10] F.E. Brightman, *The English Rite* (2 vols., London, 1915), i, lviii–lxviii, 174–85.

[11] H.P. Liddon, *The Divinity of Our Lord and Saviour Jesus Christ* (fifteenth edn, London, 1891), 531–43 (Note G); Judith Anne Merivale (ed.), *Autobiography of Dean Merivale with Selections from his Correspondence* (London, 1899), 262–3 (letter of Dean Merivale, 3 October 1866; a letter on this aspect of the Litany from Bishop Colenso was printed in *The Times* of 26 September 1866, and Liddon's Note begins by rebutting it).

[12] For the five collects mentioned below see Brightman, *The English Rite*, i, 208–209, 226–7, 234–5, 294–5, 438–9.

[13] On the provisions for these festivals noted below see Brightman, *The English Rite*, i, 59 (Proper Psalms and Lessons), 82–9 (Kalendar), 220–21 (Christmas); ii, 564–71 (Purification), 574–9 (Annunciation), 684–5 (Proper Prefaces); [William Bright (ed.)], *The Prayer-book of Queen Elizabeth, 1559* (London, 1890), 25 (Proper Lessons).

[14] The earlier Prayer-books (taking the Gospel from the Great Bible) had followed the reading 'their purification', which reappeared in modern times in the Revised Version and the New Revised Standard Version.

[15] *Book of Discipline* of 1560, reproduced in book iii of John Knox's *History of the Reformation in Scotland*; see D. Laing (ed.), *The Works of John Knox* (6 vols., Edinburgh, 1895), ii, 185–6 ('The Explication of the First Head').

[16] Brightman, *The English Rite*, ii, 744–5.

[17] C. L. Feltoe & E. Minns, *Liber Vetus Archidiaconi Eliensis* (Cambridge, 1917), 9, 215–17.

[18] A modern English rendering, from Middle English, is given (in view of a possible attribution of the Middle English version to Richard Rolle) in Geraldine E. Hodgson, *Some Minor Works of Richard Rolle* (London, 1923), 94–147.

[19] Brightman, *The English Rite*, ii, 794–5.

[20] The Confirmation office from a fifteenth-century Sarum Pontifical is reprinted in F. Procter & W. H. Frere, *A New History of the Book of Common Prayer* (London, 1911), 603–4.

[21] Brightman, *The English Rite*, ii, 894–7.

[22] B. McGinn, *The Mystical Thought of Meister Eckhart* (New York, 2001), 40–41.

[23] C.F.D. Moule, *The Holy Spirit* (London, 1978), 19–21: 'In the New Testament … so far from the Spirit's being cosmic in scope (as Christ, the *Logos* of God, is), the Spirit is scarcely mentioned except as among Christians and as the agent of the "new creation" – the bringing persons to new life in Christ'.

6
THE MAKING OF THE AUTHORIZED VERSION:
KING JAMES'S TRANSLATORS
AND THEIR PROBLEMS

The translators who made King James's version of the bible represented the two universities of his new English realm.[1] Their tasks are approached here through some recollection of the Cambridge involvement in the process, from the antecedents of the translation project to the making of the English version, and its early reception. Following this thread, I seek to discover the tasks of biblical translation in something of their roughness and particularity.

Antecedents
The translators' task was shaped by the work of their predecessors. The project for a new translation had arisen at the Hampton Court Conference convened by the king in 1604, soon after his accession, to consider difficulties felt by the Puritan party in the Church of England in conforming to the Book of Common Prayer. Among these difficulties was acceptance of the Prayer-book's use of the English version of scripture by Miles Coverdale, based on translations by William Tyndale and others, and presented in the Great Bible of Henry VIII; they called it 'a most corrupted translation', according to the preface of 'The Translators to the Reader' in the 1611 Bible. The king sponsored the suggestion of a new translation which was made by the Puritan leader John Rainolds, President of Corpus Christi College, Oxford.

The king's translators, as represented in their preface, were themselves unwilling to echo condemnation of their predecessors. They claimed only that, thanks to the efforts of earlier translators, they might sometimes do better. They had in fact been commanded, not to make an entirely fresh version, but to revise the Bishops' Bible of 1568, the translation of which had been overseen by archbishop Matthew Parker, formerly Master of Corpus Christi College, Cambridge. Parker's Preface stressed the value of earlier versions, in the manner which the 1611 translators would follow.[2] The Bishops' Bible was itself a revision of Henry VIII's Great Bible of 1539–40, which incorporated the work of Tyndale, John Rogers, and Coverdale, all associated with Cambridge in different ways, and it received a preface on the perils as well as benefits of bible reading – still reprinted in the Bishops' Bible – from archbishop Thomas Cranmer, formerly fellow of Jesus College, Cambridge.

The Cambridge line running from Cranmer's Great Bible through Parker's Bishops' Bible directly to the Authorized Version is completed under King James by his two first Archbishops of Canterbury, both originally singled out for advancement by queen Elizabeth. John Whitgift, at Cambridge formerly Master of Pembroke and Trinity, as archbishop in the 1590s had known the complaints about variation and suspected inaccuracy in English bibles which accompanied requests for a fresh translation, and he led the bishops at the Hampton Court Conference in the last year of his life. Then Richard Bancroft, educated at Christ's, as Bishop of London formulated the translators' rules according to the king's wish, and as archbishop made some last changes in the completed translation. Both were scholar-archbishops as well as ecclesiastical statesmen, and their biblical interests are symbolized by two of Whitgift's own books now in Cambridge, a transcript of Codex Bezae, an important manuscript of the Greek text of the gospels and the Acts, which he left to Trinity, and a Complutensian Polyglot bible – the first printing (1514 onwards, at Alcalá de Henares, Latin Complutum) of all the Hebrew, Greek and Latin biblical texts in parallel – which he left to Pembroke.

In queen Elizabeth's time, however, the new translations which became current together with the Bishops' Bible group themselves in the contemporary debate on order in church and state. Eight years before the Bishops' Bible, the Geneva Bible was dedicated to queen Elizabeth in 1560. It had been translated mainly in queen Mary's

time by William Whittingham and other English exiles under
Calvin's wing in Geneva, among them the Cambridge Hebraist
Anthony Gilby of Christ's. Its informative notes were outspoken on
the reformed side. Matthew Parker initially saluted its achievement,
but in 1571 he was having to arrange for both Whittingham and
Gilby to be interviewed as suspected offenders against church
discipline.[3] They belonged to the party now being called 'puritan',
who opposed the wearing of the surplice and wanted government
by elders, 'presbytery', alongside or instead of government by
bishops, in line with the much debated appeal on this point to the
New Testament and St Jerome which Calvin had mounted in later
editions of his *Institutes* (1559, iv 3, 8; 4, 2).

Then in 1582, after the Bishops' Bible, the first printed English
version to be approved by Roman Catholic authority appeared in
Rheims, under the auspices of the English College in exile founded
at Douai in 1568, which had moved to Rheims ten years later. It
was a New Testament only; the Old Testament was finished, but
not printed until 1611, too late for James I's translators. This New
Testament continued a small series of Roman Catholic versions
in modern European languages which were probably sometimes
valued simply as translations, but were justified by their sponsors
as helps for disputation.[4] The English was translated from the Latin
Vulgate, with reference to the Greek and with defensive notes, by
Gregory Martin, formerly scholar of St John's College, Oxford. At
the same time he issued a lively short polemic against the earlier
Tudor versions, touching the sore point of their variations, under
the title *A Discoverie of the manifold corruptions of the Holy Scriptures
by the Heretikes of our daies, specially the English Sectaries, and of their
foule dealing herein, by partial and false translations to the advantage of
their heresies, in their English Bibles used and authorised since the time of
Schisme*. Martin received a reply in a substantial work by William
Fulke, Master of Pembroke College, Cambridge, with the counter-
title *A Defense of the sincere and true Translations of the holie Scriptures*

into the English tong, against the manifold cavils, frivolous quarels, and impudent slaunders of Gregorie Martin ... (1583).[5]

It is in the light of the close bond between the bible and disputation that Matthew Parker had prohibited polemical notes in the Bishops' Bible, perhaps thinking especially of Geneva, and that, in extension of his rule, King James's translators were allowed no annotations at all. As far as possible, their version was to be for unity.

The thread of Cambridge association with the Tudor and Stuart series of English biblical versions thus runs from Henry VIII to James I through the Bishops' Bible and in touch with two other Elizabethan translations. It shows up the importance of the bible for debate on ecclesiastical and civil polity. At the same time it exhibits two less-frequently discussed concerns of public opinion, both of them vital for King James's translators: philology on the one hand, and the special status of the biblical books on the other.

Philology and the Special Status of the Bible
The names of Tyndale, Parker and Gilby hint at the international humanist philological engagement with Greek and Hebrew as well as Latin which informs the whole series of translations, including King James's. Gilby as a Fellow of Christ's had shared a concern with Greek and Hebrew which went back in his college to bishop John Fisher in the early sixteenth century. Then and earlier, humanists could appeal to the decree of the Council of Vienne in 1311–12 which had ordained chairs in Hebrew, Greek and other languages at Paris, Oxford and elsewhere. The steady sixteenth-century continuance of philological concern is seen in Cambridge in the succession of new colleges at this time which require from all Fellows or scholars study of and sometimes converse in Hebrew and Greek as well as Latin: see the statutes of St John's under Henry VIII (1516, 1524), Trinity under Edward VI (1552), and Emmanuel and Sidney Sussex under queen Elizabeth (1584, 1596). The series of statutory trilingual provisions was continued in the early seventeenth century by Trinity College, Dublin, founded in 1592 and closely linked with Cambridge.[6] The

primacy of the three tongues was also shown by king Henry's chairs of Greek and Hebrew at Oxford and Cambridge, and in older college foundations by benefactions like the Thomas Watts scholarships endowed in 1571 at Pembroke, involving examination in Latin, Greek and Hebrew. These provisions are matched in Oxford and continental Europe, and mirror the humanist ideal, dear to Erasmus, of a trilingual college.

Philology is also one clue to the widespread sense that a new translation was needed. The advance of learning had brought attention to freshly-known manuscripts like Codex Bezae, already mentioned, and new editions of primary biblical texts. Thus Erasmus's Greek Testament and the pioneering Complutensian Polyglot were followed in 1555 by the first edition of a Syriac text of the gospels, by J.A. Widmanstadt, named in the 1611 translators' preface, in 1565 by Beza's Greek Testament, dedicated to queen Elizabeth, and then, unfortunately just after the Bishops' Bible had appeared, by the great Antwerp Polyglot of Arias Montanus (1569–72), dedicated to Philip II of Spain and at once a standard resource; thus Matthew Parker, Lancelot Andrewes and the early library of Emmanuel each owned a copy. Then in 1587 Pope Sixtus V printed the Septuagint according to the fourth-century Codex Vaticanus, a landmark in study of the Greek bible.

Again, new biblical translations by individual Hebrew and Greek scholars brought light from sources including mediaeval Jewish commentary and wide classical reading. Influential examples are the Latin bible of 1528 translated by the Dominican Hebraist Santi Pagnini, known to the English less melodiously as Pagnine or Pagnins, whose early Hebrew studies in Florence were moved forward by Savonarola, and the Latin Old Testament of the former Franciscan Sebastian Munster, of Basle, dedicated to Henry VIII in 1535.[7] Pagnine was reprinted and revised by Arias Montanus in the Antwerp Polyglot, and again issued simply with the Hebrew in 1584; and in 1569 Immanuele Tremelli (Tremellius), the Italian Jewish Protestant who had been Regius Professor of Hebrew in

Cambridge under Edward VI, dedicated to queen Elizabeth and Matthew Parker a Latin New Testament translated from both Greek and Syriac, followed by widely-used new Latin translations of the entire bible. New modern-language versions, such as A. Brucioli's Italian bible of 1532, were also important. At the time of king James's translation, new English versions by individuals, Ambrose Ussher in Ireland and Hugh Broughton, formerly Fellow of Christ's, were already in progress.

At the same time the affirmation of the authority of the Vulgate at the Council of Trent in 1546 had been followed by efforts to correct the printed Latin biblical texts, notably in the edition of Louvain, 1547 and then in Sixtus V's unsuccessful 1590 edition, rapidly superseded under Clement VII in 1592 by another, the so-called Sixto-Clementine Vulgate. The variations between editions sponsored by two successive popes did not fail to attract in England the kind of notice which those between the earlier English versions had just received in Rheims – see the critique by Bodley's Librarian, Thomas James, under the title 'The War of the Popes', *Bellum papale* (1600, 1611). Yet the efforts made to correct the printed Latin Vulgate – the version which educated members of the Church of England still often quoted rather than any English version – did underline the need for corrected English bibles which could also have had the benefit of the many new instruments of biblical study which were available by the end of queen Elizabeth's reign.

Philology then was a passion of the age, but it might be in tension with the special status of the bible. Soon after the Hampton Court Conference, Francis Bacon, a former pupil of Whitgift and a friend of Lancelot Andrewes, issued his review of the whole field of human inquiry, *The Advancement of Learning* (1605).[8] Here (book ii, dedication, 5) he notes the need for 'new editions of authors, with more correct impressions' – printings – 'more faithful translations, more profitable glosses, more diligent annotations, and the like'. 'More faithful translations', 'more profitable glosses', and 'more correct impressions', were at the heart of the 1611 translators' concerns. But, although Bacon holds that human wisdom and learning, including natural science, are from God and lead to him, he distinguishes them from revelation apprehended through faith. 'I do much condemn', he writes (book ii, 25.17), 'that interpretation of the scripture which is only after the manner as men use to interpret a profane book.' He enlarges here on modes of exegesis, but considerations about translation itself are also implied. These two dicta of Bacon, one endorsing the philological approach to good literature and the other suggesting that, in the case of the bible, this approach is not enough, highlight a tension which the 1611 translators shared with their predecessors in the ancient as well as the contemporary world.

The sacred and authoritative character of scripture has indeed tended from ancient times onwards to encourage an unusually literal style of translation, often designed to keep open all or much of the whole range of meaning hitherto attached to the text. So the polymath lawyer and Hebraist John Selden, aged twenty-seven in 1611–12, said later

> There is no book so translated as the bible for the purpose. If I translate a French book into English, I turn it into English phrase, not into French English. I say it is cold, not, it makes cold; but the bible is rather translated into English words than into English phrase. The Hebraisms are kept, and the phrase of that language is kept.[9]

This joke of course does apply to 1611, which elsewhere he praises, as well as its predecessors. Without entering into the literary problem of translation, we may simply add that the argument does not stop when literalism is seen to be unusual. At the same time as the twentieth-century revolt against literalism in biblical translation, the view was also being expressed that good translation paradoxically requires there to be some impact of the alien syntax and idiom of the original on the language of the translation – in this case some Hebraism, as Selden put it, in English.[10] Part of the interest of the Authorized Version lies in the ingenuity with which a close translation, itself revising the Bishops' Bible, is made to serve both philology – my main concern here – and English.

Translators

To come now to the work of translation, over fifty of king James's translators are known by name. Cambridge can claim twenty-nine of them. This number for such an enterprise was perhaps unrivalled since pre-Christian times, when the translation of Hebrew biblical books into Greek known as the Septuagint was credited to seventy-two translators sent by the Jewish high priest Eleazar to Alexandria at the request of the bibliophile Greek king of Egypt, Ptolemy II. The making of the Septuagint is mentioned in the prefaces of both the Bishops' Bible and the Authorized Version, and was doubtless in the mind of the learned king James and his advisers.

At any rate, they divided six companies of translators between Westminster, Oxford and Cambridge, setting one Hebrew and one Greek company in each centre, and also inviting comments from scholars not in the companies. To follow the Cambridge thread, the first Westminster company, led by the Dean of Westminster, Lancelot Andrewes, was composed almost entirely of Cambridge members, and charged with the books from Genesis to II Kings. Just under half the second Westminster company were from Cambridge; led by William Barlow, of St John's and Trinity Hall, Dean of Chester, it undertook the New Testament Epistles. Then the two companies in Cambridge took in Hebrew the books from I Chronicles to the Song of Solomon, and in Greek the Apocrypha, respectively.

Within the high general linguistic standard of these translators, noted scholars included Lancelot Andrewes, William Bedwell the Arabist, Edward Lively the Regius Professor of Hebrew (died 1605), Andrew Downes the Regius Professor of Greek, and a star pupil of his, John Bois, rector of Boxworth and formerly fellow of St John's; a surviving copy of some of Bois' notes forms a help to study of the 1611 translation. Typically of the age, Bois learned Hebrew as a child from his father (he was writing in Hebrew characters by the age of six or thereabouts), and then, again after initial instruction from his father, became at the university (which he entered aged fourteen) an outstanding Grecian who, when appointed to a philosophical lectureship, could sometimes fill the schools by his lectures on Plato's *Timaeus*. From Boxworth he used to ride into Cambridge to carry on hearing the lectures of Downes and Lively. No doubt in connection with the translation, he wrote notes on the New Testament, comparing the older English translation (? the Bishops' Bible) with more recent versions.[11]

The Cambridge contingent also shows the diversity of church opinion among the translators, from friends of episcopacy and ordered ceremonial like Lancelot Andrewes to puritan sympathizers like Laurence Chaderton, Master of Emmanuel.

Within Cambridge strongly represented colleges are Trinity, in the lead with nine translators (including John Overall, Master of St Catharine's), followed by Emmanuel with five (including three who became college heads elsewhere), in turn nearly bumped by St John's and Pembroke, each with four. The high places therefore go not simply to large colleges, although size was probably a factor, but rather to three of the four trilingual Tudor foundations mentioned above (the fourth, Sidney, is represented by its Master Samuel Ward, formerly Fellow of Emmanuel); the single older college in a high place, Pembroke, is also one with a Tudor trilingual benefaction, the Watts scholarship which most or all of its translators had held.

A general revision committee, including Downes and Bois, reviewed the whole translation. Finally it was submitted to two bishops, Thomas Bilson of Winchester, and Miles Smith of Gloucester (from the second Oxford company; author of the translators' preface), and to archbishop Bancroft. The work then went to the printers. It was soon issued not only in the imposing folio size suitable for lecterns but also, often bound up with the Book of Common Prayer and the metrical psalms, in handier quarto volumes which could be used at home and taken to church (see Plate 7).

Two Non-Translators

Two Cambridge non-translators cast light on the enterprise. The rôle of gadfly was performed by the slight and fiery Hugh Broughton of Christ's, whose independent translation has been mentioned already.[12] Living mainly in London and Germany, in a somewhat F.R. Leavis-like fashion he held no chair or fellowship, but was famous for rabbinic learning, imaginative teaching (he knew how to teach a small boy Hebrew attractively through the spoken language), and pungent criticism – directed not least at Edward Lively, 'thirty years Professor of Hebrew', as Broughton delighted to say when noting what seemed to him Lively's mistakes. He had lobbied in the 1590s for a new translation, but believed that the way had been blocked by Whitgift. Now he accompanied the translators' efforts with pamphlets on their progress and with his own continuing biblical translations. In the end he contributed indirectly to the 1611 version, as compiler of the series of genealogical tables issued by John Speed which were inserted in early editions; his characteristic reference to the Talmud on the descent of Jesus in the introduction may have brought before some younger bible-readers the name of the Talmud for the first time (the last of these tables [Salathiel (I Chron. 3:17) to Christ] can be seen, opposite the title-page of the translation, in Plate 7). Broughton was perhaps the earliest critic of the Authorized Version, and he influenced another Cambridge critic, his academic grandson John Lightfoot, Master of St Catharine's and among the greatest English Hebraists; Lightfoot as a young man was chaplain to Sir Rowland Cotton, the Staffordshire squire who had once been the little boy who learned Hebrew from Broughton, and who now led Lightfoot to deepen his Hebrew study.

Another non-translator scholar was Andrew Willet, Rector successively of Childerley and Little Gransden in Cambridgeshire and then of Barley, just over the border in north Hertfordshire. A master of synthesis, from 1605 onwards he in effect complemented the translators' efforts by supplying the need for full biblical commentary in English, in volumes on Genesis, Exodus, Leviticus,

I–II Samuel, Daniel, and Romans. His interpretation is based on a translation process very like that followed by the king's translators. See his characteristic book title *Hexapla in Genesin*: that is, A sixfold commentarie vpon Genesis: wherein sixe seuerall translations, that is, the Septuagint, and the Chalde, two Latin, of Hierome and Tremellius, two English, the great Bible, and the Geneva edition are compared, where they differ, with the originall Hebrew, and Pagnine, and Montanus interlinearie interpretation … (Cambridge, 1605). Compare the 1611 translators' preface: using 'the Hebrew text of the Old Testament, the Greek of the New', we did not think it too much 'to consult the Translators or Commentators, Chaldee, Hebrew, Syrian, Greek, or Latin, no nor the Spanish, French, Italian, or Dutch …'. Willet indicates the setting of the translators' work in what might now be called a kind of research culture, a large public who could make a reasonably informed judgment on what they were doing, and had an appetite, to which the much debated biblical annotations had catered, for reliable information on the problems of interpreting scripture.

The Translators' Tasks

Cambridge translators, including among them here the first Westminster company, were charged with all the Old Testament apart from the

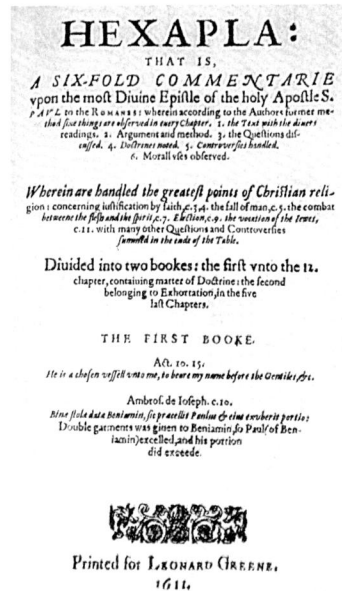

Figure 6.1: Title-page of Andrew Willet's *Hexapla* or sixfold commentary, on Romans (1611); one of a number of English-language commentaries which he wrote in this format, it illustrates the widespread interest in biblical translation and interpretation taken at the time of the publication of the 1611 King James Bible.

111

Prophets. To follow the conventional English names and order of the books, they had to render from Hebrew all the Pentateuchal law and narrative, all the histories which follow (Joshua–Esther) and four poetical books (Psalms to the Song of Songs). Their problems included the mannered prose style of the books of Chronicles, which they mirrored in a more literal translation than Geneva had favoured, as in the famous 'thine, O Lord, is the greatness, and the power, and the glory, and the victory, and the majesty' (I Chron. 29:11), which unlike Geneva translates all the Hebrew articles and suggests the almost incantatory or liturgical quality of the original. Then there were the poetical books, including Job, with its grandeurs and obscurities.

Then in the Apocrypha they were confronting directly the Greek texts of the Septuagint, ranging in style from simple representations of Hebrew narrative and verse to what Jerome called, in the case of the book of Wisdom, 'Greek eloquence'. The results are still valued, as when the sonorous 'Let us now praise famous men' in Ecclesiasticus modulates to 'such as found out musical tunes, and recited verses in writing' – although there has been more controversy over the close rendering of the ornate but deliberately abrupt Greek prose of II Maccabees: Lysias 'persuaded, pacified, made them well affected, returned to Antioch' (II Macc. 13:26) – I like it myself, but you can see why Geneva and others add more words.

In the New Testament Epistles, which Cambridge translators shared, the Second Westminster Committee's rendering of Ephesians has brought strong reactions. Here the habitually close 1611 translation reproduces the vast sentence-paragraphs of the Greek, whereas modern translators break them up into short units for comprehensibility, but, in Henry Chadwick's view, at the same time forfeit their impact. He adds mordantly: 'the Authorized Version, with all its portentous obscurity, conveys something of the right total effect'.[13]

Shape of their Bible
The arrangement and titles of the books in an English bible are closely associated with the Authorized Version. It is then worth recalling that already under James I they were largely inherited. Thus Cambridge translators tackled the Apocrypha as a single group of books, but the Bishops' Bible and the Great Bible had already gathered these books, which Jews did not recognize as authoritative and for which no Hebrew original was then available, from their various places among the books translated from Hebrew into one place together at the end of the Old Testament. This custom goes back to the 1520s in the reform movement; it followed St Jerome's statement, in his Prologue to the books of Kings, that such books 'should be set apart among apocrypha', a dictum which had also been echoed in the Middle Ages.[14]

The application of the title Apocrypha to these books, also inherited from Coverdale's Bible, goes back to common mediaeval usage, following St Jerome. By 1611, however, the name as well as the place of these books had become controversial; the new term deuterocanonical had been coined among Roman Catholics after the Council of Trent, and the Thirty-Nine Articles in 1562 had simply used the phrase 'other books' – but the 1611 bible still followed its Tudor predecessors, including Geneva, with the old title 'the books called Apocrypha' which a hundred years before had been less controversial.

A Cambridge translator was however to be involved in discussing the place of the Apocrypha when English delegates sent to the Dutch reformed Synod of Dort (Dordrecht) in 1618, including Samuel Ward (who described the translation process to the Synod), said that these books were best set with the Old Testament as in the English Bible, following the example of antiquity and the present reformed churches.[15] Yet Dutch Synod members wanted either to move them right to the end of the bible or to leave them out altogether. Many disliked (as did Broughton in England) that the Apocrypha should seem to be at the heart of scripture. The English delegates' opinion in favour was however echoed later by Selden, probably under Cromwell, with his dictum 'The Apocrypha is bound with the Bibles of all Churches that have been hitherto. Why should we leave it out?'[16]

The 1611 titles of individual books are also conservative, as in the case of a New Testament epistle with which Cambridge translators engaged, Hebrews. In the Geneva Bible the title was simply 'The Epistle to the Hebrews', with a note that, although Hebrews is fully authoritative, the author hides his name and anyway is unlikely to be St Paul. The 1611 bible, by contrast, follows the Bishops' Bible and Coverdale with 'The Epistle of Paul the Apostle to the Hebrews'. Was this a response to Gregory Martin, who, while admitting that the authorship was doubted in the early church, urged that the credit of the book was lessened by the Geneva title? Perhaps his appeal to expediency was one consideration, but, even if so, the 1611 title here was still of a piece with the general 1611 fidelity to Bishops' Bible titles.

Specimen Translations
Two individual passages may exemplify the Cambridge translators' engagement with passages where the desire to maintain the consistency of scripture, or what is regarded as the general drift of its teaching, might impinge on philological choices. Thus Genesis on the emergence of bird-life presents a problem. Gen. 1:20 in the Authorized Version, slightly modifying but still following the Bishops' Bible, forms one continuous sentence, 'Let the waters bring forth abundantly the moving creature that hath life, and fowl that may fly above the earth.' In this rendering the birds emerge from the primaeval waters. Yet the clause on the birds can be separated, and rendered, as noted in the 1611 margin, 'and let fowl fly above the earth' – now suggesting a separate creation of the birds. For the interpreter interested in the general consistency of the bible this has the advantage of agreeing better with Gen. 2:19, where the birds are formed from the earth, not the waters. The reading tradition

indicated by the accents added to the Hebrew text supports this second rendering, and so there is a fair philological argument for it, and it was adopted by Pagnine, Geneva, the Antwerp Polyglot, Tremellius, and Andrew Willet.

The first rendering, however, despite its seeming contradiction with Gen. 2:19, has a very long history, appearing in the Jewish community in the Septuagint in the third century before Christ and also in part of the ancient Aramaic translation tradition and in the Talmud (Hullin 27b). It was followed in the Latin Vulgate, so familiar in sixteenth-century Europe, before it reached Coverdale and the Bishops' Bible. It is likely that the two different understandings of the verse both go back to pre-Christian times. A present-day interpreter might judge that the rendering preferred by the 1611 translators is commended to some extent by its very inconsistency with Gen. 2:19; seeming harmony is sometimes secondary.

The 1611 translators, in this case Lancelot Andrewes and his company, were not allowed a note, but they silently explained themselves by putting the second translation, suggested by the Hebrew accents, in the margin, showing that although not preferred it was considered and thought worthy of record, and by continuing from Coverdale a cross-reference to II Esdras 6.47, from a Jewish apocalypse included in the Apocrypha, which says that the waters were commanded to bring forth living creatures, birds and fishes, and so supports the translation given in their text. This may well be one of the passages which caused Hugh Broughton, a devotee of the reading tradition recorded in the Hebrew accents, to say exasperatedly that the king's translators usually placed the true rendering in the margin. At any rate, here the 1611 translators stick to a rendering which may query biblical consistency, and had become unfashionable for philological reasons too, but which did have strong ancient Jewish precedent; and through the margin they also give you notice that all this needs thinking over. Compare the question in their preface: 'Doth not a margin do well to admonish the reader to seek further?'

An example showing somewhat greater change is given by the Greek of the Apocrypha, for which John Selden tells us that Andrew Downes took the lead. King Solomon in the book of Wisdom recalls his youth, without any false modesty, in the crisp Authorized Version words 'I was a witty child, and had a good spirit' (Wisd. 8:19). The final words might be rendered still more closely 'I received for my lot a good spirit'. The 1611 'had a good spirit' differs, however, from Coverdale, 'and had a good understanding', followed in the main text of the Bishops' Bible, and from Geneva, which similarly has 'was of a good spirit'. These earlier translations muffle the most disquieting implication of the Greek, namely that Solomon speaks in Platonic fashion as if his spirit or soul were pre-existent, not brought into being specially for him. The 1611 text follows, with abbreviation, the margin of the Bishops' Bible, 'and had a good spirit with me'. 1611 is particularly close to the Greek, and also comes nearest to allowing the Platonic implication, although it can still be read in accordance with customary church teaching. The king's translators in this instance allow philology to have some impact by a very neat abbreviation of the Bishops' Bible margin – and they also, I think, achieve literary success in conveying the epigrammatic quality of the Greek.

These two instances of translation from Hebrew and Greek, in their concern with philology as well as the status of the bible, must stand for hundreds of other similarly scrupulous translators' decisions. They remind us first that the 1611 bible was indeed an event in Hebrew and Greek scholarship as well as in the history of English language and literature. It opened a golden age of biblical study, marked by Brian Walton's London Polyglot bible of 1655–7 and great interpreters like John Lightfoot, and not matched again in England until the late nineteenth century.

Secondly, however, both the chosen passages show a discriminating fidelity to the Bishops' Bible tradition. They are indeed from parts of the bible – the historical and poetic books, on the one hand, and the Apocrypha, on the other – where 1611 has been judged in general to draw far less on Geneva than is the case in the Prophets, translated by the first Oxford company.[17] At least, however, these examples bring out the significance of Selden's most famous comment on the Authorized Version: 'The English Translation of the Bible is the best Translation in the World, and renders the Sense of the Original best, taking in for the English Translation, the Bishops' Bible as well as King James's.'[18] Selden, familiar with the Bishops' Bible before he could know King James's, saw readily how close the king's translators did keep – in obedience to royal command – to the Bishops' Bible; and yet, how considerable they were as translators.

Endnotes

[1] Based on a contribution to talks in Cambridge organized by Professor Robert Gordon to mark 'Four Hundred Years of the Authorized Version'.

[2] Parker's Prefaces to the Old and the New Testament in the Bishops' Bible are reprinted in J. Strype, *The Life and Acts of Matthew Parker* (1771; repr., 3 vols., Oxford, 1821), iii, 236–57 (Appendix, nos. 83–4).

[3] Letter of 28 August 1571 from Edmund Grindal, Archbishop of York, to Parker, in W. Nicholson (ed.), *The Remains of Edmund Grindal, D.D.* (Parker Society; Cambridge, 1843), 326–8.

[4] Elizabeth Morley Ingram, 'Dressed in Borrowed Robes: The Making and Marketing of the Louvain Bible (1578)', in R.N. Swanson (ed.), *The Church and the Book* (Studies in Church History, 38; Woodbridge, 2004), 212–21; Alexandra Walsham, 'Unclasping the Book? Post-Reformation English Catholicism and the Vernacular Bible', *Journal of British Studies* xlii (2003), 141–66 (152–6).

[5] On Fulke and Martin as biblical interpreters see W. McKane, *Selected Christian Hebraists* (Cambridge, 1989), 76–110.

[6] R.B. McDowell & D.A. Webb, *Trinity College, Dublin, 1592–1952* (Cambridge, 1982), 5–6.

[7] U. Cassuto, *Gli ebrei a Firenze nell' età del Rinascimento* (Florence, 1918, repr. 1965), 324; T.M. Centi, 'L'attività letteraria di Santi Pagnini (1470–1536) nel campo delle scienze bibliche', *Archivum Fratrum Praedicatorum* 15 (1945), 5–51 (7–9).

[8] For the passages quoted below see Sir Francis Bacon, *The Advancement of Learning*, ed. W. Aldis Wright (2nd edn, Oxford, 1880), 77, 264.

[9] *The Table-Talk of John Selden*, with a Biographical Preface and Notes by S.W. Singer (London, 1847), 8 ('Bible, Scripture', para. 3).

[10] W. Benjamin, 'Die Aufgabe des Uebersetzers' (1923), reprinted in M. Opitz (ed.), *Walter Benjamin. Ein Lesebuch* (Frankfurt am Main, 1996), 45–57 (56–7), discussed by G. Hammond, *The Making of the English Bible* (Manchester, 1982), 2–3.

[11] For these details on Bois see Anthony Walker, *Life of John Bois*, repr. in Ward Allen (ed. & transl.), *Translating for King James: Notes made by a translator of King James's Bible* (Nashville, TN: Vanderbilt University Press, 1969, repr. 1993), 131, 133, 135, 137–8, 146.

[12] See now Kirsten Macfarlane, *Biblical Scholarship in an Age of Controversy. The Polemical World of Hugh Broughton (1549–1612)* (Oxford, 2021).

[13] H. Chadwick, 'Ephesians', in M. Black & H.H. Rowley (edd.), *Peake's Commentary on the Bible* (London & Edinburgh, 1962), 980–81 (paragraph 857c).

[14] A twelfth-century instance is Hugh of St Victor, *On the Sacraments*, i, Prologue, 7 'There are moreover in the Old Testament certain other books which are indeed read, but are not written in the body of the text or in the canon of authoritative books (*qui leguntur quidem, sed in corpore textus vel in canone auctoritatis non scribuntur*). Such are Tobit, Judith, the books of the Maccabees, that which is entitled the Wisdom of Solomon, and Ecclesiasticus.' For further mediaeval statements see J. Cosin, *A Scholastical History of the Holy Scripture* (London, 1657; repr., ed. J. Sansom, Oxford, 1849), chapters xi–xvi.

[15] A. Milton (ed.), *The British Delegation at the Synod of Dort (1618–1619)* (Church of England Record Society, 13; Woodbridge, 2005), 133–41.

[16] *The Table-Talk of John Selden*, 12 ('Bible, Scripture', para. 14).

[17] B.F. Westcott, ed. W. Aldis Wright, *A General View of the History of the English Bible* (London, 1905), 262.

[18] *The Table-Talk of John Selden*, 7 ('Bible, Scripture', para. 2).

7
JOHN SPENCER ON THE
RELIGION OF THE BIBLE

Perhaps the most well-worn comment on John Spencer (1630–93) is still the best to begin from. In 1889 William Robertson Smith wrote in the preface of his *Religion of the Semites*: 'The value of comparative studies for the study of the religion of the Bible was brought out very clearly, two hundred years ago, by one of the greatest of English theologians, Dr John Spencer, Master of Corpus Christi College in Cambridge, whose Latin work on the ritual laws of the Hebrews may justly be said to have laid the foundations of the science of Comparative Religion, and in its special subject, in spite of certain defects that could hardly have been avoided at the time when it was composed, still remains by far the most important work on the religious antiquities of the Hebrews. But Spencer was so much before his time that his work was not followed up ...'.[1]

Spencer attained this stature as a student of ancient religion by a route now little known, although in the seventeenth century it was a main road: the study of the post-biblical as well as the biblical Hebrew literature of the Jews. His book 'on the ritual laws of the Hebrews, and the reasons for them' – *De Legibus Hebraeorum Ritualibus et earum Rationibus* – was first issued in three parts, folio (Cambridge, 1683–5). Its presentation in Latin rather than English meant that it could immediately be read internationally. It was at once reprinted at The Hague, 1686 (in handier form), and again at Leipzig, 1705. Spencer, preparing a revised edition in 1691–2, added a fourth book to the existing three, but when he died in 1693 the revised edition had not appeared. Soon afterwards Isaac Newton reported on plans for its publication to the editor of a learned journal in Leipzig.[2] Spencer's executor Thomas Tenison, archbishop of Canterbury from 1694, caused the work to be prepared for the press, but he had not yet arranged for it to be printed when he died in 1715. 'I have been prevented in it', he wrote in his own will, 'by the death of Mr Mortlock Senr' – probably the London bookseller Henry Mortlock, who distributed Edward Stillingfleet's *Origines Sacrae*, cited below – 'and by divers other accidents'.[3] Tenison therefore left the relevant papers to the university of Cambridge, with a legacy to provide for an editor. The revised text was finally issued in two volumes folio (Cambridge, 1727 see Plates 8 and 9), edited by Leonard Chappelow, the Professor of Arabic (references below are to this edition). Once again there was a continental reprint in a handier form (Tübingen, 1732), and it was reprinted again in parts at Venice between 1757 and 1767, in seven out of the thirty-four volumes of the *Thesaurus* of works on biblical and Jewish antiquity issued by Blasio Ugolini.

Spencer's contrasting lack of influence late in the following century, underlined by Robertson Smith, can be put down partly to increasing neglect of works in Latin, but it may owe something too to Spencer's use of post-biblical Hebrew writings. This entirely suited the taste of the age when the book appeared, but in later biblical study it had become a specialized interest. What evoked the fascination and anxiety which surrounded the book at the time when it was issued, revised, and reissued?

Perhaps essentially it is this: Spencer undertook an old task in a new way which was compelling, yet disturbing. The old task was that mentioned in the title, to determine reasons for the biblical commandments and institutions, including sacrificial worship, the sabbath day, and the dietary laws. The assignment of reasons begins in the biblical books themselves; thus, within the Decalogue, Exodus and Deuteronomy offer two differing reasons for the sabbath commandment, 'For in six days the Lord made heaven and earth ...' (Exod. 20:11) or 'And you shall remember that you were a servant in the land of Egypt ...' (Deut. 5:15). The process of finding reasons was highly developed among Jews in the Greek world before the rise of Christianity, and remained important whenever the bible was known in an atmosphere of rational inquiry, throughout the ancient, mediaeval and later periods and among both Jews and Christians – for their differences in custom did not exclude a common loyalty to biblical institutions.

Symbolic reasons remained popular throughout. To cite an old pre-Christian one, you can eat the meat of animals that chew the cud, as Leviticus says (11:2), because chewing the cud symbolizes the human duty of responsible recollection (*Letter of Aristeas* 153–5). Yet a sense that such explanations may not fully satisfy seems to be reflected in the currency of other lines of interpretation, exemplified in the remark in the gospels that the law for the repudiation of a wife in Deuteronomy (24:1–4) is a concession to the hardness of the human heart (Mark 10:5). Dissatisfaction with symbolic explanation seems likewise to be reflected in another interpretative theory, the view represented in rabbinic tradition that some commandments may be arbitrary. Thus the book of Numbers (19:2), using the strong terms 'this is the ordinance of the law', orders water mingled with the ashes of a red heifer for purification after contact with a corpse. According to a famous legend about R. Johanan ben Zaccai, who lived in the late first century CE, a pagan criticized the ceremony as resembling witchcraft, but Johanan answered him by comparing it with the more respectable practice of expelling a demon. The pagan left, defeated, but Johanan's pupils said to him: 'You drove this man away with a reed; what do you say to us?' 'By your life!', came the reply, 'neither does the dead defile, nor does the water purify; but the Holy One, blessed be he, says: I have ordained an ordinance, I have decreed a decree; you are not at liberty to transgress' (Midrash Numbers Rabbah, xix 8). This interpretation chimed in with devotion, but was also unsatisfactory, for it casts the Deity as one who says tyrannically, in the words of a well-worn quotation from Juvenal which Spencer repeats, 'I give no other reason but my will' (*sit pro ratione voluntas*, Juvenal vi 223). In the philosophical Jewish biblical interpretation of the Middle Ages the conception of an arbitrary lawgiver was rejected by Maimonides. His view was perhaps foreshadowed in the further rabbinic saying that Solomon knew the reasons for all the commandments except that concerning the Red Heifer – which, it seems to be implied, might have a reason if only we could find it (Midrash Numbers Rabbah xix 3, on Solomon's words [Eccles. 7:23] 'I said, I will be wise; but it was far from me').

Similarly, in Christian tradition shaped by the gospels and St Paul, you commonly find the quest for reasons. Some customs were ordained as a concession to human needs (Mark 10:5, cited already) or for a specific time now past (Gal. 3:16–4:4). These views were strengthened by the distinction between a moral law which is permanent and a ceremonial law which was temporary, a distinction based on the statement in Deuteronomy (4:13–14) that God gave the Ten Commandments himself, but also directed Moses to add further statutes or 'ceremonies' (Vulgate Latin, *caerimonias*). Analysis of the commandments on these lines could be combined with specifically Christian symbolic interpretation; thus sacrifices could be understood both as part of the ceremonial law, a concession to needs now past, and as symbols of Christ's offering of himself.

Into this relatively ordered garden of biblical interpretation Spencer now walked. He took up the old task of seeking reasons, but in such a way that it began to seem not like the old task at all, but rather, as Robertson Smith perceived it, the beginnings of the science of comparative religion. In a series of detailed studies Spencer studied customs and institutions individually, and urged that the more probable view was always that they derived from comparable institutions of the surrounding pagan world, especially but not only ancient Egypt. In this way he was able to tackle even the intractable problem of the Red Heifer. 'Unless my palate deceives me,' he remarked on this (ii 26, 2; p. 488), 'no explanation advanced hitherto has had one single grain of salt in it'; whereas he could argue, with some show of plausibility, that this ordinance formed a blow at the Egyptian cult of Typhon, who was a red god to whom red cattle were sacrificed. (Spencer's contemporary Simon Patrick, bishop of Ely from 1691, rebuts this explanation at some length in his commentary on Numbers, without naming Spencer.) The added book iv supports the general position taken in books i–iii by arguing that many ancient Jewish customs which are not, or not clearly, commanded in scripture likewise derive from pagan usage. Here he includes treatment of such varied subjects as women's assemblies, funeral rites, temple music, barefoot worship, and phylacteries (Deut. 6:8, Matt. 23:5).

You can see here in his treatment of music in worship, a subject even more controversial in the seventeenth century than it is to-day, how annoying he will have been to anyone trying either to attack or to defend organs and choirs on biblical grounds. Spencer accepts that the temple music was a biblical institution, founded by king David, but adds that reason shows that David adopted pagan usage for the needs of the time. Spencer was Dean of Ely Cathedral as well as Master of his college. While he was Dean the cathedral's choral service was fully restored (1682) and the organs were extensively repaired and renewed (1683–4, 1688–9, 1691–3).[4] You might not guess this, however, when he writes, perhaps not without irony, that 'Reason alone will readily judge that that great sound of musicians (*ingens ille musicorum strepitus*)', instituted by David for the temple, 'first of all had its place in the rites and usages of the gentiles' (iv 3, 3; p. 1104). He argues, in fact, that these choirs and instrumentalists were instituted not by any commandment of God, although they were divinely permitted in order to elevate the minds of the worshippers, but by king David. David was aware – as Spencer says in late seventeenth-century manner – how much his people needed greater elegance (*elegantia*) in their forms of worship. 'David judged that God should be worshipped with greater elegance than before, for new times seemed to require new customs, and more elegant and polished usages of divine service' (iv 3, 2; p. 1103). Spencer's supremely elegant marble font for Ely Cathedral, expelled from the cathedral in the nineteenth century perhaps because it was just too elegant in a late seventeenth-century way, shows that he went along with this argument himself. His words on David indeed sound like a moderate person's apologia for the Prayer-book restored in 1662;

his leaning in this direction overall led a German Lutheran critic to say sardonically that Spencer's audacity could not be excused even by a wish to defend the notoriously unreformed customs of the Church of England (C.M. Pfaff, in his preface to the Tübingen, 1732 text of *De Legibus*). Yet, may this passage in Spencer, in which reason alone will readily judge that the great sound of the temple musicians was pagan in origin, also reflect some nostalgia for the commonwealth austerity in which he was bred when young?

The value of Spencer's work to students of Jewish and non-Jewish religion of course lies especially in the review of ancient evidence in detailed investigations such as these. Spencer himself, however, wanted also to perform the old task of indicating reasons. It had once again become urgent, because of the general drive in the late seventeenth century, for example in the early work of the Royal Society, towards bringing new observations and new knowledge into accord with a conviction of the rationality of true religion. Spencer's interpretation of his conclusions on the history of religion in ancient Israel was therefore not only the continuation of a Jewish and Christian theological tradition; it was also a systematization comparable with Isaac Newton's theological interpretation of his mathematics, or the argument of the botanist John Ray that his study of nature led to perception of *The Wisdom of God in Creation*, to quote the title of a famous book by Ray issued in 1691.

Spencer interpreted the results of his historical inquiry on lines taken over from Maimonides, but much extended.[5] Maimonides, in the twelfth-century Egyptian Jewish community, had boldly argued that the sacrificial laws were indeed divine accommodations to the limited capacity of the ancient Israelites, who lived among and expected such rites; the biblical version of these rites formed an implicit attack on idolatry, and weaned the people from unworthy practices. Like Spencer later on, he had justified this position by historical inquiries, in his case into Arabic descriptions of the idolatry of the Sabaeans, which he assumed was the pagan religion encountered by Abraham (see his *Guide to the Perplexed*, iii 29–32).[6]

Spencer extended this interpretation from the sacrifices to a great many other rites and usages; and although, as in his discussion of the Red Heifer, he echoed the view that divine accommodation to human capacity struck a blow against idolatry, he laid more emphasis simply on the accommodation itself: God took over the devil's rites (Spencer followed the old view that pagan religion evinced the work of evil spirits), and adapted them for his own people.

Spencer's development of Maimonides was not unprecedented. Early Christian writers, from Justin Martyr in the second century onwards, had maintained that God commanded sacrifices not because he needed them, but in order to keep the Israelites from idolatry (Justin Martyr, *Dialogue with Trypho the Jew*, 19.6, 67.8). The similar view of Maimonides on sacrifice was taken up by mediaeval and later Christians. Thus in 1640 Hugo Grotius urged, citing Maimonides, that many Jews hold the sacrifices to have been less a primary divine ordinance than an accommodation to ward off idolatry; and Grotius's later annotator J. Le Clerc, a friend of Locke, added a reference to Spencer as copiously illustrating this point. In Spencer's own generation, Edward Stillingfleet (1635–99) had in 1662 explicitly cited Maimonides on the Sabaeans, together with Grotius, in order to show that many ceremonial laws were only intended as temporary preventative measures.[7] In Spencer's much more extended treatment, however, this view sounded less like a buttress for the ancient claim that the ceremonial law was temporary, than like an assertion that biblical ordinances were imitations of pagan idolatry. His title, 'On the *ritual* laws', used a traditional designation of the ceremonial law, and thereby suggested the time-honoured Christian view; but his arguments and instances tended much more towards a bolder title which was drafted for the second edition but not adopted: *On the customs of the Hebrews drawn from the usage of the Gentiles, as is often mentioned in canonical and apocryphal scripture*.[8] The title-page motto would have been Psalm 106:35: 'they were mingled among the heathen: and learned their works'.

Biblical Voices and Echoes

It can readily be seen that a defence of the rationality of the biblical laws with this particular emphasis would have been disliked. Indignation was expressed with zest by John Edwards (formerly a fellow of St John's College, Cambridge) in 1699. Spencer 'makes the true God most diligently and precisely tread in the steps of the false Gods and Idols'; he maintains

> that God raked up all the Vain, Ludicrous, Superstitious, Impure, Obscure, Irreligious, Impious, Profane, Idolatrous, Execrable, Magical, Devilish Customs which had been first invented and afterwards constantly used by the most barbarous Gentiles, the Scum of the World, the Dregs of Mankind, and out of all these patched up a great part of the Religion which he appointed his own people.

Finally, in the unkindest cut of all, Edwards concludes, 'But I hope the learned Doctor, before he left the world, corrected his error, and entertained other thoughts of these things'.[9] Weightier authors sympathized with such criticisms at least in part. On the other hand, in the eighteenth century the redoubtable William Warburton, bishop of Gloucester, brought in Spencer to support his paradoxical argument that the law of Moses must be of divine origin, for it was accepted even though it was issued without the socially necessary teaching on rewards and punishments in an after-life; this outcome indicated the workings of an extraordinary divine providence. 'The table is always full, Sir', said Dr Johnson of Warburton, and Spencer is part of the ample menu offered in Warburton's *Divine Legation of Moses* (1737–41).[10]

Within the international atmosphere of the seventeenth-century Christian Hebraism, in which Christian scholars devoted themselves to Hebrew literature of all periods, Spencer's literary achievement stirred his European contemporaries, but is rooted in England. Thus in his debt to rabbinic literature and to Maimonides Spencer followed a trend which was international, yet strongly represented in this country. Annotated translation from the *Mishneh Torah* of Maimonides (book i, 5, on the laws of repentance,

126

Hilkhoth Teshubhah) had been issued in Spencer's university by William Norwich, *Canones Poenitentiae* (Cambridge, 1631).[11] Then translation from the Mishnah with commentary (the treatise *Yoma*, on the Day of Atonement) appeared from Robert Sheringham, *Joma* (Cambridge, 1648).[12] Later, Spencer himself was one of those appointed to read and review the translation of the Mishnah being prepared in Restoration Cambridge by the Jewish scholar Isaac Abendana.[13] At the same time work on the Mishnah, rabbinic study and Maimonides was advancing at Oxford (see the following chapter). In view of the increasing seventeenth-century accessibility of Jewish literature through translation one should note the tribute to Spencer paid by Julius Guttmann (n.6, above): Spencer used the Latin translations of post-biblical Hebrew books when available, but the greater part of his citations of Hebrew literature are taken directly from the originals.

Further, Spencer was one of a recognized and particularly versatile group of scholars and Hebraists in late seventeenth-century Cambridge. This point emerges from a printed commendation of the eighteenth-century Hebraist, J.A. Danz of Jena. As a young man in 1684 he had visited Cambridge, and met: Ralph Cudworth (Professor of Hebrew) and Henry More – two of the Cambridge Platonists; John Spencer; Isaac Newton; and Edmund Castell (Professor of Arabic and pioneering lexicographer in several Semitic languages) – scholars then described collectively, in this admittedly laudatory composition, as 'those lights of England, who illuminate the whole world of letters by their splendour'.[14]

Then, the naming of Spencer here together with Newton recalls not only the link between them seen in Newton's letters, but also Spencer's association with some who, like Newton, differed in particular respects from the norms of belief or practice followed in the Restoration settlement. Thus Spencer continued his friendship with his old tutor Richard Kennet, who could not conform to the Prayer-book of 1662 and was ejected from his benefice of East Hatley in west Cambridgeshire. Such links with dissenters were one of the hallmarks of those then called in praise or blame 'men of latitude' or 'Latitudinarians'. Spencer's friend and executor, archbishop Tenison, was known, comparably, for moderation towards dissenters. Somewhat similarly, Spencer was said to have given a friendly reception to the Socinian antitrinitarian writer Samuel Crell, on a visit to England from Holland.[15] This seems in character; as was also suggested by his remarks on music, he went with the times, but understood some of those who could not bend. Brought up in times of doctrinal strife, he may have cared more for the general concord of religion and reason, less for precision in doctrine. He may then, like Newton, have had Crell-like views which he did not publicize, or, like Newton and the aged Milton, he may have regarded Socinian dissent from an Athanasian view of the Trinity as an interpretation of scripture which was admissible in principle in a Christian commonwealth.[16] At any rate, he represented the moderation with regard to norms of Christian doctrine and custom which was one characteristic aspect of opinion in later seventeenth-century England.

Finally, Spencer's large-scale literary work, like other achievements of English Hebraists, rested on the general importance of Hebrew teaching and study in seventeenth-century academic life, as much in England as overseas. Colleges often sponsored Hebrew lectureships. A glimpse of some of the duties attached can be seen in a bequest (will dated 24 May 1700) made to Corpus Christi College, Cambridge, by a former fellow and colleague of Spencer, Samuel Chapman; he had forfeited his fellowship for nonconformity in 1662, but he later conformed and became rector of Thorpe-by-Norwich. He left £150 for the foundation of three Hebrew exhibitions or scholarships. He laid down that the exhibitioners should show their work to the Hebrew lecturer. The exercises Chapman prescribed were grammatical analyses of chapters or psalms from the Hebrew bible.[17] The simple but potentially far-reaching nature of these exercises appears from a Cambridge text-book of the period, a reprint (printed by Elizabeth Flesher in London, 1679; for sale from the Cambridge bookseller William Morden) of Victorinus Bythner's *Lyra Prophetica Davidis Regis, sive Analysis critico-practica Psalmorum.* The book, originally printed by James Flesher in London (1650), had already been reprinted once by him (1664) for sale at Cambridge by the booksellers Edmund Beechinoe and William Morden. In an analysis of each psalm the beginner is encouraged by transliteration of the Hebrew, but is given further systematic guidance which would eventually allow profitable use of much of the material from the ancient versions of scripture set out in the London Polyglot Bible of 1657. The book also includes an introduction to both Hebrew and Aramaic; the introductory Hebrew grammar had at first been issued by Bythner at his own expense (Cambridge, 1645). The learned author, of Polish origin, taught at both Oxford and Cambridge, and his career and publications show that although there was room for the encouragement of Hebrew, there was also a clear demand in the universities for Hebrew instruction.[18]

Spencer's achievement in the history of biblical religion is thus marked by an academic approach and also a political and religious outlook, so far as it can be traced, which belong to his English environment. Yet his academic approach, made through Hebrew literature, belongs also to the international movement of Christian Hebraism. International interest fosters the vigour and extent of response to, and attack on, his work. At the same time, however, it highlights the individuality of his achievement. He had precedent for his position in the church fathers and in later Christian use of Maimonides, but stands out for the cumulative force of his arguments for deriving particular rites and ceremonies from Egyptian and other gentile worship.

His work was fiercely opposed, but was in the end admired as a pioneering contribution to the history of religion and to historical interpretation of the bible. This contribution was achieved, however, through typically seventeenth-century devotion to Hebrew and post-biblical Jewish tradition and literature. Spencer made a venturesomely creative use of Hebrew sources in an argument on the origins of the Jewish laws; he brought rabbinic and mediaeval Hebrew writings together with a range of Greek and Latin testimonies to ancient Jewish and pagan religion, but he found in Hebrew texts from the bible onwards both his matter and his interpretative theory. The contribution to the history of religion for which he is specially remembered was thus also a contribution to the study of biblical and post-biblical Jewish literature – the contribution of a scholar who, rising to the height of a great argument, shows the value and vitality of the texts to which he appeals.

Endnotes

[1] W. Robertson Smith, *Lectures on the Religion of the Semites* (Edinburgh, 1889), vi.

[2] Newton to Otto Mencke, editor of the Leipzig *Acta Eruditorum*, 22 November 1693, in H.W. Turnbull (ed.), *The Correspondence of Isaac Newton*, iii, *1688–1694* (Cambridge, 1961), 291–3, no. 416.

[3] Extract of Tenison's will, MS. Cambridge University Library, Add. 2610 (2); H.R. Plomer et al., *A Dictionary of the Printers and Booksellers who were at work in England, Scotland and Ireland from 1668 to 1725* (Oxford, 1922), 211 (1709 the last year of Henry Mortlock's recorded activity).

[4] José Hopkins, 'Organs in Ely Cathedral before 1851', *Journal of the British Institute of Organ Studies* 21 (1997), 4–19 (5–7). Catherine Hall kindly drew this article to my attention.

[5] J. Guttmann, 'John Spencers Erklärung der biblischen Gesetze in ihrer Beziehung zu Maimonides', in *Festskrift i Anledning af Professor David Simonsens 70-aarige Fødelsdag* (Copenhagen, 1923), 258–76.

[6] M. Friedländer, *The Guide to the Perplexed by Moses Maimonides translated from the original Arabic text* (2nd edn, London, 1904, repr. New York, 1956), 315–27. Spencer will have used the Hebrew translation by Ibn Tibbon, itself translated by J. Buxtorf II (1629).

[7] H. Grotius, *De Veritate Religionis Christianae* (Oxford, 1827), 240–41 (book v 8); in this edition Grotius's text and notes (Paris, 1640) were reprinted together with Le Clerc's annotations (The Hague, 1724); E. Stillingfleet, *Origines Sacrae* (1662; repr. Cambridge, 1702), 146-8 (ii 7). In 1691 Spencer had considered a specimen of a projected Latin translation of the Old

Testament by Le Clerc, transmitted by Newton (Newton to Locke, no. 378 in Turnbull, *Correspondence of Isaac Newton*, iii, 185).

[8] 'De moribus Hebraeorum e Gentium usu sumptis, ut a Scriptura Canonica vel Apocrypha plerumque memoratur', MS. Cambridge University Library, Add. 2610 (2), f. 13a.

[9] John Edwards, POLYPOIKILOS SOPHIA (London, 1699), 249, 251–2.

[10] James Boswell, *The Life of Samuel Johnson, Ll.D* (3rd edn [1799] repr., 2 vols. in 1, London, 1927), ii, 367 (on the year 1781).

[11] S. Levy, 'English Students of Maimonides', in *Miscellanies of the Jewish Historical Society of England,* iv, *Essays presented to E.N. Adler,* i (London, 1942), 61–84 (66–7).

[12] See now T. Roebuck, 'Ancient Rabbis Inspired by God: Robert Sheringham's Surprising Edition of Mishnah Tractate Yoma (1648)', in Piet van Boxel, Kirsten Macfarlane & Joanna Weinberg (edd.), *The Mishnaic Moment: Jewish Law among Jews and Christians in Early Modern Europe* (Oxford, 2022), 193–214.

[13] I. Abrahams, 'Isaac Abendana's Cambridge Mishnah and Oxford Calendars', *Transactions of the Jewish Historical Society of England* 8 (Sessions 1915–1917; London, 1918), 98–121; on Sheringham, 103, 116–17; on Spencer, 100; 108 (he signs after reviewing the translation of three Mishnah-tractates, 2 August 1671); and 110 (he transmits payments to Abendana, 31 October 1674 and 7 June 1675). See now T. Dunkelgrün, 'The First Complete Latin Translation of the Mishnah: Isaac Abendana and Rabbinic Erudition in Restoration England', in van Boxel, Macfarlane & Weinberg (edd.), *The Mishnaic Moment*, 89–113.

[14] J.F. Budde, Dean of the Jena theological faculty, in the biography concluding his printed invitation to the lectures and inaugural disputation of J.A. Danz: *Ioann. Franciscus Buddeus … ad lectiones cursorias, quas vocant, et disputationem inauguralem … Io. Andreae Danzii … theologiae bonarumque artium patronos atque cultores … invitat* (Jena, 1710).

[15] M. Mulsow, 'Orientalistik im Kontext der sozinianischen und deistischen Debatten um 1700: Spencer, Crell, Locke und Newton', *Scientia Poetica* ii, ed. L. Danneberg and others (Tübingen, 1998), 27–57 (kindly brought to my notice by D.R. Hedley).

[16] On this point in Newton see M.F. Wiles, *Archetypal Heresy: Arianism through the Centuries* (Oxford, 1996), 78; 84–5 and M. Goldish, *Judaism in the Theology of Sir Isaac Newton* (Dordrecht, 1998), 133–40, 170–71.

[17] J. Lamb, *Masters' History of the College of Corpus Christi and the Blessed Virgin Mary in the University of Cambridge, with additional matter and a continuation to the present time* (Cambridge, 1831), 210, 361–2.
[18] On Bythner see D. McKitterick, *A History of Cambridge University Press*, i, *Printing and the Book Trade in Cambridge, 1534–1698* (Cambridge, 1992), 369–70.

Plate 1: Virgil's Tomb (see pp. 2–3), Sun breaking through (Joseph Wright of Derby, 1785) © National Museums of Northern Ireland, Ulster Museum Collection.

Plate 2 (above): St Paul, Magdeburg Cathedral pulpit, Christoph Kapup (1595); see p. 18. Photograph: © Raymond Faure.

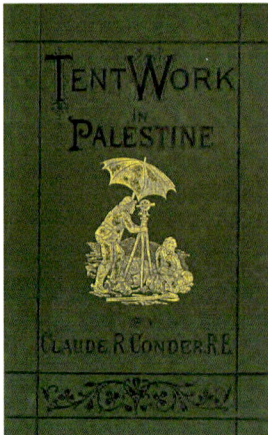

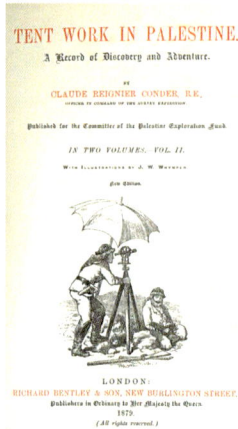

Plates 3 and 4 (left): Cover image and title page from C.R. Conder, R.E., *Tent Work in Palestine* (2 vols., London: Richard Bentley & Son, 1879), showing work for the survey of western Palestine (1871–7, see p. 33 above).

Plate 5 (right): St Raymond of Pennafort (*c*.1180–1275; see p. 65), Master General of the Order of Preachers, promoter of Hebrew and Arabic study, and a leading figure in the Barcelona Disputation (1263); copy of roundel from Fra Angelico, *Crucifixion with Dominican Saints*, fresco at the friary, now museum, of S. Marco, Florence.

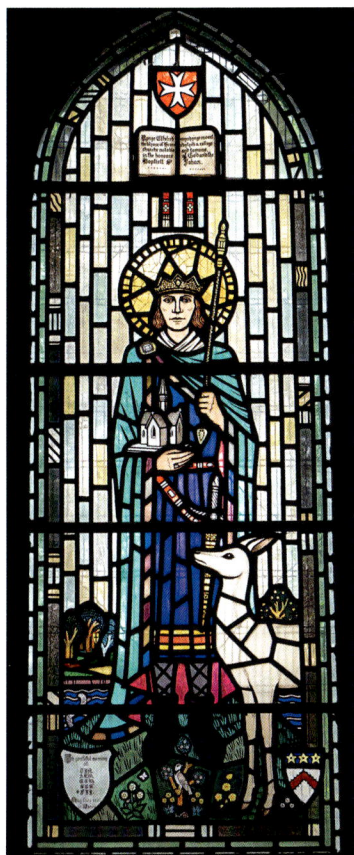

Plate 6 (left): King Ethelred of Mercia (ruled 675–704) finds the site for the foundation of the church of St John Baptist, Chester, guided by a white hart, perhaps symbolizing Christ ('like a roe or young hart', Song of Solomon 2:17); window by Trena Cox, St John's, Chester (see p. 79). The story of the foundation appears in the thirteenth-century chronicle of St Werburgh's abbey in Chester (*Annales Cestrienses*, ed. R.C. Christie [1887], 11); see T. Pickles, 'The Christian Landscape of Early Mediaeval Chester and the Wirral', in Sharon M. Varey & Graeme J. White, *Looking at the Landscape: Glimpses into the History of Cheshire and Beyond* (Chester, 2022), 9–30 (13–15).

Plate 7 (above): Title-page of King James Bible, quarto, bound up with the Prayer-book and the metrical psalms (Cambridge, 1633); see p. 109.

Plates 8 and 9 (left and below): John Spencer (1630–93), Dean of Ely and Master of Corpus Christi College, Cambridge, see p. 120; details of engraving by George Vertue, forming frontispiece of John Spencer, *De legibus Hebraeorum et earum rationibus* (2 vols., Cambridge, 1727).

Plate 10 (right): Narcissus Marsh (1638–1713), archbishop successively of Cashel (1690), Dublin (1694), and Armagh (1703); detail of portrait attributed to Hugh Howard, see p. 133 (photograph © Fennell Photography, Dublin).

Plate 11 (above): Interior of Marsh's Library, Dublin, showing a window looking towards St Patrick's Cathedral, see p. 133; (photograph by Tristan Hutchinson; © Marsh's Library, Dublin).

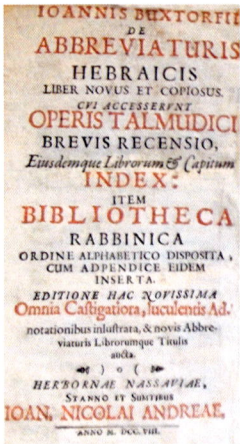

Plate 12 (left): Title-page of Johann Buxtorf I & II, *De abbreviaturis hebraicis*, etc. (2nd edn, Basle, 1640, small octavo; reissued with additions, repr. Herborn, in Nassau, 1708). This handbook, first issued by Johann Buxtorf I (Basle, 1613, small octavo), was enlarged in the second edition by his son Johann Buxtorf II, see p. 148. It contains three works: on Hebrew abbreviations; an outline of the contents of the Talmud; and *Bibliotheca rabbinica*, a bibliography of post-biblical Hebrew literature. Herborn at the time of reissue was the home of the university-like Nassau Academy.

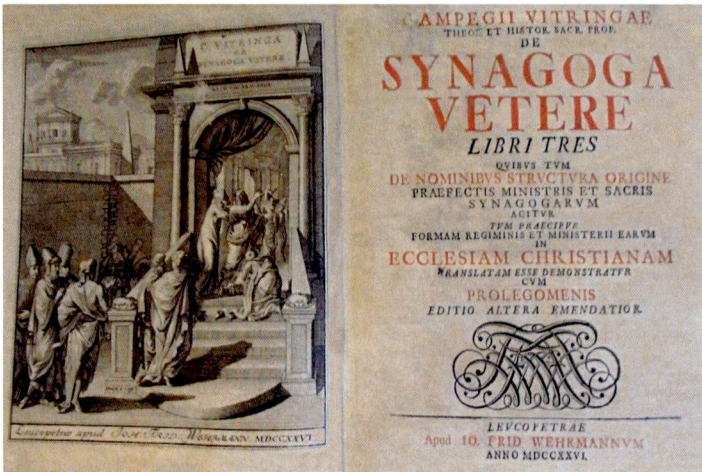

Plate 13 (above): Frontispiece and title-page of Campegius Vitringa, *De Synagoga vetere* (1696; 2nd edn, Weißenfels, 1726), on the ancient synagogue, see p. 153; the engraving illustrates Zech. 8:23 'Ten persons from the nations of every tongue shall take hold of the robe of a Jew, saying, Let us go with you, for we have heard that God is with you.' The scene represents the attraction of the synagogue in the ancient world for non-Jews, but also evokes the prestige of Hebrew in early modern Christian Hebraism.

Plate 14 (above): The house in Abbey Square, Chester, occupied by Charles Kingsley as canon of Chester, see p. 170.

Plates 15 and 16 (left and above): window depicting St Bernard of Menthon in the cloisters of Chester Cathedral, with inscription below commemorating George Leigh Mallory and Andrew Comyn Irvine, who lost their lives in the 1924 Everest expedition (full text and detail of inscription on pp. 186–7).

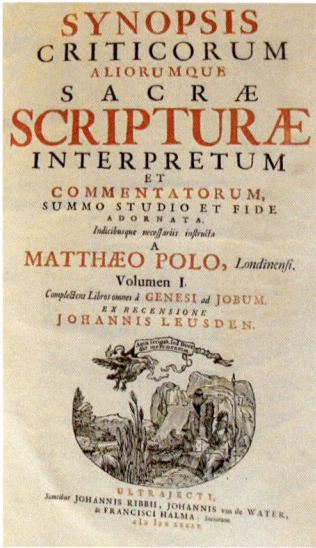

Plate 17 (above): Title-page of Matthew Pole, *Synopsis criticorum*, vol. i (repr. Utrecht, 1684); see p. 258.

Plate 18 (right): King Edgar rowed by vassal-kings (pp. 258–9); west window (1887–90) by Edward Frampton, St John's, Chester; see Pickles, 'The Christian Landscape of Early Mediaeval Chester and the Wirral', 13–15.

8
CHRISTIAN HEBRAISM IN THE
MIRROR OF NARCISSUS MARSH'S
BOOK COLLECTION

Narcissus Marsh (1638–1713), born at Hannington in Wiltshire, will have been christened after the Narcissus named by St Paul (Rom. 16:11).[1] After an Oxford career ending with service as principal of Alban Hall he became provost of Trinity College, Dublin (1679–83), bishop of Ferns, and then archbishop successively of Cashel, Dublin and Armagh, in the reformed Church of Ireland (see Plate 10). Yet he is probably best known as a benefactor and book collector. His personal collection became well-known, and he enlarged it by purchasing the printed books from the equally famous collection of his contemporary Edward Stillingfleet (1635–99), bishop of Worcester; the two together form Marsh's collection, as considered here. His aim was to provide for and found a public library in Dublin, covering, as he put it in a letter to his friend Thomas Smith in London, 'each faculty and science'.[2] Smith, cut off as a non-juror from the facilities he had formerly enjoyed in Oxford, wrote when the plan came to fruition that 'Dublin will now infinitely exceed London in this particular'.[3] This library is the present-day Marsh's Library, still in its original building on part of the site of the former archbishop's palace of St Sepulchre, south-east of St Patrick's Cathedral (see Plate 11).[4] The Stillingfleet books formed the basis of the library, but Marsh also left to it all the printed books from his own private library which were not in it already.[5] The combination brought together, within the wide range of the Library, a noble assembly of books on biblical and Hebrew learning.[6] They represent a field to which Marsh had been devoted since his undergraduate years in Oxford, and which was also a lifelong concern of Stillingfleet. These books have always been of interest to Jews as well as non-Jews. Their writing and collection, however, primarily reflect a phenomenon of

Christian study, the Christian Hebraism which flourished above all in the seventeenth century.

The Phenomenon of Christian Hebraism
Christian Hebraism can be described as western Christian interest in post-biblical as well as biblical Hebrew literature, but it also has something of the quality of a movement in European scholarship. Like Greek, Hebrew kindled a philological passion which awoke lively esteem and enthusiasm for the writings in the language. The two great periods of Christian Hebraism extend from the twelfth to the fourteenth century, and then again from the late fifteenth to the eighteenth century. In each case this brought great benefit to biblical study. Perhaps the last eminent Hebraist in this mould was Giovanni Bernardo de Rossi of Parma, at the end of the eighteenth century, renowned not only as a scholar but also as a collector of Hebrew manuscripts and printed books.

These Hebraists navigated a vast sea of literature. From the biblical books they moved, through the Greek Jewish writers contemporary with the rise of Christianity, to the later Hebrew texts which became classical in Jewish tradition. At the heart of these were the legal dicta and discussions of the Mishnah, compiled in Galilee at the end of the second century, and their expansion and further discussion as attested down to the fifth century in the Jerusalem (Palestinian) Talmud, and down to the early seventh century in the vast and influential Babylonian Talmud. Biblical interpretation from the time of the Mishnah and Talmud is also presented in collections under the general name of Midrash, and in the series of Aramaic biblical translations known as the Targums. The Hebraists of course did not stop here, but went on to the great literary monuments of mediaeval and later Judaism, including biblical commentaries by Rashi, David Kimchi and others, the philosophical presentation of Judaism and Jewish law by Maimonides, and also mediaeval mystical writings which were taken in the second great period of Christian Hebraism to hand down old mystical tradition, the Kabbalah. Outstanding among these mystical works is the Zohar, which has the form of a midrash-like commentary on the Pentateuch, containing discourse attributed to the second-century R. Simeon ben Yohai and his contemporaries.

Marsh's collection falls squarely in this second period of Christian Hebraism, towards its climax at the end of the seventeenth century. Hebrew study had then moved to the centre of biblical and theological work, and had claimed the allegiance of scholars in other areas. Thus two outstanding Hebraists were the great lawyers Hugo Grotius in the Netherlands, and John Selden in London; and in Marsh's own circle, Robert Boyle, famous for 'Boyle's Law' in physics, was skilled in Hebrew, Aramaic, Syriac and Arabic as well as the natural sciences. Indeed, a late seventeenth-century English observer wrote that the study of post-biblical Hebrew, since its revival, 'hath had somewhat the fortune of Chymistry, and hath been by degrees inspected, improved, and used not only by men of whimsy, memory, or vanity, but by the more Wise, Judicious and Philosophical'.[7]

The wealth of books on Hebrew and Jewish studies in Marsh's collection is therefore an outstanding instance of a characteristic feature of seventeenth-century scholarly libraries. Many college libraries were then augmented in this field. Thus at Oxford in 1676 Christ Church obtained 'a very good collection of Hebrew books' simply by buying duplicate copies from the Bodleian Library.[8] Sometimes the augmentation was from scholars who gave their collections. Humphrey Prideaux (1648–1724) gave to Clare College, Cambridge the magnificent Hebrew collection which he had assembled, probably mainly at Oxford in the 1670s.[9] John Spencer (see chapter 7) likewise gave books to his own Cambridge college, Corpus. A non-university parallel with Marsh's Library is Chetham's Library in Manchester, comparably founded for public use in 1653, and also rich in Christian Hebrew scholarship.

Yet Marsh's books extend into other fields of oriental learning, especially but not only Arabic. Marsh wrote that as an undergraduate (1655–8) 'I betook myself seriously to the study of old Philosophy, Mathematicks, and oriental languages.'[10] This too is a widespread interest of the time. In 1669 Edmund Castell of Cambridge (1606–85), in the Preface of his great heptaglot lexicon of Hebrew, Syriac, Arabic and other languages, pictured in an extended metaphor 'the splendour of oriental knowledge, that is the best knowledge', as shining ever more and more into western and northern Europe over a period of four jubilees. Hebrew study from about 1500, with Johann Reuchlin and Sebastian Munster, gave a first glimpse of a greater light, from 1550 Syriac too beamed forth through J.A. Widmanstadt, after 1600 Arabic was most happily displayed through William Bedwell and Thomas Erpenius, and since 1650 the constellation of Ethiopic, Persian and Malay had appeared in brightness over England, and still other eastern languages manifested themselves in the Low Countries.[11] All the scholars and languages named here by Castell figure in Marsh's collection. Yet within this broad oriental field the weight of his collection lies in the area of Christian Hebraism.

Estimates of Christian Hebraism
Chronologically, Marsh and his contemporaries just overlap with the earliest writing reviewed at length by Edward Said in his critical study of 'Orientalism', Barthélemy d'Herbelot's *Bibliothèque Orientale*, published in 1697. Viewing Christian Hebrew study in the broader 'oriental' linguistic context in which Marsh pursued it, should one not enlarge and alter the sketch of Christian Hebraism as ardour for Hebrew learning, on the lines followed for Orientalism by Said? Western oriental scholarship, in Said's presentation, is a collusion with western colonialism, and a kind of triumph over a potentially hostile culture.[12] Was not Christian Hebrew study, comparably, a triumph over the biblical yet troublingly divergent

Jewish culture, and a co-operation with large-scale western attempts to baptize or exclude or discredit the Jewish population?

The answer is perhaps not an unconditional Yes, but Hebraists were repeatedly involved in such attempts, in both the mediaeval and the early modern periods. Great scholars of whom this is true include the Dominican Raymund Martini in the thirteenth century. His *Pugio Fidei* has formed a treasury of rabbinic literature for gentile inquirers, but was originally envisaged as a handy 'dagger of faith', in the words of the title; for he sought to show through copious quotation of post-biblical Hebrew texts (which Jewish communities had to submit for examination by royal command) that Christian biblical interpretation corresponded to the best and most ancient insights of Jewish tradition. His approach was followed in public disputations intended to promote the baptism of Jews in Spain and France, but it also gave grounds for the defence of the Talmud as a work of value for Christians, an argument which would be classically expressed by Reuchlin in the early sixteenth century. Raymund Martini's work significantly received both its first and second printed editions in the seventeenth century; Marsh's Library has both, and its copy of the former (Paris, 1651) comes from Stillingfleet, and of the latter (Leipzig, 1687, with additional material) directly from Marsh. Among seventeenth-century authors, a partly comparable place was held by J.C. Wagenseil (1633–1705), Professor of Oriental Languages in the university of Altdorf, near Nuremberg. His works include an edition, translation and rebuttal of mediaeval Hebrew writings against Christianity, collected as 'fiery darts of Satan', *Tela Ignea Satanae* (Altdorf, 1681). Stillingfleet's copy of the book is in Marsh's Library. The title, like that of Raymund Martini, echoes Eph. 6:16 on the Christian's armour and shows that this work of Hebrew scholarship is also intended, by its clarification and confutation of Jewish argument, to serve Christian apologetic writing and mission. Wagenseil advocated humane treatment of Jews in the state, coupled with a more informed and kindly type of mission, and he defended the Talmud from charges of blasphemy.[13]

He was, however, also sometimes felt by Jews to have behaved as their enemy, by publishing works which brought them into ill repute.[14]

To move accordingly from apologetic and mission to defamation, publications purporting to give an 'exposure' or 'unveiling' of the Jews could not always claim the scholarship of the Hebraists, but they formed part of their reading and sometimes affected their sentiments. The most famous or infamous attempt to convict Jews of blasphemy in this period, through copious quotation of the Talmud and Jewish literature, did indeed come from a Hebraist of the university of Heidelberg, J.A. Eisenmenger (1654–1705), in his two-volume *Entdecktes Judenthum*. The first edition (Frankfurt am Main, 1700) was confiscated by imperial order, and a second did not appear until 1711, too late for acquisition by Stillingfleet or Marsh. The Library owns, however, Stillingfleet's copy of an interesting example of comment by another Hebraist of the same period on earlier attempts both to discredit and to defend the Jews, in the form of J. Wülfer, *Theriaca Judaica, ad examen revocata* (Nuremberg, 1681) – 'The "Jewish Antidote" examined'. S.F. Brenz's pamphlet *Jüdischer abgestreiffter Schlangenbalg*, 'the Jewish snakeskin sloughed' (Nuremberg, 1614), had charged the Jews with poisonous blasphemy against Christ, but it quickly received its 'Jewish antidote' in a Yiddish response by Zalman Zevi (or Hirsch) Uffenhausen, *Jüdischer Theriak* (Hanau, 1615). Wülfer (1651–1724), over sixty years later, reprinted both texts, with a Latin translation of the response and copious notes on it (often but not always endorsing Zalman's answers), and with a reprint of Isaac Vita Cantarini's later short book in answer to the blood libel, *Vindex Sanguinis* (originally issued at Groningen, 1675). Wülfer had visited Oxford in 1676, and was in touch there with at least two members of the group of Hebrew scholars to which Marsh belonged, Edward Bernard and Thomas Hyde.[15]

Raymund Martini, Wagenseil and Wülfer are among many names represented in Marsh's Library which straddle the border between Hebrew study and Jewish–Christian relations. They vary in attitude and ecclesiastical background, but they can suggest that Christian Hebraism was indeed in cooperation with western Christian mission to the Jews, and in this respect comparable with oriental study under the aegis of empire, as presented by Said. They also in some ways fit the notion of a discursive formation as outlined by Michel Foucault.[16] Thus, the literature of Christian Hebrew study can be said to show, irrespective of individual scholarly options, an overall tendency – in this case, to domesticate or rebut the post-biblical Hebrew writings; it is closely bound up with practice – practice in church and state concerning the status of Jews; and it is associated with a particular group – a western Christian readership, for taken as a whole Christian Hebraism has indeed enabled western Christians not only to learn Hebrew but also somehow to cope with the phenomenon of Jewish tradition.

Yet there would be grounds for hesitation over an account of Christian Hebraism which solely followed the lines of Foucault or Said. The relationship between Christian Hebrew study and defamation has already received scrutiny over a long period. Appraisals have varied in a way which underlines the variety within Christian Hebraism itself. Thus in the early twentieth century there was a contrast in overall judgment between two eminent gentile Hebraists, George Foot Moore of Harvard and his younger colleague Herbert Danby, of Jerusalem and Oxford. Moore wrote a fundamental account of ancient Judaism up to the completion of the Mishnah; Danby produced the first complete English translation of the Mishnah.[17]

Moore was impressed and depressed by the constant link between Hebrew study and anti-Jewish argument and invective, from the times of the first Dominicans and Franciscans through to the Hebraists of the seventeenth century, and beyond them. In a lucid, extensive and mordant review of the history of scholarship he presented Christian interpretation of Hebrew literature as repeatedly distorted by apologetic and polemic.[18]

Moore's view won renewed prominence in later twentieth-century inquiry into St Paul and his interpreters on Jewish religion, and into Christian antisemitism.[19] Some years after Moore's article appeared, however, it received a complement in the equally clear-eyed but somewhat more positive appraisal of Christian Hebraism offered by Danby. Danby – here very close to Moore – put first in a list of motives for Christian study of post-biblical Hebrew the desire to bring Jews into the Christian fold, and the endeavour to expose the Jews to obloquy; the latter, he wrote, 'is (at least to Jews) the motive that is most familiar – that of exciting and feeding anti-Semitism'. On the other hand he brought out the ardour, skill and toil with which the Hebraists studied so vast a range of Hebrew literature of all kinds, and he noted that Hebraists had sometimes been ready to defend the Jews, not simply to attack them. He urged also that some Christian study of this literature had indeed been illuminating, especially through the edition and translation of texts and the recognition that post-biblical Hebrew sources were essential for biblical interpretation and the study of Christian origins.[20] An approach simply in the wake of Moore, Foucault and Said would then perhaps do too little justice to the variety of Christian Hebraism, and notably to those occasions evoked by Danby when the text does appear to have grasped the scholar.

The impression of a variety which deserves further characterization is deepened if one turns back from these two discussions to the Hebraism of Marsh's time. Said, with all his debt to Foucault, urged that at least in the case of oriental studies Foucault's perspective unduly minimizes the significance of individual scholars and their variety of approach.[21] This observation applies also to Christian Hebraism, a movement on which particular scholars have left marked and differing impressions. Its links with apologetic have now been underlined, in complement to that philological ardour which was noted initially; but the comments of Danby and also Said have suggested that still other aspects deserve notice, and that the individuality of scholars should not be neglected. Three aspects can be picked out here: Jews contributed in various ways to the Hebraists' discussion; the habit of comparison with other oriental languages and religions brought a degree of detachment; and there was never lacking a sense of the greatness of Hebrew literature, post-biblical as well as biblical. Are these likewise reflected in Marsh's collection?

Marsh and his Hebraist Circle, 1658–83
Coming back to Marsh's books with this question in view, I should like first to link the books with his own personal entry into the world of Christian Hebraism. His formative years as a collector and scholar were probably the quarter-century from 1658, when in Oxford at the age of nineteen he graduated as a member of Magdalen Hall, to 1683, when in Ireland at the age of forty-four he became bishop of Ferns. In these twenty-five years he had been fellow of Exeter College, Oxford (from 1658), then principal of Alban Hall, Oxford (from 1673), and finally had moved to Ireland as provost of Trinity College, Dublin in January 1679, shortly after his fortieth birthday.

Marsh therefore had over twenty years of contact with Oxford Hebraists, above all Edward Pocock(e) (1604–91), the revered Regius Professor of Hebrew and Laudian Professor of Arabic, who had earlier served in Aleppo as chaplain to the English Factory. In the immediate past when Marsh graduated was Pococke's *Porta Mosis*, an edition and translation of parts of the Arabic introduction to the Mishnah by Maimonides (Stillingfleet's copy is in the Library).[22] Pococke and Oxford were deeply involved in a British and European movement to edit, translate and comment on Maimonides.[23] The stream of Pococke's Oxford publications continued through and beyond the twenty-five years under review, leading eventually to his long-awaited commentary on the Minor Prophets (1677–91). Marsh's heart was in his 1702 tribute to Pococke, on 'the rare Endowments of this admirable Man, with whom I had the honour to be very intimately acquainted for many Years'; and in 1680 Pococke for his part, when Marsh had left for Dublin, had written to him

141

expressing (in the words of L. Twells) 'his great want of Dr Marsh's good converse and company'.[24]

Other foci of Hebrew and oriental scholarship in Marsh's early Oxford years were formed by the writing and manuscript collecting of archbishop Ussher (died 1655), and by the great London Polyglot Bible edited by Brian Walton (Stillingfleet's copy is in the Library). In the last years of Ussher's life his publications concentrated on biblical history and textual criticism, notably in his famous *Annals*, his epistle to L. Capellus, of the French Reformed academy at Saumur, on variant readings in the Hebrew bible (1652), and his dissertation on the Septuagint (1655). He lent manuscripts, including a celebrated copy of the Samaritan Pentateuch, to Walton for the Polyglot. The sixth and last folio volume of the Polyglot appeared in 1657, with contributions from Pococke and the Irish orientalist Dudley Loftus; but it had inspired further philological work of the kind which fascinated Marsh, and some projects in this area gravitated to Pococke's Oxford and its press.

There were other developments in British biblical and Hebrew study in the 1650s. John Selden (d. 1654) had been working on his last great book, on the councils and courts of justice – sanhedrins – of the Jews, *De synedriis Judaeorum*, issued between 1650 and 1655 – unfinished, but over 1,400 pages quarto in the 1696 reprint. John Lightfoot in Cambridge had started to publish an epoch-making series of commentaries on the New Testament books from rabbinic texts. Both works are in Marsh's Library. It was, however, in an atmosphere formed especially by Pococke, Ussher and the Polyglot that Marsh and his Oxford contemporaries began their Hebrew and oriental studies.

In 1658, when Marsh was elected fellow of Exeter College, Oxford, the Hebraist Samuel Clarke of Merton College (1625–69) became the Oxford Architypographus, with oversight of the university press. The years in which Marsh emerged as a gifted oriental linguist were therefore also years in which Hebrew and oriental publication was central to the work of the press. Clarke had learned from Pococke, had worked on Hebrew, Aramaic and Persian texts for the Polyglot, and together with A. Huish was collaborating with Edmund Castell on the great 'Heptaglott Lexicon unto the Polyglot Bibles' mentioned already. (Clarke later withdrew, without breaking his friendship with Castell.) He issued his own translation of the Mishnah tractate Berakhoth, with a Hebrew text (Oxford, 1667), and had also copied and translated the still inedited Targum on Chronicles from a Cambridge fourteenth-century manuscript which had formerly belonged to the collection of the Dutch Hebrew and oriental scholar Thomas Erpenius.[25] Under Clarke's auspices further Arabic work by Pococke was issued, notably (with financial aid from Robert Boyle) an Arabic translation of Grotius 'On the Truth of the Christian Religion', *De veritate Religionis Christianae* (1660) – this famous work discusses Islam as well as Judaism and paganism – and a collection of Arabic poetry, *Carmen Tograi* (1661), with an appendix by Clarke himself on Arabic versification; Marsh's copies of both books are in the Library. Clarke was preparing for Oxford publication a seventh volume of the Polyglot Bible, to include the Targum of Chronicles and other unpublished ancient biblical versions.[26] After he died prematurely in 1669 this projected volume never appeared. In the same year, however, Castell's lexicon was issued, uniform with the Polyglot which it subserved, and from the same London printer, Thomas Roycroft; the preface includes thanks for materials supplied by Clarke (Targum) and Dudley Loftus (Syriac). Marsh's copy of the Lexicon, mentioned already, is interleaved and annotated.[27]

Marsh was one of a noteworthy group of Hebraists who shared this background and were inspired by Pococke. Four other members of the group were almost exactly contemporary with Marsh. Robert Huntington (1637–1701), fellow of Merton, ultimately bishop of Raphoe and famous as a collector of oriental manuscripts, served like Pococke in Aleppo and succeeded Marsh in Dublin as Provost of Trinity; his visit to the Samaritans in Nablus in 1671 formed the occasion of their celebrated correspondence with Oxford, for 'they mistook Mr Huntington, who told them there were Hebrews here, he meaning Jews, and they their own Sect'.[28] Huntington wrote that he had tried in vain to undeceive them.[29] A copy of a Samaritan letter of 1672 to their brethren in England is among the Library's portion of Marsh's manuscripts. The Oxford Samaritan correspondence is part of a longer history of letters between Samaritans and western scholars.[30] Then Marsh's friend Edward Bernard (1638–96), fellow of St John's and in 1673 Christopher Wren's successor as Savilian Professor of Astronomy, shared with Marsh a love of both mathematics and Semitic languages. Thirdly, Thomas Smith (1638–1710), who has already been cited, a fellow of Magdalen College ejected under James II, and then a non-juror, was Marsh's lifelong friend and adviser. Much of our knowledge of this group is due to Smith, who published lives of Ussher, Huntington and Bernard; but he began his publishing career as a biblical scholar and Hebraist, with a treatise on the Aramaic Targums, *Diatriba de Chaldaicis Paraphrastis* (Oxford, 1662); Marsh's copy is in the Library. Lastly, Thomas Hyde (1636–1703), originally of King's College, Cambridge, worked on Syriac and Arabic texts in Walton's Polyglot, and entered the Queen's College, Oxford in 1658; Bodley's Librarian from 1665, he eventually succeeded Pococke as Laudian Professor of Arabic (1691). It will be noted that Marsh and these four contemporaries entered a scholarly tradition in which Irish participation was significant (Ussher, Loftus, Boyle) and that two of the five (Huntington as well as Marsh) were promoted into Ireland in middle life, thanks to recommendations by their patron John Fell, dean of Christ Church and from 1676 also bishop of Oxford, to James Butler, first Duke of Ormond and also chancellor of the university of Oxford.[31]

Older members of the group of Marsh's Hebraist friends included Thomas Marshall (1621–85), Rector of Lincoln College, Oxford and Dean of Gloucester, who carried on the Samaritan correspondence. A younger member was William Guise, an exceptional Arabist and Hebraist, who died of smallpox in 1683 at the age of thirty-one; he stood out as a member of a landed family who chose to continue life in Oxford from 1680 as a married man, and to devote himself to learning and the service of the church.[32] Friends of Huntington who benefited from his zeal for manuscripts are named by Smith as Marsh himself, Pococke, Marshall, Bernard, Hyde and Guise, together with Dr Fell, who among many other achievements would renew the Oxford press in 1688-9 through the establishment of printing at the Sheldonian Theatre with the new 'Fell types' (bought in Holland by Thomas Marshall, who had been chaplain in Dordrecht).[33]

Another prominent younger disciple of Pococke was Humphrey Prideaux, Student of Christ Church and later dean of Norwich, already mentioned as a book collector. In 1675 Pococke asked Prideaux, then twenty-six, to read the unpublished commentary on the Minor Prophets for the press; soon thereafter Pococke was taken ill, and Prideaux wrote that his death would 'deprive me of the best friend I have in this place, and utterly spoile me for a linguist … If he liveth, we designe great things, and I am resolved to labour hard to bring them to passe'.[34] Some part at least of them may consist in Prideaux's work 'on the law of the poor and the stranger among the Jews', *De jure pauperis et peregrini apud Judaeos* (Oxford, 1679), comprising text and translation, with comment, of portions from Maimonides, *Mishneh Torah*; Stillingfleet's copy is in the Library. The characteristic concern of Hebraism at this period with subject-matter as well as language is seen in Prideaux's equal care for philology and exegesis; he notes the esteem given to the commentary *Keseph Mishneh* by the great sixteenth-century interpreter of legal tradition, Joseph Caro.

Prideaux's published letters to John Ellis (1674 onwards) make no mention, so far as I can see, of Marsh, who was now governing Alban Hall and left for Dublin in 1678; but their cheerful Oxford gossip gives some impression of Marsh's circle from the angle of a Hebraist ten years junior to Marsh. Prideaux admired, supported and claimed kinship with the still younger Guise, but he was perhaps not so close to Marsh as Guise and his friends; his references to Thomas Smith in London do not suggest much acquaintance. In 1675, however, Prideaux writes warmly of Bernard, 'to whom I have been beholden for reveweing all my papers before they have gon to the presse'. Huntington, again, was liked and esteemed by Prideaux, who saw him in 1682 as his obvious rival for the Hebrew chair (not in fact vacated until 1691); but Hyde is bluntly characterized as one 'who doth not understand common sense in his own language, and therefore I cannot conceive how he can make sense of anything that is writ in another. And beside, he hath ye least skil in this language [Arabic] of any that pretend to it in the University; in the Persian language he can doe something, as having been bred to it when young ...'. This reluctant concession chimes in fact with the specification in Marsh's salute to Hyde as 'my friend rightly esteemed highly cultivated in oriental languages, especially Persian and Turkish' – words inscribed in the copy of Pococke's Arabic version of Grotius, *De veritate* which Hyde gave Marsh in 1669.[35]

Prideaux's comments on Pococke and on Marsh's friends can perhaps fairly be taken to suggest that by the later 1670s, whatever might have been the case in the 1660s, Marsh did not stand out in Oxford as an oriental scholar – this despite his friendship with Pococke and other prominent Hebraists, his known linguistic ability, and his zest for teaching Hebrew (see his later letter to Pococke, quoted below). Marsh did not publish in the oriental field, though it might perhaps have been hoped that he would edit a portion of Maimonides, like Prideaux; a copy of the *Mishneh Torah* was among his early acquisitions (see below). By this time, however, he was playing a full part, perhaps including teaching in such subjects as logic and mathematics as well as Hebrew, as head of a Hall. Yet he remained a committed Hebraist. This point is confirmed by accessions to his books in the quarter-century under review, together with a letter he wrote towards the end of it, as provost of Trinity.

Five at least of the accessions form hints on his linguistic studies and the esteem he won in them. First, in the year of his ordination, 1662, the rector of Exeter (J. Maynard) gave him the Venice (C. Adelkind for M.A. Giustiniani) 1550–51 edition of the *Mishneh Torah* of Maimonides, whose work was at the heart of current scholarship, as seen already; John Worthington, sometime master of Jesus College, Cambridge, was trying to procure a Maimonides early in 1666.[36] In 1662 Maynard also gave Marsh a copy of Edward Brerewood's *Enquiries touching the Diversities of Languages and Religions* (1614; repr. London, 1635). This early essay in comparative study was often reprinted, and translated into Latin, French and German; in the 1670s the Oratorian scholar Richard Simon prepared an extensive supplement to the French translation.[37] Marsh's annotated copy suggests what his book collection as a whole confirms, his share in contemporary awareness of this broad context of linguistic work – and the way in which the regular association of other oriental languages with Hebrew at this period encouraged such awareness.

These copies of Maimonides and Brerewood together form a context for a book inscribed by Marsh in the following year (1663), his copy of Moses Kimhi's *In Introductorio Grammaticae* (Hagenau, 1519; from the workshop of Thomas Anshelm) – a book entirely in Hebrew apart from the dedicatory letter. This renowned mediaeval Hebrew grammar, entitled *mahalakh shebhiley ha-da'at*, 'a journey on the paths of knowledge', is introductory, as both the Hebrew and the 1519 Latin title suggest. Perhaps it was bought with a view to Marsh's teaching of Hebrew as well as his own studies. In any case, in the Christian Hebraism of Marsh's time, as his copies of Maimonides and Brerewood suggest, it opened the door not only to the biblical books but also to post-biblical Hebrew and to a breadth of religious as well as linguistic comparison. Moses Kimhi's grammar was in fact a fundamental work for sixteenth- and seventeenth-century Hebraism. It had received a Hebrew commentary from the Jewish humanist Elias Levita.[38] It was issued three times with this commentary but without Levita's name by the great Hebrew printer Girolamo (Gershom) Soncino (1508, 1517, 1518); Anshelm's printing soon followed, and the many further issues of the grammar include a Venice, 1546 printing with the commentary, now supervised by Levita himself (in Marsh's Library), and a text with a translation by the Christian Hebraist Constantijn L'Empereur (1631); Stillingfleet's copy of the latter is in the Library.

Then in 1666, when he was twenty-seven, Marsh was given a beautiful 16° Hebrew Bible (Venice, 1615; *Wisdom of the East*, no. 21) by the young J.J. Buxtorf (1645–1704). The donor was third in the family succession of Basle professors of Hebrew (see Plate 12), and had been elected to the chair by the city magistrates, despite his youth, after the sudden death of his father and teacher, Johann Buxtorf II (1664). Samuel Clarke and Thomas Smith had contributed memorial poems.[39] The occasion of the gift to Marsh was the young Buxtorf's departure after a stay in Oxford during his visit to England in 1666, when he met the principal Hebraists, including, outside Oxford, John Lightfoot and Edmund Castell.[40] The warm and graceful Latin dedicatory inscription, under a Hebrew motto on the manifold significance of the Torah, praises Marsh for his learning, above all in oriental philology (*Philologia Orientalis*), and for his friendship while Buxtorf was living in Oxford. It seems then that Marsh had helped to look after Buxtorf during his stay, and his choice for this office, probably by Pococke, betokens his repute as a linguist as well as a kindly host.

Lastly, between 1671 and 1673 comes his acquisition of Castell's lexicon, a book which was the foundation of much subsequent Semitic lexicography. The cover in which it was sent, addressed to 'Dr' Marsh at Exeter College, and later hanging, framed, in Marsh's Library, sets the despatch of his copy within these years; Marsh proceeded to the D.D. degree on 23 June 1671, and became principal of Alban Hall in 1673. When the lexicon was published in 1669 Dr Fell had promised Castell to write to the Vice-Chancellor (Peter Mews) in order that every college, at least, should buy a copy.[41]

Marsh's annotation of his copy suggests, however, that he needed no official encouragement towards its purchase.

These five accessions to his collection take one with Marsh as a Hebraist and oriental linguist from his early years at Exeter into the 1670s, near the time when he moved to Alban Hall (1673) and Prideaux's surviving comments begin (1674). As suggested above, Marsh, who had still not published in the field in his second decade after graduation (contrast Prideaux), was perhaps now not obviously to the fore among Oxford Hebraists. It might also be thought that his philological ardour could have waned in the 1670s in view of his new administrative concerns at Alban Hall, which were of course redoubled when he moved to Dublin in January 1679. In fact, however, he will have continued to study and to accumulate books in the field. Thus his copy of I. Tremellius's 1569 Syriac New Testament, originally owned by Erpenius, was acquired in 1678. Two years later the student of Moses Kimhi's grammar, the friend of J.J. Buxtorf and the annotator of Castell are all still there in the person of the provost of Trinity. In his second spring in Ireland, on 29 April 1680, Marsh writes to Pococke, full of cheerful determination to promote Hebrew:

> We have not many, that can judge of the Original [Hebrew text of the bible]; but I hope to breed up good Store that way, since we have an Hebrew Professor's place lately settled on the College, to which Lecture I make all the Bachelors of Arts attend, and be examined thrice every Week, and they are likewise to be publickly examined in Hebrew, before they can take their Degree of Master in Arts, which I sometimes do myself.[42]

The good spirits which this subject clearly evoked in Marsh contrast with his understandably gloomy reaction to some of his administrative tasks at Trinity. Twenty-five years later Marsh, the loyal lover of Hebrew, would probably still have hoped that Hebrew would be or become familiar to the graduates for whom his new library was largely intended. The college statutes at Trinity then restricted study in the Trinity College Library itself to the Provost and Fellows; any other member of the college had to be accompanied by one of them throughout the visit. 'And 'twas this, & this consideration alone,' wrote Marsh to Bernard in 1705, 'y^t at first mov'd Me to think of building A Library in some Other Place (y^n in the College) for publick use, where all might have free access, seeing They cannot have it in the College; nor are our Booksellers Shops furnisht any thing tolerably with other Books than new Triffles and Pamphletts, & not well with Them also.'[43]

Christians and Jews in Christian Hebraism
How far do the books of this scholar with a consistent care for Hebrew and oriental philology reflect those further aspects of Christian Hebraism which were mentioned above? The attempt just made to follow hints of his path in Hebrew and oriental studies between 1658 and 1683 has certainly touched on the aspects which were singled out at the very beginning. He has displayed something of the philological passion which was taken to be a cardinal feature, and the apologetic dimension has also appeared, for instance in the Arabic translation of Grotius, *De veritate*. Yet Marsh's collection can also suggest that Christian Hebraism did indeed have greater complexity.

The first of the further aspects which were named to illustrate this point is formed by the contribution of Jews to Christian Hebraism. It goes almost without saying that Jews who had received baptism played an important part, often in apologetic and polemic but also in Hebrew teaching; thus Emanuele Tremelli (Tremellius) of Ferrara (1510–80), Marsh's copy of whose Syriac New Testament has just been mentioned, was baptized about 1540 and eventually became professor of Hebrew in Cambridge and Heidelberg, and a noted biblical scholar. Yet there was also pervasive participation by non-Christian Jews.

Perhaps their most prominent mode of participation was through teaching, advice, and the making and transmission of books.

Thus Elias Levita can almost be called the official grammarian of sixteenth-century Hebraists, through personal teaching as well as the printed book. In the seventeenth century, although it had long been possible to learn Hebrew from Christian teachers, Jewish teaching continued to be highly valued, as in the case of Isaac Abendana in the Netherlands and England.[44] With regard to advice and consultation, the friendship which grew up at Constantinople between Pococke and Jacob Romano, 'second to none for learning and ingenuity among the Jews whom I have known', is mentioned with warmth and gratitude by Pococke and his biographer.[45] Then, without Jewish printers and press-revisers the second great age of Christian Hebraism could not have flowered as it did; Marsh's collection is typical in representing printers' names such as Soncino and Foa in Italy, Isaac ben Aaron of Prossnitz (Cracow) and Immanuel Benveniste (Amsterdam), as well as the Christian printers like Daniel Bomberg in Venice and Froben in Basle who issued rabbinic works with the cooperation of Jewish scholars and craftsmen. One such co-worker was Cornelius Adelkind, printer for M.A. Giustiniani in Venice of Marsh's 1550-1 Maimonides, *Mishneh Torah*. Conversely, Christian Hebraist participation in Jewish book production has now been highlighted in the case of Willem Surenhuis, discussed below, for example in connection with the edition of Maimonides, *Mishneh Torah* printed by Immanuel ben Joseph Athias (4 vols. folio, Amsterdam, 1702).[46] Lastly, book transmission was also exemplified in Marsh's time by Jewish bookselling. Portuguese catalogues of Hebraica and Judaica were issued by Menasseh ben Israel in the 1650s, and one was used by John Selden; while a member of the Athias family supplied Edmund Castell in the 1660s, and Marsh himself bought books through his correspondent Aron Moses, perhaps to be identified with Aaron Moses of Dublin and London, who was elderly but still active as a communal scribe under Queen Anne.[47]

Another mode of Jewish participation was indirect but significant. Jews spoke with much freedom through their mediaeval

Biblical Voices and Echoes

and later Hebrew apologetic and polemical works, and Christian Hebraists edited and answered these writings, as Wagenseil did in his 1681 collection mentioned already. Publications like this express Christian apologetic, but also transmit a Jewish voice, a voice moreover which has been thought to demand a reply. Thus in England a little later, perhaps in the 1690s, when Richard Bentley was writing Christian apologetic for his Boyle Lectures, Edward Bernard asked him if he should not consider Jewish objections; but he answered that it was better to leave them in the decent obscurity of Hebrew or Latin.[48] Bernard's point was accepted, however, by another Boyle lecturer, Richard Kidder, bishop of Bath and Wells, in his extensive *Demonstration of the Messias against the Jews* (3 parts, 1684–1700). He had studied the Hebrew polemical texts in Wagenseil and elsewhere, and the printed and manuscript writings of contemporary Jews in Latin and Portuguese. Yet Kidder too felt to some extent with Bentley, for he divided up his statement of Jewish objections lest they be read as a body without his replies.[49] The hesitations of Bentley and Kidder are a testimony to the freedom and force of the Jewish writings, and their convergence at times with contemporary Deist and Socinian argument, a point made by Kidder to show the utility of his work.

Kidder's reading as just described also indicates, however, a third mode of Jewish participation in Christian Hebraism, this time direct literary contribution by contemporary Jews. In the seventeenth century, Jews had begun not only to circulate handwritten apologetic in the vernacular and in Latin (two such manuscripts were used by Kidder), but also to print apologetic and scholarly treatises in Latin and in modern western languages, both independently and through Christian editors like Philip à Limborch (through whom Kidder read Orobio de Castro). Examples of defence against defamation include Cantarini's *Vindex Sanguinis*, mentioned already. On the other hand, strong assertion of Jewish principles mingled with biblical scholarship marks the printed writings of Menasseh ben Israel, notably his *Conciliator* of apparently inconsistent biblical

152

texts (1632) and his *Spes Israel* (1650), on messianic hope; both are among Stillingfleet's books, and in his *Origines Sacrae* Stillingfleet both followed the *Conciliator* and argued against it (on the eternity ascribed to Mosaic law).[50]

Christian Hebraism was clearly marked by the absorptive or hostile tendencies noted above; but it also stands out for the degree to which personal as well as textual knowledge of Jews is present, the degree to which textual knowledge derives from Jewish writing or printing in European languages as well as Hebrew, and the degree to which Jews are encountered, both in person and through their writings, as teachers, fellow-workers and respected disputants.

Religious and Cultural Comparison
A second further aspect of Christian Hebraism is formed by the tendency to religious and cultural comparison noted already in connection with Brerewood. This tendency was not absent from the mediaeval literature of triple debate between Jews, Muslims and Christians, exemplified in the twelfth century in Judah ha-Levi's *Kuzari*; but it is particularly characteristic of the later seventeenth century. Thus two Hebraists of this period, John Spencer (see the preceding chapter) and Richard Simon in Paris, have been hailed as pioneers of the study of comparative religion, through their description of Jewish and gentile rites and ceremonies, past and present. Research into Jewish customs could suggest guidance on Christian origins, as in the study of the Dutch Hebraist Campegius Vitringa on the ancient synagogue, *De synagoga vetere* (Franeker, 1696), preserved among Marsh's books in the Library (*The Wisdom of the East*, no. 29); the title-page engraving of a synagogue porch illustrates the prophecy of Zechariah (8:3) that 'ten men out of all languages of the nations shall take hold of the skirt of him that is a Jew, saying, We will go with you, for we have heard that God is with you'. (See Plate 13.)

Then, comparison of both Judaism and Christianity with other religions was encouraged by the perception of Hebrew study as part of a broader *Scientia Orientalis* or *Philologia Orientalis* (the terms are those noted above from E. Castell and J.J. Buxtorf, respectively), a perception which was fully shared by Marsh. Lastly, as George Bright's parallel between the progress of Hebrew study and chemistry suggests, the Hebraists' comparison of languages and religions went hand-in-hand with comparison of the advancement of learning in the several sciences. This step was easy when so many scholars, including Marsh, concerned themselves with a number of sciences at once.

A conspicuous salute to this manifold comparative tendency was given by the Dutch rabbinic scholar Willem Surenhuis (Surenhusius), editor (1698–1703) of the first complete Latin translation of the Mishnah and its principal Hebrew commentaries (Marsh's copy is in the Library).[51] Surenhusius regarded his age as a time when quarrels over religion had lost their vehemence, contacts with the Jews had been re-established, and all sciences had been recognized as inter-connected.[52] Without over-assimilating Marsh to the Enlightenment, one may suppose that current views of this kind helped to form his book collection and his conception of a library – strong in Hebrew and oriental philology, yet representing every science. At any rate, the broad comparative tendency in contemporary Christian Hebraism is important as bringing a certain detachment and sense of proportion to complement the devotion which these studies evoked.

Devotion to Hebrew Literature
Lastly, a third further aspect of Christian Hebraism is the Hebraists' sense for the greatness of Hebrew literature. It emerges in Marsh's collection perhaps especially in argument for the value of Hebrew study, as interpreted by the books acquired, and through some of the larger literary projects of Marsh's time.

Argument on behalf of Hebrew study was intertwined with Christian apologetic and with claims for academic attention, but could hardly have been sustained without a measure of admiration for the texts. This can sometimes be detected as the argument counters current objections to Jewish literature, mainly those which had been familiar from mediaeval times in connection with the Talmud. Theological response merged in the seventeenth century with more pragmatic considerations.

The Talmud was publicly burnt in both the great ages of Christian Hebraism, notably at Paris in the 1240s and at Rome, Venice and elsewhere in Italy in the 1550s. It was condemned in both periods not only as a book of fables and blasphemies, but also as in effect a replacement of the Mosaic law for Jews, and a hindrance to their seeking baptism. This criticism was matched on its own theological ground, however, by a contrasting Christian affirmation that parts of rabbinic literature do indeed belong to a divinely-originated tradition deriving ultimately from Moses, as rabbinic teaching itself asserts.

This affirmation appeared in the thirteenth-century Raymund Martini, who urged that precisely these parts of the literature confirm Christianity, however misleading other parts may be. With an indirect or direct debt to him it reappeared in the Christian Hebraism of the sixteenth and seventeenth centuries; diverse witnesses to it in Marsh's collection are the Italian Franciscan Petrus Galatinus (Pietro Colonna Galatino), a supporter of Reuchlin, on 'the hidden riches of catholic truth' gathered, against the perfidy of the Jews of our time, from the Talmud and other Jewish books – *De arcanis catholicae veritatis*, first printed by Gershom Soncino (Ortona, 1518), and often reprinted – and later the royalist Cambridge divine Robert Sheringham (1648; see chapter 7, above, n.12), and the Dutch scholar Willem Surenhuis (1698), already mentioned. In Sheringham and Surenhuis (see below) aggressive apologetic application recedes, and it becomes easy to see that this claim, however applied, expresses and encourages deep esteem. Christian Hebraists thus regularly give some endorsement to a position which can be called characteristically Jewish rather than Christian, the treatment of rabbinic tradition as deriving from divine revelation.

155

Yet most often, perhaps, disapproval of parts of the Talmud was incorporated in the defences of Hebrew. Thus in John Lightfoot (1658) a sense for the literature emerges precisely as he wrestles with his conviction (here he was at one with mediaeval criticism) that the Talmudic authorities led the Jews to destruction. 'There are no Authors do more affright and vex the Reader; and yet there are none, who do more intice and delight him.' Later Humphrey Prideaux, mainly concerned with reasoning and style, contrasts the elegance and strength of Maimonides with the wretchedness of his Talmudic sources. A stylistic defence of their fables had to wait until the Romantic movement a century later (see p. 72 above). Occasionally, however, the regular objections were set aside. Sheringham coolly contends that fables and blasphemies do not affect the credit of the Talmud, for they also occur in Greek and Roman historians, and these authors keep their reputation. Surenhuis urges that the Mishnah faithfully renders the genuine Mosaic revelation mediated in the Talmudic literature.[53]

Among the most forceful of the more pragmatic arguments was a simple statement of the value of these texts for both Old and New Testament interpretation. As John Lightfoot said drily at the Westminster Assembly (1643), when Samuel Rutherford of St Andrews seemed to impugn the rabbis, 'There are divers things in the New Testament, which we must be beholden to the Rabbins for the understanding of, or else we know not what to make of them.'[54]

These diverse arguments almost all suggest a real sense for the rabbinic literature as a whole as well as other later Hebrew writings. Prideaux, however, represents a recognizable tendency to reserve full admiration for Hebrew works other than the Babylonian Talmud itself. Praise could more readily be accorded to the Mishnah, the foundation document of the Talmud, and to Maimonides, the philosophical systematizer of rabbinic texts. Both showed a clarity and elegance which appealed to the later seventeenth century. Nevertheless, this tendency should in turn be viewed in the light of the published work of the Hebraists and the books they collected (in the case of the Babylonian Talmud, at no small price). Prideaux himself owned the Palestinian and Babylonian Talmuds as a whole, and many aids to their study, of course including Maimonides; and the same is true of Marsh. The Library has his personal copies of the Babylonian Talmud with commentaries in two editions (Amsterdam, 1644; Frankfurt an der Oder, 1697), the Palestinian Talmud (Cracow, 1579; from Guise's books), and separate study aids in Hebrew including the index of biblical quotations in the Talmud by Aaron Pesaro (Amsterdam, 1652), the compendium of Talmudic legal material by Isaac Alfasi (Basle, 1602), and the compendium of non-legal material by Jacob ibn Habib (Amsterdam, 1684).

The Hebraists' sense of the greatness of Hebrew literature can be briefly confirmed, in conclusion, by reference to three ongoing projects of Christian Hebraism. Between them they show how the post-biblical Hebrew writings touched characteristic tastes or concerns of the age. At the same time they allow further glimpses of Marsh's own life and interests. They indicate the value which he and others set on differing literary streams: mystical, rational, and, once again, rabbinic.

Among the mystical writings of the Kabbalah the Zohar stood out, as noted already. It puts itself forward as the work of great rabbis of the second century, and was widely revered as such. In the seventeenth century it was near the heart of much Jewish piety, including the mystical enthusiasm which surrounded the messianic movement of Sabbatai Zevi (1665 onwards). Ever since Pico della Mirandola and Reuchlin at the end of the fifteenth century and the beginning of the sixteenth, the Zohar and associated works had been equally revered by Platonizing Christian Hebraists.[55] The short *Book of Formation* (*Sepher Yetsirah*) found a series of Christian editors and translators, including in Marsh's time J.S. Rittangel (1642). These texts seemed to show that, not long after the time of Christ, Judaism had a mystical theology of divine intermediaries. The Zohar could suggest (against the Jews) that Trinitarianism reflected ancient Jewish tradition, but also (against more dogmatically inclined Christians)

that Platonic Christian mysticism represented true primitive Christianity. Hebraists who studied Kabbalah for apologetic and devotion include Reuchlin and Galatinus, mentioned already, and contemporaries of Marsh such as Rittangel in Amsterdam and Cambridge Platonists like Ralph Cudworth (for whom it was part of his *True Intellectual System of the Universe* [1678]). All are present in Marsh's collection. Cudworth's friend John Worthington, when he wanted to obtain a Maimonides in 1666, already had at least one folio copy of the Zohar (which he was willing to exchange, as he says in the letter to Lightfoot cited above). Marsh owned three different editions of the Zohar (1568, 1684, 1701), together with the Latin translation of much of it by Knorr von Rosenroth (1677). The Zohar was theologically in vogue, at least in Cambridge, if also in dispute there and elsewhere (Bentley, in the letter to Bernard cited above, called argument from it 'Juggle'); but possibly it appealed also to Marsh's warm piety, as evinced in the first of his recorded dreams, with its near-mystical focus on the love between Christ and those that are his – part of 'an intense and immediate spirituality', in Raymond Gillespie's phrase.[56]

Christian study of Kabbalah foundered in the end on the late date of the Zohar, but was not wholly misconceived, for mediaeval mystical texts have antecedents in older Jewish writings. Among these is the Targum, brought to the fore again in Marsh's time by Walton's Polyglot. Conceptions of divine mediation in the Targums form a topic for Marsh's friend Thomas Smith in his 1662 Targumic handbook, mentioned above, and for many other contemporary names in his collection, such as Rittangel, Kidder, and Peter Allix.

Secondly, a stream of literature which can be called rational for its appeal to reason is summed up in the twelfth-century interpretation of the bible and Jewish law in harmony with Aristotle by Moses Maimonides. Marsh found himself in the midst of Oxford and European efforts to edit, translate and study the Arabic and Hebrew works of Maimonides. As seen already, their style suited the age as well as their subject-matter. The work of the Hebraists on Maimonides found its echo in late seventeenth-century integration of religion with reason, as exhibited by Stillingfleet and, among specialist Hebraists, John Spencer in his interpretation of the ritual laws of the Hebrews (see the preceding chapter). Spencer's collection, like that of Marsh, has the relevant works by Pococke, Prideaux and many others.

Lastly, there was a Europe-wide project to edit and translate the Mishnah and its traditional commentaries. Again this text appealed for its style as well as its fundamental character. In Cambridge Isaac Abendana was preparing a translation in the 1670s, under the joint review of Spencer, Cudworth and Bright (chapter 7, p. 127, above). In Oxford the brilliant William Guise completed the translation of almost seven tractates, with substantial notes, before he died in 1683. He was judged by a modern critic to show a real genius for translation, in comparison with other translators of the Mishnah.[57] In 1690 Edward Bernard printed his work, and prefaced it with a long dedicatory letter addressed to Narcissus Marsh, then bishop of Ferns. 'You know above all others', Bernard wrote, 'how to estimate his contribution – and indeed, as much as the care of the churches allows you, how to restore it to us through similar studies.' Guise was like Marsh, Bernard goes on, in his love both of mathematics and of languages. 'Farewell', the letter ends, 'O venerable prelate; you excel in all the learning displayed by Guise, but you prefer to be adorned by the glory of a holy life.'

Marsh and Christian Hebraism
Marsh's collection thus mirrors those further aspects of Christian Hebraism which I have tried to highlight: the participation of Jews, the tendency towards religious and cultural comparison, and the sense of the greatness of post-biblical Hebrew literature. They can be viewed together with the aspects noted earlier: the philological passion on the one hand, and the tendency towards absorption or exclusion of the Jews and their literature on the other. Something of the complexity of Christian Hebraism in the seventeenth century

is then suggested. For all its conscious and unconscious apologetic tendency, it was in a sense a Jewish as well as a Christian movement. For all its theological intensity, it was pursued with keen awareness of linguistic and religious comparison, and the advancement of all the sciences. It showed a true philological passion; at the same time it was at the heart of integrations of religion with both mysticism and reason. Not insignificantly, it set beside the customary metaphor of triumph in a field of study another commonplace, Edmund Castell's metaphor of increasing awareness of a light.

This survey has afforded glimpses of Marsh himself, up to the time when he had become bishop of Ferns. It now closes with Bernard's dedicatory address to him, when he was soon to become archbishop of Cashel. It happened that this dedication was reproduced in the Latin translation of the Mishnah and its commentaries as finally achieved by Surenhuis, for he opened his six volumes with a reprint of Guise on the first section (*seder*) of the Mishnah.

Marsh's name therefore stands at the head of the work which can be regarded as the crown of seventeenth-century Hebrew study. In this fitting position he is praised as one who might have himself advanced Christian Hebrew scholarship. His books have now helped to present him as Bernard knew him; the dedicatory letter was laudatory, but not untrue. Through attention to the phenomenon of Christian Hebraism his library has emerged as the creation of a scholar who used his books. Archbishop Marsh's library is something different from the learned publishing of an archbishop like Ussher, but like Ussher's works it has issued from dedication to the biblical books and Hebrew, oriental languages and the sciences more broadly. It attests a founder who stood for the contribution to biblical and Hebrew study made by those who are not known for interpretative writing, but have studied, taught, and collected books. Marsh exemplifies the reader and teacher who persists in learning, and is enabled to become, as was said of Marsh, 'a great encourager of learning in others'.[58]

Endnotes

[1] This chapter is reproduced with revision from 'Christian Hebraism in the Mirror of Marsh's Collection', in Muriel McCarthy and Ann Simmons (edd.), *The Making of Marsh's Library: Learning, Religion and Politics in Ireland, 1650–1750* (Dublin, 2004), 256–79, based on a lecture in the Library.

[2] Marsh's letter to his friend Thomas Smith, of 5 July 1704, printed in R. Mant, *History of the Church of Ireland* (2 vols., London, 1840), ii, 113.

[3] T. Smith's letter of 7 August 1707, printed in Mant, *History*, ii, 119.

[4] On the Library building see E. McParland, 'Building Marsh's Library: The Architecture of Marsh's in its European Context', in McCarthy and Simmons (edd.), *The Making of Marsh's Library*, 41–50.

[5] Funeral sermon for Marsh (6 November 1713) by William King, archbishop of Dublin, quoted by R. Gillespie, *Scholar Bishop: The Recollections and Diary of Narcissus Marsh, 1638–1696* (Cork, 2003), 81.

[6] For general description see Muriel McCarthy, 'Introduction', in A.P. Coudert, S. Hutton, R.H. Popkin, & G.M. Weiner (edd.), *Judaeo-Christian Intellectual Culture in the Seventeenth Century: A Celebration of the Library of Narcissus Marsh (1638–1713)* (Dordrecht, Boston & London, 1999), viii–xiv, and the exhibition catalogue by M. McCarthy & C. Sherwood-Smith. *The Wisdom of the East: Marsh's Oriental Books* (Dublin, 1999) – cited by short title below.

[7] G. Bright (ed.), *The Works of the Reverend and Learned John Lightfoot* (2 vols., London, 1684), i, Preface by Bright [8].

[8] Letter from H. Prideaux of 31 October 1676, in E. Maunde Thompson (ed.), *Letters of Humphrey Prideaux, sometime Dean of Norwich, to John Ellis, sometime Under-secretary of State, 1674–1722* (Camden Society, London, 1875), 54. On Prideaux see the following note.

[9] On Prideaux and his collection see now S. Mandelbrote, 'The Significance of Historical Judaism and the Career of Humphrey Prideaux', in Piet van Boxel, Kirsten Macfarlane & Joanna Weinberg (edd.), *The Mishnaic Moment: Jewish Law among Jews and Christians in Early Modern Europe* (Oxford, 2022), 255–77.

[10] Marsh's Diary, in Gillespie, *Scholar Bishop*, 17.

[11] E. Castell, *Lexicon Heptaglotton* (2 vols., London, 1669), i, unpaginated Preface. For Marsh's copies of this Lexicon and grammars by Munster and Erpenius, and Stillingfleet's copies of works by Bedwell and Widmanstadt, see *The Wisdom of the East*, nos. 3, 65, 72; 35, 85.

[12] E.W. Said, *Orientalism: Western Conceptions of the Orient* (1978; reprinted with new Afterword, London, 1995), especially 1–25, 330–40.

[13] See now Piet van Boxel, 'Johann Christoph Wagenseil: From Scholar to Missionary', in van Boxel, Macfarlane & Weinberg (edd.), *The Mishnaic Moment*, 215–34.

[14] Letter of reproach (1683) to Wagenseil from Haggai Levi (Hönig Fränkel), noted by P. Blastenbrei, *Johann Christoph Wagenseil und seine Stellung zum Judentum* (Erlangen, 2004), 98.

[15] Joanna Weinberg, 'Jewish Commentaries in Christian Interpretation of the Mishnah in Seventeenth-Century Northern Europe', in van Boxel, Macfarlane & Weinberg (edd.), *The Mishnaic Moment*, 301–19 (311–12, noting Wülfer's signature on 18 August 1676 in the admissions book of the Bodleian Library).

[16] The three aspects mentioned below figure for example in M. Foucault, *L'archéologie du savoir* (Paris, 1969), 91–3, 95–101.

[17] G.F. Moore, *Judaism in the First Centuries of the Christian Era: The Age of the Tannaim* (3 vols., Cambridge, MA, 1927–30); H. Danby, *The Mishnah, translated from the Hebrew with Introduction and brief explanatory Notes* (Oxford, 1933).

[18] G.F. Moore, 'Christian Writers on Judaism', *Harvard Theological Review* 14 (1921), 197–254.

[19] E.P. Sanders, *Paul and Palestinian Judaism* (London, 1977), 33–6, began his influential fresh approach to Paul and Judaism by recalling Moore's article, and noting in subsequent biblical interpretation the survival of apologetic and polemic like that recorded by Moore.

[20] H. Danby, *Gentile Interest in Post-biblical Hebrew Literature* (Jerusalem, n.d. [1930]) (quotation from p. 11); also published as an article in N. Bentwich & H. Sacher (edd.), *The Jewish Review* 3 (December 1932–March 1933), 18–34.

[21] Said, *Orientalism*, 23.

[22] See now Benjamin Williams, 'Bringing Maimonides to Oxford: Edward Pococke, the Mishnah, and the *Porta Mosis*', in van Boxel, Macfarlane & Weinberg (edd.), *The Mishnaic Moment*, 157–76.

[23] S. Levy, 'English Students of Maimonides', in *Miscellanies of the Jewish Historical Society of England*, iv, *Essays presented to E.N. Adler*, i (London, 1942), 61–84 (67–74).

[24] L. Twells (ed.), *The Theological Works of the learned Dr Pocock* (2 vols., London, 1740), i, 74 (Pococke's letter to Marsh), 82–3 (Marsh on Pococke).

[25] Bright (ed.), *The Works of the Reverend and Learned John Lightfoot*, i, p. xxi; letters of Castell to Clarke, and other documents, in J.E.B. Mayor, *Cambridge under Queen Anne* (Cambridge, 1911), 492–3, 529; N. Barker, *The Oxford University Press and the Spread of Learning, 1478–1978* (Oxford, 1978), 14, and plates 39–40 (G. Langbaine's letter to Clarke on the Lexicon).
[26] Bright, as cited in n.19, above.
[27] *The Wisdom of the East*, no. 3.
[28] E. Bernard's letter of about 1673 to John Lightfoot, in Bright (ed.), *The Works of the Reverend and Learned John Lightfoot*, i, p. xxi.
[29] Letter of Huntington to Job Ludolph, Ascension Day 1675, in T. Smith, *Admodum Reverendi et Doctissimi Viri, D. Roberti Huntingtoni … Epistolae: praemittitur De ejusdem D. Huntingtoni vita … Hypomnemation* (London, 1704), 55; late seventeenth-century or early eighteenth-century copy of letter from Huntington to Pococke (no date reproduced), in M. Gaster, *The Samaritans* (London, 1925), 160.
[30] Gaster, *The Samaritans*, 3, 159–80; M. Delcor, 'La correspondance des savants européens, en quête de manuscrits, avec les Samaritains du XVIᵉ au XIXᵉ siècle', in J.-P. Rothschild & G.D. Sixdenier (edd.), *Études samaritaines* (Louvain & Paris, 1988), 27–43.
[31] Gillespie, *Scholar Bishop*, 5; M. Hunter, 'Robert Boyle, Narcissus Marsh and the Anglo-Irish Intellectual Scene in the Late Seventeenth Century', in McCarthy & Simmons (edd.), *The Making of Marsh's Library*, 51–75 (63, n.46).
[32] Letter of October 1681 in Maunde Thompson, *Letters of Humphrey Prideaux*, 109–10; see now A. Hamilton, 'William Guise: The Application of Arabic to the Interpretation of Mishnah Zera'im', in van Boxel, Macfarlane & Weinberg (edd.), *The Mishnaic Moment*, 177–92.
[33] Smith, *De … Huntingtoni vita*, vi–vii; Barker, *Oxford University Press*, 15–17.
[34] Letter of 2 September 1675 in Thompson, *Letters of Humphrey Prideaux*, 43.
[35] *The Wisdom of the East*, 65.
[36] Worthington to John Lightfoot, 13 February 1666, in Mayor, *Cambridge under Queen Anne*, 518.
[37] *The Wisdom of the East*, no. 70; J.A. Fabricius, *Delectus Argumentorum et Syllabus Scriptorum qui veritatem religionis Christianae … asseruerunt* (Hamburg, 1725), p. 472; G.G. Stroumsa, 'Richard Simon: From Philology to Comparatism', *Archiv für Religionsgeschichte* 3 (2001), 89–107 (94).
[38] G.E. Weil, *Élie Lévita, Humaniste et massorète* (Leiden, 1963), 42–7.

[39] J. & B. Prijs, *Die Basler hebräischen Drucke (1492–1866)* (Olten & Freiburg i.B., 1964), 472.
[40] Castell's letters to Lightfoot of 13 June 1666 and 8 July 1667 [? 1666], in Mayor, *Cambridge under Queen Anne*, 502–503; Bright in Bright (ed.) *The Works of the Reverend and Learned John Lightfoot*, i, p. xxi.
[41] Castell to S. Clarke, 23 December 1669, in Mayor, *Cambridge under Queen Anne*, 493.
[42] Marsh's letter printed in Twells, *The Theological Works of the learned Dr Pocock*, i, 75.
[43] Marsh to Thomas Smith, 19 January 1705, edited from Bodleian Library, Smith MS. 45, ff. 121–5 in Gillespie, *Scholar Bishop*, 58–67 (60).
[44] T. Dunkelgrün, 'The First Complete Latin Translation of the Mishnah: Isaac Abendana and Rabbinic Erudition in Restoration England', in van Boxel, Macfarlane & Weinberg (edd.), *The Mishnaic Moment*, 89–113.
[45] Pococke, *Porta Mosis*, Appendix, 90, in C. Roth, 'Edward Pococke and the first Hebrew Printing in Oxford', *Bodleian Library Record* 2 (1948), 215–20, repr. in C. Roth, *Studies in Books and Booklore* (Farnborough, 1972), 31–5 (34); Twells, *The Theological Works of the learned Dr Pocock*, i, 11.
[46] D. van Miert, '"To the Advantage of the Republic of Letters"? Guilielmus Surenhusius's Projects, Plans and Collaborations beyond the Mishnah', in van Boxel, Macfarlane & Weinberg (edd.), *The Mishnaic Moment*, 359–77 (360–65).
[47] Roth, 'Edward Pococke and the first Hebrew Printing in Oxford', 35 (n.2) and A. Yaari, *Studies in Hebrew Booklore* (Hebrew; Jerusalem, 1958), 430–49 (433–7, with facsimile of 1652 catalogue) (on Selden and Menasseh ben Israel's printing business); Mayor, *Cambridge under Queen Anne*, 518 (Worthington to Lightfoot, 1666, on Castell); on Aaron Moses, M. McCarthy, *Marsh's Library, All Graduates and Gentlemen* (2nd edn, Dublin, 2003), 62 and (on Aaron Moses the scribe), I. Abrahams, 'Anglo-Judaica in the Catalogue of the British Museum Hebrew Manuscripts', *Miscellanies of the Jewish Historical Society of England*, i (London, 1925), 75–80; L. Hyman, *The Jews of Ireland* (Shannon, 1972), 24–6.
[48] J. Wordsworth & C. Wordsworth (edd.), *The Correspondence of Richard Bentley, D.D.* (2 vols., London, 1842), i, 39.

[49] R. Kidder, *A Demonstration of the Messias* (2nd edn, three parts in one volume, London, 1726), Preface to Part II [first issued 1699], i–iii; Preface to Part III [first issued 1700], iii–iv. Marsh's Library has the first edition, in three separate parts.

[50] E. Stillingfleet, *Origines Sacrae: Or, A Rational Account of the Grounds of Natural and Revealed Religion* ([1662]; 7th edn, Cambridge, 1702), 105, 144 (book ii, chapters 4 and 7).

[51] On aspects of Surenhusius see now van Boxel, Macfarlane & Weinberg (edd.), *The Mishnaic Moment*, 12–43 (editors' introduction), 301–400 (essays by Joanna Weinberg, R.I. Cohen, D. van Miert, and Kirsten Macfarlane).

[52] P. van Rooden, 'The Amsterdam Translation of the Mishnah', in W. Horbury (ed.), *Hebrew Study from Ezra to Ben-Yehuda* (Edinburgh, 1999), 257–67 (259–60).

[53] For passages cited in this paragraph see J. Lightfoot, *In Evangelium S. Matthaei Horae Hebraicae et Talmudicae* (1658), dedicatory letter as translated in Bright (ed.), *The Works of the Reverend and Learned John Lightfoot*, ii, 94; Prideaux, *De Jure Pauperis et Peregrini apud Judaeos*, preface; R. Sheringham, *Joma* (London, 1648), preface; Surenhuis, as cited and discussed by van Rooden, 'The Amsterdam Translation of the Mishnah', 262, 265–7.

[54] Bright (ed.) *The Works of the Reverend and Learned John Lightfoot*, i, p. xxvii.

[55] On this aspect of Surenhusius's Christian Hebraism, see van Boxel, Macfarlane & Weinberg, 'The Mishnah between Jews and Christians in Early Modern Europe', 330–33.

[56] Marsh's Diary, 24 December 1690, on a dream of about twenty years before, in Gillespie, *Scholar Bishop*, 26–7, discussed further by Gillespie, 'Narcissus Marsh and his God', in McCarthy and Simmons (edd.), *The Making of Marsh's Library*, 85–98 (phrase quoted from p. 98).

[57] E. Bischoff, *Kritische Geschichte der Thalmud-Übersetzungen aller Zeiten und Zungen* (Frankfurt am Main, 1899), 29.

[58] Twells, *The Theological Works of the Learned Dr Pocock*, i, 74.

9
CHARLES KINGSLEY ON ASCETICISM, MYSTICISM AND SCRIPTURE

Waves of energy still radiate from the name of Kingsley.[1] They can already be sensed in efforts made to describe him during his lifetime (1819–75). 'Charles Kingsley stammered in impassioned tête-à-tête' – with his friend and nephew-in-law Max Müller, the student of comparative mythology (an Oxford memory of William Tuckwell); 'the fiery zeal of Mr Kingsley ruffling the dead calm of the comfortable and respectable classes' (Kingsley's publisher Daniel Macmillan); 'it [Kingsley's novel *Westward Ho!*] has more of the life and vigour and enjoyment of life that the Iliad shows than any book I ever read' (the New Testament scholar F.J.A. Hort, then aged twenty-six).[2]

Kingsley's energy did indeed divide my mind when I was asked to discuss him. Initially I recoiled from his hostility to the Tractarian movement in Anglicanism ('my horror of popery and tractarianism', he called it himself[3]), and his advocacy of muscular Christianity (as it was called by others).[4] Both positions form part of his thought and feeling on asceticism, in its broad sense as training in virtue. Prominent in Greek philosophy, it has been biblically commended to Jews and Christians by the book of Proverbs and related writing on discipline, gospel precepts on perfection, and Pauline athletic metaphors.

Asceticism and Muscular Christianity
To think first of Kingsley's anti-Tractarianism in this connection, he was himself drawn to ascetical discipline; but he vehemently rejected its special manifestation in religious orders and a celibate clergy. The Tractarians or Oxford Movement were led in Kingsley's youth in the 1830s by Keble, Newman and Pusey at Oxford, and had many sympathizers elsewhere (they took their nickname 'Tractarian' from their widely read tracts). Continuing earlier High

Church tradition, they looked for a pattern above all to the first six centuries of Christianity, and issued a new Library of the Fathers in English translation. In Christian thinking they gave a recovered freshness and centrality to the idea of the church. Kingsley admired their high tone of thought, reverence, self-discipline and care for the poor, he had his own high idea of the church, and he could indeed call himself 'an old-fashioned High Churchman' (no doubt in resistance to being given a liberal Broad Church label);[5] but he deplored what he saw as the Tractarian tendency, not least in the revival of religious orders, to exalt a celibate form of holiness. This, he felt, divided the church and the sacraments from ordinary human relationships.

In much of this reaction he was close to his mentor, the theologian and Christian Socialist F.D. Maurice; but his hostility went back to his arguments when he was twenty with his fiancée, Fanny Grenfell, who held Tractarian views and might herself have become a nun. 'My own heart', Kingsley wrote to her afterwards, 'strangely yearned towards them [the Oxford tracts] from the first … if they had not struck at the root of wedded happiness, I too had been ensnared!'[6] Something of the couple's debate emerges also in his early writings. The verse *Saint's Tragedy* (1848) treats the young royal widow St Elizabeth of Hungary (1207–31), her ascetic zeal, and the stern renunciations asked of her. His first novel *Yeast*, written 1848–51, reflects his Christian Socialist identification with Chartism, but also includes argument between the energetic, stuttering and Kingsley-esque hero Lancelot, and Argemone ('wind-rose'), the Tractarian-inspired woman whom he loves.

Perhaps Kingsley's most effective counterweight on these subjects was another novelist, his contemporary Charlotte M. Yonge (1823–1901), a disciple of John Keble. Her books show the capacity of Tractarian teaching to permeate ordinary family and daily life with the leaven of training, not just to commend a monastic ideal. Kingsley himself was typically wholehearted in a generous letter to her (and his) publisher John Parker, praising her 1854 novel

Heartsease (which does in fact condemn headstrong as opposed to wise ascetic devotion).[7] Kingsley and Yonge continued to share a publisher (later Macmillan), and their novels, divergent in outlook but comparably popular, were often advertised on the same page.

Within Kingsley himself, as noted already, the other side of opposition to celibate asceticism was his muscular Christianity, that form of Christian discipline which takes positive account of our need for and enjoyment of physical exertion, sport, and the relief of pugnacity.[8] In Kingsley it can recall the nobility of a soldier's religion, and it is balanced by his sympathy with sickness and weakness; but it is inevitably linked too with the aggressiveness which can appear when he writes on erotic love or defends harshness in subduing opposition to imperial power.[9] In any case, for reasons which had at least as much to do with my personality as with his, muscular Christianity – or at any rate its mutation into insistence on sport[10] – was uncongenial to a laggard footballer or cricketer like myself.

Yet as I recoiled from the anti-Tractarian and muscular manifestations of Kingsley's energy I felt mean and ungrateful. It wasn't just that Kingsley's prejudices weren't quite the same as my prejudices. It was also that I'd had pleasure and instruction, ever since childhood, from his historical novels and their poetic and pictorial insight. In them he made landscapes as well as history live: the imagined ancient Egypt of *Hypatia* (1853), and also – both known from his boyhood – the north Devon of *Westward Ho!* (1855), and the Peterborough and Cambridgeshire fenland of *Hereward the Wake* (1866).

Then I thought, besides, how attached I had always been to the character of Tom Brown in the novels *Tom Brown's Schooldays* (1856) and *Tom Brown at Oxford* (1861) by Kingsley's friend Thomas Hughes. But in the second book (chapter 11) Hughes approved the view that Tom Brown could be taken to represent muscular *Christianity*, as opposed to the mere cult of muscle. And in Kingsley himself, wasn't muscular Christianity modified by his feeling for Christian mysticism? Hadn't it some parallel in the adaptation, by Kingsley's learned contemporary Mark Pattison, of asceticism as the pattern of the life of the scholar?[11] Wasn't Kingsley, in his own way, continuing the strenuous and mystical pursuit of virtue commended to Sir Walter Raleigh and his group of Elizabethan adventurers by Edmund Spenser (Kingsley's favourite author) in *The Faerie Queen*?[12] Didn't muscular Christianity even suggest some response in advance to Nietzsche's attack on Christianity as the cult offered by the weak to a degraded 'God of the sick'?[13]

Historical Narrative and Scripture in Kingsley
And now, after this flux and reflux of feeling, it struck me that Kingsley's historical novels and his writings as an historian, marked as they are by his critique and reshaping of asceticism, also have links with the traditionally biblical theme of these Chester talks. Asceticism has been intertwined with biblical exposition since Philo of Alexandria and Origen, but Kingsley also touches biblical interpretation simply as historical narrator.

Thus in some novels he was rewriting the narrative of church history – in *Hypatia* that of the age of biblical and doctrinal interpretation in the late fourth and early fifth centuries, in *Westward Ho!* that of reception of the Elizabethan settlement. Yet the history of the community of faith is inevitably a continuation of the biblical narrative. As Kingsley found, its retelling can evoke almost as strong a reaction as biblical criticism.

Then a clue to Kingsley's own thoughts on biblical interpretation is offered in *Hypatia*. Here he presents ascetic training in virtue as it is taught in pagan Greek philosophy, in Philo's Jewish-Greek philosophy, and in early Christianity. In each case, he shows the teaching of asceticism is focused on spiritual exposition, whether of Homer or the scriptures. With his own mystical instinct, he shows how such exposition is bound up with a mysticism which reads both nature and literature as symbolic. His characters represent and comment on the traditional modes of interpretation, literal and allegorical, which through the Tractarians were being debated again in his own time.

Finally, the moral enthusiasm of Kingsley's historical narration is bound up with biblically-shaped views of divine providence and judgment.

These links of historical narrative in Kingsley with scripture stand against the background of his revised asceticism and his degree of sympathy for mysticism. Their appearance in his historical novels will be considered shortly. Meanwhile, a glance at his work as a teacher of history may relate them also to his professedly historical writing.

Kingsley as Professor of History (1860–69)
Kingsley came to Chester as a canon in 1869 (see Plate 14), when he was fifty and had just resigned his historical chair. To look back from this point is to see the historical strand of Kingsley's writing first as it stands out when he himself, in his forties, was Regius Professor of Modern History in Cambridge (1860–69). Neither his chair nor his canonry required full-time residence. Each in turn (the canonry was better paid) was a post which Kingsley could properly combine with being Rector of Eversley in Hampshire.

In 1860 the Prime Minister (Lord Palmerston), having made three unsuccessful attempts at filling the Cambridge chair, took up a suggestion from Prince Albert, the Prince Consort, and nominated Kingsley.[14] Kingsley had not long before been appointed a royal chaplain. Queen Victoria and Prince Albert both esteemed him.

The question now posed by his professorship was whether he was truly an historian. This was a question which the modest Kingsley was always asking himself, despite the numbers who flocked to hear him. He was best known as poet, novelist and social reformer. Within Cambridge especially, he was the writer who, in the Christian Socialist novel *Alton Locke*, had attacked the university for its seeming servitude to wealth and rank.

His moral ardour was not unsuited to the task of an historian, especially as that task was conceived in the 1860s, but he was obviously different from younger scholars like William Stubbs or Lord Acton, who had given much of their lives to historical research. He looked like a brilliant amateur. The Cambridge Roman historian Charles Merivale (1808–93), later Dean of Ely, not wholly sharing objections to his appointment, wrote 'I should have thought him an acquisition in many ways – ignorant, no doubt – but his ignorance more eloquent than most people's knowledge'.[15]

From the first many asked whether Kingsley was not really just a novelist. They told the story that Palmerston, when reproached for appointing a Professor who knew no modern history, had exclaimed 'Why! He wrote [the novel] *Two Years Ago*, and if that is not modern history, what is?'[16] In 1864 his lectures published as *The Roman and the Teuton* were called by the historian E.A. Freeman, who shared his fascination with the Teutons, 'history … brought down to the lowest level of the sensation novelist'.[17] Stubbs's appointment to the Oxford History chair in 1866 evoked further comment on the 'popular novelist' who was his opposite number at Cambridge.[18] At the same time Kingsley's reputation had been suffering as a result of his 1864 controversy with Newman. In the 1990s Christopher Brooke, writing as historian of the university of Cambridge, judged that 'None of the holders of the chair … have commanded wider audiences, or done less to win respect for history as a scholarly subject, than the novelist Charles Kingsley'.[19]

This verdict implicitly rejects the rehabilitation of Kingsley as professor made at the centenary of his death in 1975 by Owen Chadwick, who himself held the same chair.[20] Chadwick urged that there was a genuinely historical strand in Kingsley's writing. When Kingsley became professor he had published at least one serious historical contribution, the short book *Alexandria and her Schools* which forms an historical companion-piece to *Hypatia*. It traces continuity between the thought of pagans and Christians who were alike devoted to Neoplatonism – the resurgence, in such pagan teachers as Plotinus and Porphyry, of a deeply religious philosophy inspired by Plato. Then, Kingsley's arduously prepared lectures did do something for history, not simply by drawing large numbers, but also by insisting on the study of original sources. His hearers were found to be asking for books which undergraduates had never before requested at the University Library.[21] The works he mentioned included some which the conventional might avoid. Chadwick notes that Kingsley's *The Ancien Régime* (1867) was the first book by an English professor of history to call for reconsideration of Voltaire.[22] One of Kingsley's hearers wrote: 'He made us read too. He taught us how to read.'[23]

Kingsley's failure was rather, Chadwick suggests, his lack of organizing capacity, made worse by illness which ruled out the long periods of residence in Cambridge which he had managed at first. In 1866–7 he allowed Honours examinations in modern history – taken only by a very few candidates – to be discontinued. This step was proposed by F.D. Maurice, whose antipathy to examinations as hindering true and free inquiry Kingsley may well have shared.[24] (Maurice had just returned to Cambridge, partly on Kingsley's initiative, as Professor of Moral Philosophy.) The change, however, combined with Kingsley's absences, meant that Kingsley's successor J.R. Seeley had to build up undergraduate study of history afresh.

Brooke's negative verdict is followed by an account of this episode, but also once more calls Kingsley 'the novelist'. Criticism of Kingsley as professor has been linked with a firm distinction between historians on the one hand, and novelists on the other. As historian his contribution, though genuine, as Chadwick urged, was modest; but the distinction between historian and novelist invoked by his critics was hardly crystal-clear. Palmerston's jesting defence perhaps had something in it. In Kingsley's time the historical novel had ascended far up the heights occupied by history. Sir Walter Scott in his Scottish historical novels had been recognized, for all his freedom with the record of events, as the historian of a vanishing Highland civilization which overlapped in time with the modern mercantile life of Glasgow and Edinburgh. Then in France Honoré de Balzac, an admirer of Scott, sought to build up in his novels, by painstaking observation, an historical picture of a quickly-passing early nineteenth-century society.[25] The near-contemporary novel also was recognized as a kind of historical document. Kingsley as professor comparably carried on research not only on the subjects of his lectures, but also on the eleventh-century setting of *Hereward the Wake* and the natural history of *The Water Babies*. He took pains to keep historical romance true to what is suggested by surviving histories and records. Correspondingly, however, he stressed that the life of a period is illuminated historically by its own imaginative narratives; in his inaugural lecture he says that he himself has learned about the Middle Ages especially 'from the thumbing over, for years, [of] the semi-mythical saints' lives of Surius and the Bollandists'.[26]

Kingsley's career as professor thus underlines the measure of continuity between history and historical romance, as conceived by Kingsley and practised in his time. As historian he emphasized accordingly the conviction of human responsibility and divine judgment which penetrates his novels – and defended it with care. In his inaugural lecture he engaged sympathetically with the view that history is determined by social or economic laws. He sought to leave room for the significance of individuals and their choices, and for the element of the unknowable in character and motive; he affirmed one law – not leading to an *inevitable* historical sequence – that of 'the everlasting judgments of God' (Ps. 119:52, Prayer-book version).[27] Comparably, in the opening chapters of *Hypatia*, he had presented the world of the later Roman empire into which the monastic hero ventures from the desert as a 'dying world', doomed by persistence in wrongdoing.

A Young Writer who Looked like a Lion (1848–59)
To see Kingsley's chief activity as a novelist means going back, however, from the 1860s into the 1850s, when he was in his thirties.

In the years 1848–57 he published *The Saint's Tragedy* and five novels. Daniel Macmillan, already quoted, was describing him to undergraduates in his bookshop in Cambridge as a young writer 'who looked like a lion'.[28]

One group of these books, the series *Hypatia* (1853), *Westward Ho!* (1855) and *The Heroes* (1855), seems to me to excel in those Homeric qualities of life and vigour and enjoyment of life which Hort discerned in *Westward Ho!* Close in time, they all present asceticism and muscular Christianity. These related disciplines are displayed among monks, pagans and Jews in *Hypatia*, by Spanish Dominicans and Elizabethan sea-captains in *Westward Ho!*, and, in pagan but implicitly Christian forms, by Perseus and Andromeda, Jason and the Argonauts in the retelling of their myths in *The Heroes*.

The limpid prose of *The Heroes* slips now and then into Homeric metre. Perseus and Andromeda die, but Athena takes them up into the heavens to shine as stars. 'All night long they shine, for a beacon to wandering sailors: but all day they feast with the Gods, on the still blue peaks of Olympus.'[29] These lines recall Kingsley's mystical acceptance of patristic teaching on the 'deification' of the disciple, attached to the psalmist's words *I have said, Ye are gods* (Ps. 82:6), quoted by Christ in St John's Gospel (10:34).[30]

Among these three books, *Hypatia* stands out. It links, more explicitly, the ascetic theme with mysticism as well as scripture. The Platonist New Testament scholar Alexander Nairne called it 'a great book, with solid learning behind it'.[31] Not overwhelmed by propaganda, it still hints plainly at a way of life to pursue.

The Novel Hypatia *and a Way of Christian Life*
Socrates the church historian, *c*.450, says that Hypatia in early fifth-century Alexandria 'surpassed all the philosophers of her time, following the Platonic teaching as carried on by Plotinus'. In Kingsley she seems as beautiful and wise as Athena. Like Plotinus she is a mystic, seeking the vision of the One. Yet, as Socrates relates, fanatical Christians dragged her to a church (the

Caesareum, the former temple of Augustus near the sea), stripped her of her clothing, and murdered her with oyster-shells (*ostraka*). They were under the aegis of Cyril, bishop of Alexandria, revered for his doctrinal teaching but a violent represser of heretics, pagans and Jews. In political power he rivalled Orestes, the governor of Egypt. Driving out the Alexandrian Jews, he allowed the plunder of their goods.[32]

This story of Cyril and 'the sacrifice of a virgin, who professed the religion of the Greeks' was retold by Gibbon with an echo of Iphigenia, sacrificed to meet the demands of religion.[33] In the 1830s the freethinking couple Richard Carlile and Eliza Sharples had named their first child Hypatia.[34] In Kingsley's novel twenty years later, by contrast, the deeply religious character of Hypatia's own philosophy reappears.

The *Ecclesiastical History* of Socrates supplied Kingsley with the characters of Hypatia, Cyril and Orestes. Cyril, supported by militant monks, encroaches on the civil power in the belief that he is advancing the kingdom of God. Kingsley the Christian Socialist stresses, however, that Cyril's care for the poor and his modest way of life also represent the essentially democratic nature of Christianity. In pagan philosophy, by contrast, despite its similar religious focus, Kingsley finds an exclusive and aristocratic tendency. Further historical characters who come on stage include Synesius, bishop of Ptolemais in Cyrenaica and Hypatia's former pupil. As a bishop with wife and children and a lover of dogs and hunting (in his case ostrich-hunting) as well as Plato and Plotinus he is a Kingsley-esque figure described, like Lancelot in *Yeast*, in such a way ('the squire-bishop') as to poke some quiet fun at the author.

The young monk Philammon, a veritable Apollo in beauty, falls in love with Hypatia. The wealthy young Jew Raphael, who goes to her lectures, is full of wit and disdain, but is picked out as co-hero with Philammon by his ownership of a dog – a mastiff bitch, Bran, not the least memorable member of a strong cast of female characters in *Hypatia*. Raphael cheerfully bears the plunder of his goods at the expulsion of the Jews, and becomes an ascetic in the philosophical tradition, a Diogenes-like figure wandering with Bran. She rescues him from drowning, but when he is on the run she delays him by producing a litter of nine puppies. The once elegant Raphael has to flee with her new-born puppies slung in a blanket over his shoulder.

Pagan–Christian controversy is now matched by Jewish–Christian debate, arising in the course of Raphael's conversion to Christianity. He emerges as a representative of Kingsley's own views and experience. He has found himself in an abyss of doubt, 'disporting myself', he muses sardonically in chapter 13, 'on the firm floor of the primeval nothing'. He is drawn to the church not initially by his seemingly kindred philosophic asceticism, but by Bran's life-affirming example and by the muscular and practical Christianity of the Roman commander Majoricus and his daughter Victoria. Raphael the student of Philo now recognizes a good knowledge of Plato in the Epistle to the Hebrews. Eventually, with Clement of Alexandria, he will accept Plato on the inevitable execution of a truly righteous man as a hint at Christianity.[35] He can begin to think Paul right 'in his theory that the Church was the development and fulfilment of our old national polity'. Yet now he is appalled at Majoricus's view that Victoria should become a nun. He cannot believe that the God of Adam and Eve, Abraham and David could find 'delight in seeing his creatures stultify the primary law of their being'.

It takes meetings with another muscular but also philosophical Christian, Synesius, and with St Augustine, and it takes a service attended by soldiers in a church ruined by war, where psalms are sung, the Proverbs are read, and Augustine expounds a psalm, for Raphael to draw near to Christianity – and marriage with Victoria. Once again Kingsley's own story seems to show through, but the plot, discussed in detail with Maurice, sketches a non-Tractarian approach to Christian discipline. Kingsley perhaps recalled how in Oxford *The Saint's Tragedy* alienated the High Church party, but enthused those seeking a liberal alternative to Tractarianism.[36]

Asceticism in Hypatia
The spiritual Greek ascetic teaching of Hypatia, carried out most thoroughly by Raphael, is depicted as noble but, in the end, not enough. On the other hand, the Christian ascetic common life of the desert fathers in Egypt is praised in chapter 1 as happy and fundamentally biblical: 'for the common good each man had toiled' (early Christian communism had helped to inspire Christian Socialism). Their celibacy is of course excepted. Philammon nonetheless returns to the desert in the last chapter and becomes an abbot, but he now takes the broad-minded Clement of Alexandria as his favourite church father. He has discovered his lost sister Pelagia living among a group of Gothic warriors (here the theme of *The Roman and the Teuton* is anticipated), and she also becomes a desert ascetic. Before they die, however, her brother seeks her out and administers Holy Communion to her, in a typically Kingsleyan association of the sacrament with familial love.

There is then a measure of approval for Christian ascetic life in *Hypatia*, despite the personal importance of anti-celibacy to Kingsley. His mixed position is in good part, however, inherited from earlier writers, including the Gothick novelists of the eighteenth century. Alison Milbank shows how the ruins of abbeys and priories were continuously interpreted, from the sixteenth century onwards, within a partly positive Anglican response to the ascetic discipline and prayer which they represent.[37]

Sympathy with Mysticism in Kingsley
Yet Kingsley stands out for his sympathy with mysticism. He was cautious about it, yet also affirmed it.[38] He himself was recognized by W.R. Inge as a witness to 'objective' or externally-directed mysticism, as opposed to a 'subjective' search in the depth of inner consciousness. 'The great mysticism' (he wrote to Fanny Grenfell) 'is the belief which is becoming every day stronger with me that

all symmetrical natural objects are types of some spiritual truth or existence ... Everything seems to be full of God's reflex. Oh to see, if but for a moment, the whole harmony of the great system!'[39]

Reactions to mysticism had often, like abbot Pambo in the desert in *Hypatia* (chapter 11), preferred this 'objective' approach to introspection. Kingsley, however, could also defend the inward mystical focus. This appears in his preface to Susanna Winkworth's translation of sermons by the fourteenth-century Strasbourg mystic Johannes Tauler. Here, in a passage reminiscent of Raphael's plight as described in *Hypatia*, he writes that Tauler 'came to find an eternal ground in the midst of that abyss' – the inward abyss of boundless doubt and a sense of the nothingness of all things – 'which belonged not to the abyss, nor to the outward world which had vanished for a moment, nor to space, nor time, nor any category of human thought, or mortal existence; and that its substance was the everlasting personal good, whose love is righteousness'.[40] Kingsley has also just urged, in another passage showing compassion for weakness, that mystical testimony found in introspection should not be dismissed as the delusion of the suffering.[41]

Kingsley's broad mystical sympathies may owe something to the influence of Coleridge and to the Neoplatonism which had begun to interest him while he was still at school.[42] They also, however, seem allied to the mythopoeic power of his imagination and the importance in his novels of dreams and visions.[43] So simply in a letter, when he touches the mystique of the railway and the steam-engine, awe and *eros* are there: '... the lines of rail in looking along a vast sweep of railway [make one feel very small]. There is an awful waiting look about them: a silent forbidden desert to all the world, except the one moment when their demon bridegrooms shall rush over them on the path which none but they must go. Does this seem real? It is because the thought is so unspeakable.'[44]

Mysticism and Biblical Interpretation
This mystical tendency brings a larger sympathy than might be

expected to Kingsley's view of biblical interpretation. In ancient biblical exegesis, as in pagan interpretation of Homer, literal interpretation contended with the spiritual interpretation which discerns a deeper meaning through types and allegories. Alexandrian Christian teachers found a spiritual sense which in turn, as already noted, formed a guide for ascetic training.[45]

This spiritual interpretation, so typical of the early church, was commended by the Tractarians. Thus while Kingsley was writing *Hypatia*, St Augustine on the Psalms was being translated for the Library of the Fathers (five volumes, 1847–57). The preface to the first volume noted the 'great value' of Augustine's 'mystical and allegorical interpretation'.[46] On the other side Susanna Winkworth, writing for Protestant homes, felt compelled to apologize for retaining the 'mystical and figurative interpretations of Scripture' in her renderings of Tauler.[47]

Kingsley favours literal and historical interpretation, but his mystical affinities give him sympathy with allegory.[48] He feelingly portrays Hypatia spiritualizing Homer: 'The soul of the book is whatsoever beautiful, and true, and noble, we can find in it. It matters not to us whether the poet was altogether conscious of the meanings which we can find in him' (*Hypatia*, chapter 8). This emphasis on the text and its reception, as opposed to the circumstances of composition, has been to the fore again in more recent debate on exegesis. Similarly, the sermon by Augustine which cheers the soldiers (and Raphael) is an allegorical exposition of a psalm. The allegory is criticized, but Augustine's mastery of it is praised, and mystical exegesis gets a place in the context of muscular Christianity.

Kingsley's own literal interpretation of the Song of Songs, put in the mouth of Raphael (*Hypatia*, chapter 21), rejects Christian and Jewish allegories of a divine bridegroom of the soul, the church or Israel. Characteristically, however, he suggests that perception of the divine ordinance for man and woman leads, in the Song, to a mystical sense of simplicity and oneness with the universe.

Solomon forgets all his seraglio and his luxury in pure and noble love for the undefiled, who is but one … as his eyes are opened to see that God made the one man for the one woman, so all his heart and thoughts become pure, and gentle, and simple; and the man feels that he is in harmony, for the first time, with the universe of God and with the mystery of the seasons; that within him, as well as without him, the winter is past, and the rain is over and gone.

This seems to illustrate Kingsley's slightly later assertion that 'a simple, literal, and historic method of interpretation … doubtless is at the same time the most spiritual'.[49] Yet it is a 'literal' reading that could only come from an interpreter in sympathy with mysticism.

Hypatia and Kingsley's Life

The breadth and sympathy with which contending modes of interpretation are presented in *Hypatia* are notable in one so strongly engaged as Kingsley. Yet it was the act of interpretation constituted by the whole narrative of *Hypatia* which proved momentous. Kingsley, like Socrates and Gibbon, condemns Cyril. Yet Cyril is venerated as a saint and a teacher of scripture and doctrine. The church's history shares the biblical aura. This early history, especially, formed the Tractarian pattern. In *Hypatia*, however, instead of church fathers unfolding apostolic truth, we see 'the shadows of night approach, with monkish fanaticism' and 'a democracy, with all its passions, transforming itself into sacerdotalism'. These phrases come from a summary of the view of early Christian history taken by the biblical and patristic scholar C.C.J. Bunsen.[50] Kingsley knew Bunsen, who was Prussian ambassador, a friend of the Prince Consort, and a follower of the mysticism of *Theologia Germanica*. Bunsen in turn admired *Hypatia*.[51]

This affinity would not improve matters in Tractarian eyes. In 1863 Kingsley was nominated for election as an honorary Doctor of Civil Law at Oxford, but it was intimated that there would be objections, for *Hypatia*, dealing so frankly with the murder of a naked woman, was immoral. Kingsley withdrew. And yet, as his wife noted, quoting A.P. Stanley, it was his moral enthusiasm, which 'has scathed with an everlasting brand the name of the Alexandrian Cyril and his followers', that brought him down.[52]

The vehemence which made him enemies was matched, however, by a corrective instinct and a capacity for breadth and affection. Through his historical writing and historical novels, *Hypatia* especially, this emerges in connection with debate over asceticism, mysticism, and modes of interpreting scripture. Systematic presentation could not be expected, but muscular Christianity is glimpsed now as part of a revised and life-affirming asceticism, with a mystical awareness which allows historical exegesis to coexist with sympathetic understanding of allegory. Grateful for Luther and Elizabeth I, noting bad as well as good in the early church, Kingsley also presents a discipleship which takes up major strands in ancient Christianity.

Endnotes

[1] This talk, reproduced with revision from the text in *Expository Times* 130.11 (2019), 485–95, formed one of a Chester Cathedral series to mark the 150th anniversary of Kingsley's installation as canon of Chester, and the bicentenary of his birth. See G. Brooke, in collaboration with Peter Bamford, *Charles Kingsley (1819–1875), Christian Socialist and Natural Historian: A Guide to the Exhibition at Chester Cathedral Library to mark the 200th Anniversary of the Birth of Charles Kingsley …* (Chester: Chester Cathedral Library, 2019).

[2] W. Tuckwell, *Reminiscences of Oxford* (London, 1901), 153; D. Macmillan, letter to J. Llewellyn Davies of 12 March 1852, in T. Hughes, *Memoir of Daniel Macmillan* (London, 1883), 240; F.J.A. Hort, reported by D. Macmillan, letter to Kingsley of 2 March 1855, in Hughes, *Memoir of Daniel Macmillan*, 261. Müller married Kingsley's niece Georgina Adelaide Grenfell in 1859; see J.M.I. Klaver, *The Apostle of the Flesh: A Critical Life of Charles Kingsley* (Brill's Studies in Intellectual History 140, Leiden & Boston, 2006), 496.

[3] Letter of August 1842 to Fanny Grenfell, in *Charles Kingsley. His Letters and Memories of his Life, edited by his Wife* [hereafter cited as *Letters and Memories*] (8th abridged edition, 2 vols., London, 1880), i, 57.

[4] On development of the 'muscular Christian' theme throughout Kingsley's writings see N. Vance, *The Sinews of the Spirit. The Ideal of Christian Manliness in Victorian Literature and Religious Thought* (Cambridge, 1985), 78–133.

[5] William Harrison, assistant curate of Eversley 1868–74, in *Letters and Memories*, ii, 216.

[6] *Letters and Memories*, i, 45.

[7] 'Never mind what the *Times* or any one else says; the book is wise and human and noble as well as Christian ...': Kingsley to John Parker, 6 July 1855, in Christabel Coleridge, *Charlotte Mary Yonge: Her Life and Letters* (London, 1903), 348.

[8] For Kingsley's defence of his attempt 'to say to the strong and healthy man ... "You too can serve God"' see for example his letter of 19 October 1858 in *Letters and Memories*, ii, 73–6.

[9] O. Chadwick, 'Charles Kingsley at Cambridge', *The Historical Journal* xviii.2 (1975), 303–25, revised reprint in O. Chadwick, *The Spirit of the Oxford Movement: Tractarian Essays* (Cambridge, 1990), 104–34 (125–7, 129–30); Jeremy Morris, *A People's Church: A History of the Church of England* (London, 2022), 227–8 and n.5.

[10] Its widespread reduction to this sense is exemplified in Matthew Arnold, *Culture and Anarchy* (1869; repr., ed. J. Dover Wilson, Cambridge, 1963), 59–61 (from chapter 1, 'Sweetness and Light'); here he mocks English reliance 'on freedom, on muscular Christianity, on coal, on wealth', but then criticizes simply 'the cultivation of bodily strength and activity'.

[11] H.S. Jones, *Intellect and Character in Victorian England: Mark Pattison and the Invention of the Don* (Cambridge, 2007), 147, 150–51.

[12] Spenser's debt to Neoplatonism was noted in Kingsley's *Alexandria and Her Schools* (1854), reprinted in C. Kingsley, *Historical Lectures and Essays* (London, 1880), 3–132 (101); for Spenser as favourite see *Letters and Memories*, ii, 298.

[13] Nietzsche's argument on these lines in his *Antichrist* (1888) was discussed by J.N. Figgis, *The Will to Freedom* (London, 1917), 105–25.

[14] On Kingsley's appointment and tenure see O. Chadwick, 'Kingsley's Chair', *Theology* lxxviii (1975), 2–8; id., 'Charles Kingsley at Cambridge'.

[15] Merivale to W.H. Thompson (then Regius Professor of Greek at Cambridge), 22 June 1860, in Judith Anne Merivale (ed.), *Autobiography of Dean Merivale, with Selections from his Correspondence* (London, 1899), 226.

[16] W.H. Thompson, reported by J. Romilly (the Cambridge University Registrary) in his diary for 18 June 1860; see M.E. Bury & J.D. Pickles (edd.), *Romilly's Cambridge Diary 1848–1864* (Cambridge, 2000), 352.

[17] E.A. Freeman in the *Saturday Review* of 9 April 1864, 446–8, quoted by Klaver, *The Apostle of the Flesh*, 557; in retrospect 'Kingsley's boyish enthusiasms seem … divided only by a hairsbreadth from Freeman's own', according to J.W. Burrow, *A Liberal Descent: Victorian Historians and the English Past* (Cambridge, 1981), 157–8.

[18] The historian J.R. Green in the *Saturday Review* of 2 March 1867, quoted in W.H. Hutton, *Letters of William Stubbs* (London, 1904), 117–18. For further negative criticisms from 1867 see Klaver, *The Apostle of the Flesh*, 570, 578.

[19] C.N.L. Brooke, *A History of the University of Cambridge*, iv, *1870–1990* (Cambridge, 1993), 228.

[20] See n.14, above.

[21] Max Müller, quoted in *Letters and Memories,* ii, 120.

[22] O. Chadwick, *The Secularization of the European Mind in the Nineteenth Century* (Cambridge, 1975), 273, n.11; see Kingsley, *The Ancien Régime* (1867), Lecture III, reprinted in C. Kingsley, *Historical Lectures and Essays* (London, 1880, repr. 1889), 207.

[23] Unnamed former pupil, later professor in the University of Capetown, quoted in *Letters and Memories*, ii, 119.

[24] Brooke, *A History of the University of Cambridge*, iv, 228. Maurice argues against examinations in general in a letter to Kingsley of 22 September 1869, printed in F. Maurice, *The Life of Frederick Denison Maurice* (2 vols., London, 1884), ii, 591–2.

[25] On early appreciation of the historical achievement of Scott, and Balzac's consciously historical aim, see G. Lukács, *The Historical Novel* ([1955]; English translation, 1962, repr. Harmondsworth, 1969), 58–62, 92–6.

[26] C. Kingsley, *The Limits of Exact Science as Applied to History. An Inaugural Lecture* (Cambridge & London, 1860), 7.

[27] Kingsley, *The Limits of Exact Science as Applied to History*, 19. H.T. Buckle's unfinished *History of Civilization in England* (2 vols., London, i, 1857, 2nd edn 1858; ii, 1861) was a widely read example of the approach discussed by Kingsley. The importance of such views is suggested again when Stubbs ends his own 1867 inaugural lecture without express mention of them, but with a similar affirmation of divine overruling, 'leading … but never forcing' (quoted by Hutton, *Letters of William Stubbs*, 116–17).

[28] D. Macmillan *c.*1850, reported in a letter quoted by Hughes, *Memoir of Daniel Macmillan*, 212.

[29] C. Kingsley, *The Heroes* (1855, repr. London, 1938), 86.

[30] C. Kingsley, preface to Susanna Winkworth (transl.), *Theologia Germanica* (1854; repr. London, 1893), xii–xiii (approving, with citation of Athanasius and Augustine, this mystical work's use of the term *vergottet*, 'deified').

[31] A. Nairne, *Poems by Charles Kingsley: A Lecture* (Chester, 1915), 10, drawn to my notice by Brooke with Bamford, *Guide* [n.1, above], 41, on item 3.24.

[32] See Socrates, *Ecclesiastical History*, vii 7; 13–15.

[33] E. Gibbon, *The Decline and Fall of the Roman Empire* (1776–88; repr. in 4 vols., London, 1895), iii, 327–8 (chapter 47). The sacrifice of Iphigenia impelled Lucretius (i 101) to his dictum: 'Such evil deeds could religion prompt.'

[34] Hypatia Bradlaugh Bonner & J.M. Robertson, *Charles Bradlaugh* (7th edn, London, 1908), 19, 93 (on Bradlaugh's early love for Hypatia Carlile; in the end he married Susannah Hooper, but their second daughter, born 1858, was also named Hypatia).

[35] Plato, *Rep.* 361E–362A, in Clement of Alexandria, *Strom.* 5.14, 108.

[36] Maurice to Kingsley, 7 and 11 February 1852, 29 September 1852, in F. Maurice, *The Life of Frederick Denison Maurice*, ii, 108–11, 139–43; on *The Saint's Tragedy* and Kingsley in Oxford (1848), *Letters and Memories*, i, 111–12.

[37] Alison Milbank, *God and the Gothic: Religion, Romance and Reality in the English Literary Tradition* (Oxford, 2018), 13–110.

[38] After the life of St Elizabeth which he wrote for his fiancée he envisaged a life of St Teresa; he told Fanny at this stage (1842) that they needed to understand asceticism and mysticism in order to eradicate them from the puritan and evangelical elements of their 'message' (*Letters and Memories*, i, 45). In the end both contributed to what he had to say.

[39] Kingsley to Fanny Grenfell, 14 July 1842, in *Letters and Memories*, i, 55, quoted by W.R. Inge, *Christian Mysticism* (London, 1899), 27, 341–2.

[40] Kingsley in Susanna Winkworth, *The History and Life of the Reverend Doctor John Tauler of Strasbourg; with Twenty-five of his Sermons (Temp. 1340)* (London, 1857), xxxix. 'Ground' perhaps echoes the use of 'ground' for innermost being or depth in Tauler and other mystics, discussed by B. McGinn, *The Mystical Thought of Meister Eckhart* (New York, 2001), 41.

[41] Kingsley in Winkworth, *Tauler*, xxxiii–xxxv; similar sympathy was expressed in his 'Hours with the Mystics', a long review of R.A. Vaughan's book of this title in *Fraser's Magazine* (September 1856), repr. in C. Kingsley, *Literary and General Lectures and Essays* (London, 1880, repr. 1898), 229–334.

[42] *Letters and Memories*, i, 16–17 (Derwent Coleridge, his old headmaster, on his reading of Porphyry and Iamblichus); i, 45; 60 (influence of S.T. Coleridge).

[43] This element in his social fiction is vividly exhibited by P.G. Scott, 'Kingsley as Novelist', *Theology* lxxviii (1975), 8–15. Visions of Philammon in *Hypatia* and Amyas Leigh in *Westward Ho!* exemplify its presence in the historical novels.

[44] Letter to J.M. Ludlow (1848) in *Letters and Memories*, i, 143.

[45] Owen Chadwick, *John Cassian* (2nd edn, Cambridge, 1968), 25, on reading of Clement of Alexandria and Origen by the desert fathers.

[46] Charles Marriott, 'Preface', in *Expositions on the Book of Psalms by S. Augustine*, i (Oxford, 1847), vi.

[47] Winkworth, *Tauler*, xiii–xiv.

[48] Kingsley, writing to Fanny Grenfell (1843), prioritizes the 'plain' meaning, but notes also that 'there may be other meanings in that book beside the plain one' (*Letters and Memories*, i, 81–2).

[49] Kingsley in Winkworth, *Tauler*, xxvii.

[50] Rowland Williams, 'Bunsen's Biblical Researches', in [F. Temple et al.,] *Essays and Reviews* (6th edn, London, 1861), 50–93 (85–6), on C.C.J. Bunsen, *Hippolytus and his Age* (London, 1852).

[51] Bunsen to Kingsley, 1853, quoted in *Letters and Memories*, i, 293–4.

[52] *Letters and Memories*, i, 292–3, quoting Stanley.

10
THE SAINTS:
FROM THE PSALMS TO EVEREST 1924

St Bernard and Everest
In the 1920s the cloister windows at Chester Cathedral, unglazed hitherto, were filled with glass depicting saints, arranged mainly in the calendrical order of their days.[1] One saint in these windows seems out of place, at first sight. St Bernard of Menthon stands with a St Bernard dog, against the background of the snowy Alps (see Plates 15 and 16). In the tenth century he was archdeacon of Aosta, on the Italian side of the Alps, and concerned for the wellbeing of travellers crossing them. He appears, surprisingly, in the south range of the cloisters, by the door into the cloister garden; surprisingly, because this is the more modern and local section of the windows. He follows Bishop Nicolas Stratford, founder of the Chester Bluecoat Hospital school in 1700. Yet he isn't local, he isn't modern, and his day is 15 June; you expect to see him further back, in the calendar order, among June saints like St Barnabas and St Alban.

The puzzle is of course solved when you look down from the saint, the dog and the Alps to the lower light of the window, with its small inset inscription:

> To remember
> two valiant men of Cheshire
> George Leigh Mallory and
> Andrew Comyn Irvine
> who among the snows
> of Mount Everest
> adventured their lives
> even unto death.
> 'Ascensiones in corde
> suo disposuit.' Ps. lxxxiv.

Figure 10.1: Inscription from the St Bernard of Menthon window in Chester Cathedral cloisters commemorating George Leigh Mallory and Andrew Comyn Irvine.

The biblical words – 'he set ascents in his heart' – are from Ps. 84:5, rendered in the Prayer-book 'in whose heart are thy ways' – the ways ascending up to Sion, on which pilgrims, as the psalm says afterwards, 'shall go from strength to strength: and unto the God of gods appeareth every one of them in Sion' (Ps. 84:8). The verse on ascents in the heart was already applied in the third century by the church father Origen to the Christian, in whose heart are some high thoughts and aspirations – ascents – given by God or the angels (Origen, *On First Principles*, iii 2, 4). The psalm-verse is strikingly apt for two men in whose heart was the love of ascents, of climbing mountains, and who, adventuring their lives to the death in the 1924 Everest expedition, can be thought to have come near to that wholehearted devotion of a life which is recognized in saints and martyrs.

In this way Dean Bennett, or another, solved the problem of commemorating among the saints two Cheshire contemporaries.[2] They are named, but not pictured, under the patronage of St Bernard. The special character attributed to the company of saints is kept, but it is suggested that others may come close to it. This window then illustrates our subject: the ideas of the saints, and their fluid boundaries. In scripture various conceptions of the saints appear perhaps most fully in the book of Psalms, wherein those who made this window found an answer, full of suggestion, to their problem.

The Saints in the Psalms

Behind our word 'saint' are two Hebrew words, Hasid, 'devout' and Qadosh, 'holy'. Hasid is more frequent in the Psalms than in any other book of the Hebrew bible, sometimes found in the singular, but most often in the plural for the group or congregation of the devout: 'Sing praises to the Lord, ye saints of his' (Ps. 30:4); 'O love the Lord, all ye his saints' (Ps. 31:23). Consistently with this plural use, Hasid has its own history in later Judaism as a word for members of pious movements, like the Hasidim of the mediaeval Rhineland or the eighteenth-century and later Hasidic movement in eastern Europe. Qadosh is used in the Hebrew psalms for holy ones who are heavenly beings – gods or angels who surround the Lord both in heaven and in his holy place on earth, the 'council of the saints' or 'congregation of saints' met in Psalm 89 (6; 8); but Qadosh is also used for the holy ones on earth, those devoted to God and set apart by adhering to him – as his priests, like 'Aaron the saint of the Lord' (Ps. 106:16), or his people: 'be ye holy, for I your God am holy' (Lev. 19:2); 'fear the Lord, ye that are his saints (holy ones), for they that fear him lack nothing' (Ps. 34:10). In post-biblical Judaism Qadosh was applied likewise to the devout, especially the chaste and ascetic, and later on to martyrs.

When the psalms were put into Greek in the Septuagint Greek version, round about the second century before Christ, Hasid was commonly represented by Greek *hosios*, 'devout', Qadosh by *hagios*, 'holy'. Some of the passages in which Qadosh was used of divine beings were now understood to refer to the human 'holy ones' or 'saints' on earth, the human 'people of God'. An example is Ps. 16:3 on the 'holy ones' in the earth, or the land. The phrase perhaps originally referred to 'the gods whom earth holds sacred', as the New English Bible put it; but in the Septuagint it is rendered 'for his holy ones' – saints – 'who are in his land, he has made wonderful all that he wills for them'.

The Latin renderings of the Greek psalms made in early Christian times often use Latin *sanctus*, 'holy', for both Greek words, *hosios* as well as *hagios*. It is *sanctus* then which, through French, gives the English word saint. 'Saint' is used accordingly in older (but not more recent) English biblical translations, including the Prayer-book psalms, which are taken from Miles Coverdale's translation. Thus Ps. 16:3 now appears with the well-known opening 'All my delight is upon the saints, that are in the earth'. 'Saint' has been used as a title for individual saints from about the fifth century, together with the title Dominus, Lord (Dom for short), which went out of use but survives in French place-names like Dammartin, Dampierre and Joan of Arc's village, Domrémy.

The use of *hagios* in the Septuagint Greek version of Leviticus and Psalms for earthly as well as heavenly saints went on increasing, as the Greek New Testament shows. Human beings appear as saints in St Matthew's Gospel, on the 'saints' asleep in their tombs who arise (27:52), and, with *hagios* now applied to present-day believers, in the Pauline epistles, on the 'saints' at Corinth or Colossae. Within the psalms, where 'holy' often appears in heavenly contexts, this human dimension of the term 'holy' makes you think of one company of saints in earth and heaven, indeed of something like a communion of saints.

The heavenly and earthly settings meet in the prayer which the Hasid, the devout saint on earth, directs towards the sanctuary, as described in Psalms 4 and 5: 'The Lord has made wonderful his saint' (following the understanding of the Hebrew attested in the pre-Christian Greek rendering in the Septuagint): 'when I call upon the Lord, he shall hear me ... Stand in awe and sin not: commune with your own heart, and in your chamber, and be still. Offer the sacrifice of righteousness: and put your trust in the Lord (Ps. 4:3–5) ... Early in the morning will I direct my prayer unto thee, and will look up ... I will come into thine house, even upon the multitude of thy mercies' (Ps. 5:3, 7). The holy place which the devout saint is facing in order to 'direct' the morning prayer is the place of the divine beings or great angels, the 'holy ones' among whom the Lord is praised and revered (Ps. 89:6–8): 'even before the gods will I sing praise unto thee. I will worship toward thy holy temple, and praise thy Name' (Ps. 138:1–2). In the temple the saints on earth approach the congregation of divine beings and are associated with them in worship.

Other aspects of the saints are picked out in their titles in the psalms. They are not only devout and holy, but also righteous: 'the congregation of the righteous' in Psalm 1. It is they who will reign in God's kingdom. So in Ps. 37 'the righteous shall inherit the land: and dwell therein for ever' (Ps. 37:29), and the company of the righteous overlaps in turn with that of the meek and those who patiently wait on God, for they also in this psalm will inherit the land (Ps. 37:9, 11). This overlap between the righteous and the meek reappears when Ps. 37 is echoed in the Sermon on the Mount: 'Blessed are the meek, for they shall inherit the earth; blessed are they which do hunger and thirst after righteousness, for they shall be filled' (Matt. 5:5–6). With a similar overlap, now with 'saints', in the psalms God 'guards the souls of his *saints*' (Ps. 97:10), but in the Wisdom of Solomon 'the souls of the *righteous* are in the hand of God' (3:1); compare the canticle Benedicite: 'O ye spirits and souls of the righteous, bless ye the Lord' (Song of the Three, 64).

One more title of the saints in the psalms is 'the friends of God'. We know it through Greek and Latin versions of Psalm 139, but it is a legitimate translation of the Hebrew. The psalm was being interpreted in the Septuagint Greek, perhaps in the second century BCE, in line with the relatively late passages of the Hebrew Bible which speak of Abraham as God's 'beloved' or 'friend' (II Chron. 20:7, Isa. 41:8), a title recalled in James 2:23. The psalmist exclaims: 'For me how greatly honoured are thy friends, O God: how steadfast are their rules' – their princedoms (Greek *archai*; in Jerome's Latin translation of the Septuagint psalter, *principatus*); compare the later title 'Lord' or 'Dom', mentioned already. 'If I reckon them, they are more in number than the sand' (Ps. 139:17–18).

The background of the understanding of saints as rulers (verse 17) here is seen in the visions of the future in Daniel: 'the kingdom and the dominion … shall be given to the people of the saints (the holy ones) of the most High' (Dan. 7:27). When the 'saints' in Daniel are understood as angels, they become the heavenly 'principalities and powers', Milton's

> Thrones, Dominations, Princedoms, Virtues, Powers

(Col. 1:16 as paraphrased in *Paradise Lost* v 600); when they are human beings, or the souls of the righteous, 'in the time of their visitation they shall shine … they shall judge the nations, and have dominion over the peoples' (Wisd. 3:7–8). So St Paul asks: 'Know ye not that the saints shall judge the world?' (I Cor. 6:2). In mediaeval and later times the psalm-verse 'For me how greatly honoured are thy friends …' (Ps. 139:17) has been an introit for feasts of the apostles, as suggested by John 15:14–15 'ye are my friends'; but in the psalm itself they are more in number than the sand, almost countless, and they seem to be the saints and martyrs of the Old Testament who form a great cloud of witnesses in Hebrews 11–12. Compare once more the book of Wisdom: in all generations entering into holy souls, [wisdom] makes them 'friends of God, and prophets' (Wisd. 7:27).

The psalter then presents the idea of a great company of saints, both heavenly and earthly, under various overlapping descriptions: the devout, the holy (and this term implicitly brings mortals near to angels), the righteous, the meek, the patient, the friends of God, the holy souls kept by God. Compare the terms used to describe old Simeon in Luke 2:25: 'righteous and devout'. But the psalms also show this company as permeated by wonderful divine energy, not only in the time to come, as in Daniel, Wisdom and Paul, but also in the present, as in the stories of Elijah and Elisha. That comes out especially in the Septuagint Greek text of the psalms and its Latin translation. 'Know that God has made his saint wonderful', Ps. 4:4, 'wonderful' there in that the saint's prayer is heard; 'for his saints who are in his land, he has made wonderful in them all that he wills', Ps. 16:2; God 'is wonderful in his saints', Ps. 68:36, words traditionally sung at the Offertory on All Saints' Day; God is glorified 'in the council of the saints', Ps. 89:8, cited already; 'praise God in his saints', Ps. 150:1, following the Greek.

Together these psalm-verses suggest the visions and miracles of the saints. Within the psalter this theme of later hagiography emerges in Ps. 68:28 in Greek. Describing the young patriarch Benjamin, at the time of a procession in the temple, the psalmist exclaims 'There is Benjamin the youth in a trance' – again this is a legitimate translation of the Hebrew – a trance in the temple like the trance later ascribed to St Paul in the Acts of the Apostles (22:17).

The representation in the Greek psalms of a vast heavenly and earthly company of saints corresponds to Jewish veneration for saints at the time of the translation. They are viewed as intercessors, for their prayer is heard, Ps. 4:4; and also as martyrs, although that term is not yet used. For what can be called a cult of saints and martyrs, compare the gospel sayings: 'You build the tombs of the prophets, and garnish the sepulchres of the righteous' (Matt. 23:29); 'O Jerusalem, Jerusalem, which killeth the prophets and stoneth them that are sent unto her' (Matt. 23:37, viewing the prophets above all as martyrs). Further back, in the second century BCE, Judas Maccabaeus is said to have had a vision of Onias the high priest and Jeremiah interceding for Jerusalem (II Macc. 15:11–16); at the same time people cherished the stories of the aged scribe Eleazar and the seven young brethren and their mother who suffered torment and death rather than sacrifice to pagan gods (II Macc. 6–7). A century later, in the 60s BCE, another Onias, renowned as a pious intercessor whose prayers brought rain (Mishnah, Taanith 3.8), was asked during civil war in Judaea to curse the party who were being besieged in the temple at Jerusalem at the feast of Passover. Onias prayed instead that God should not listen to the curses either of the attackers, for the defenders are God's priests, or the defenders, for the attackers are God's people. Immediately he was stoned to death. Yet, says the first-century Jewish historian Josephus (*Ant.* xiv 22–4), using terms we met in the psalms and St Luke, he was righteous and devout. It may be said that he was a saint, and also what would soon be called a martyr.

Martyrs and the Calendar

In the pre-Christian period, the custom of ascribing special days to individual saints is beginning. In II Maccabees the feast of Purim, commemorating the deliverance described in the book of Esther, is simply called the day of Mordecai (15:36). In the world in general, subjects keep the birthdays of their rulers. But against this background, probably the greatest impetus towards calendars of saints as we know them is given by Jewish and Christian veneration for martyrs. By the later second century after Christ the Greek-based term martyr, meaning witness, has acquired its special Christian meaning of one who bears witness by giving up life itself. The days of martyrdoms are solemnly kept, like the days of the death of members of one's family. At the same time there is a stream of ascetic devotion, already visible in I Corinthians 7 when living together in marriage has to be defended. In the third and fourth centuries the multitude of desert saints appear in Egypt, Palestine and Syria, imitated in the west by groups who withdraw to islands, forests and mountains. The days of the martyrs are therefore joined by those of virgins and abbots. Moreover, New Testament recognition of the sanctity of married life means that days of matrons, confessors and bishops are also found.

For a long time, however, the new commemorations still build on the foundation of the Old Testament saints. So St Cyril of Jerusalem in the mid-fourth century, explaining the prayers in the eucharistic liturgy, says: 'We make mention of those who have fallen asleep before us, first, of patriarchs, prophets, apostles, martyrs, that God would, at their prayers and intercessions, receive our supplication' (*Catechetical Lectures* v 9).

As seen in the cloister windows, saints remembered generally have always been combined in calendars with those who are important for a particular place. Thus the Preface to the 1549

Prayer-book, reprinted in the 1662 and 1928 revisions, mentions the diverse liturgical uses current in Tudor Britain, naming those of Salisbury (Sarum), Hereford, Bangor, York and Lincoln; the Prayer-book gives a simplified form of the Sarum calendar, and so, with that calendar, it leaves out some popular saints remembered in particular regions, like St Werburgh (February 7) in Chester and the north midlands. Sarum also reflects the retreat of Old Testament saints. As often in the story of devotion to the saints, old names are displaced by popular new ones.

Martyrs gave an impetus not only to the formation of calendars of saints, but also to the inclusiveness of the idea of sainthood. Martyrs in particular recall the jesting second couplet of one of E.C. Bentley's clerihews

> There is a great deal to be said
> For being dead –

for the main thing that can be said about martyrs is precisely that they are dead. We often know little or nothing about their lives. They may not have excelled in virtue. It doesn't matter, because in the end they suffered and gave their lives. Also, in the nature of things martyrs often suffer in a group, sometimes large. This is reflected throughout the history of martyr-remembrance, from the seven Maccabaean brothers, via the Egyptian Christian legion in Roman times who were said to have been martyred with their commander St Maurice, to the twenty-first century group of Melanesian brethren commemorated in the south transept of Chester cathedral. In such groups, we can hardly know about them all. But we probably agree with the result, as expressed by Solomon Schechter, a Jewish scholar from a Hasidic family who sympathized with both Jewish and Christian veneration of saints: 'the sufferer, far from being considered as a man with a suspected past, becomes an object of veneration, on whom the glory of God rests … by a series of conscious and unconscious modifications, [passing] from the state of a sinner into the zenith of the saint'.[3] Schechter is describing what happened in ancient Judaism, but his words apply equally to the Christian martyrs, and one thinks for a moment here again of the commemoration of Mallory and Irvine.

Heroes and Mythology
A great modern student of the traditional lives of saints and martyrs, the Belgian scholar Hippolyte Delehaye (1859–1941), distinguished what he called Epic lives from Historical lives.[4] Epic seeks to give an inspired presentation, true to the tradition as it has come down; history is concerned rather to give a true account of past events, in the light of reliable witness. In the Epic lives saints and martyrs become heroes, like ancient heroes such as Hercules, who through labours and sufferings attained a place among the gods. An example is the legend of St Katharine of Alexandria, a Christian philosopher outstanding for wisdom, learning and beauty. She confutes fifty philosophers brought to argue against her; convinced, they themselves become Christian martyrs. The emperor offers to share his throne with her, but she declines, is imprisoned, convinces further pagans including the empress Faustina, and is put to death on her famous wheel (which breaks, so that in the end she is beheaded). Angels carry her body to St Katharine's monastery at mount Sinai. She may have been pictured as a Christian counterpart to the young pagan philosopher Hypatia, murdered by monks in the fifth century, and portrayed in Charles Kingsley's novel *Hypatia*. Of course she became a patron saint of lawyers pleading in court, and academics.

A humbler 'epic' theme is the affinity of saints for animals. Thus St Peter, in Rome, sees a large dog, tightly tied by a chain. He releases it, and it speaks to him, and goes as a messenger from Peter to his adversary, the sorcerer Simon Magus. Having denounced Simon prophetically in its deep, loud mastiff's voice, it returns to Peter, tells him that he will win his contest with Simon, and then lies down at Peter's feet and dies.[5]

The poet Peter Levi wrote of the 'affinity between the ideal of pagan and primitive heroism and that of the monks' in early Britain.[6] From about the fifth century onwards the Celtic saints in Wales, Devon and Cornwall, Brittany and Ireland and Scotland, followers of the Desert Fathers, have legends which even more clearly become epics. An example is the (?ninth-century) Navigation of S. Brendan to the land promised to the saints, a work permeated by psalmody (it is almost a guide to the contemporary use of psalms in the offices of the church); reaching an island of devoted monks, Brendan hears them sing the verse following the psalm-verse from which we began: 'The saints shall go from strength to strength: unto the God of gods appeareth every one of them in Sion' (Ps. 84:7).[7] Just as the saints' lives become epics, so in the Middle Ages does the epic Arthurian legend of the knights of the Round Table turn into hagiography, in the tale of the quest of the holy Grail.

The tension between Epic and History in the lives of the saints comes to a head in the early sixteenth century. In England William Caxton had printed, about 1470, his own translation of perhaps the most popular collection of saints' lives, the *Golden Legend* of the thirteenth-century Dominican Jacob de Voragine, and then in 1485 he also printed Sir Thomas Malory's *Morte Darthur*. Nearly thirty years later the epic tradition was still being continued in Chester in Henry Bradshaw's English verse life of St Werburgh (1513); when the penitent geese are summoned before her for destroying the crops:

> Dredfully darynge comen now they be,
> Theyre winges traylynge, entred into the hall;
> For great confusion, after theyre kynde and propryte
> Mourninge in theyre maner.[8]

She dismisses them kindly in true seventh-century epic fashion with a verse from the Benedicite which also figures in S. Brendan's Navigation: 'O all ye fowls of the air, bless ye the Lord'.

But when Bradshaw was writing, Renaissance scholars like Erasmus were already making little jokes about the shrines and legends of the saints, and turning aside decisively from books like the *Golden Legend*. This new attitude preceded the Reformation and is found on both sides of the incipient religious divide. The great collections of lives of saints and martyrs printed in the sixteenth and seventeenth centuries, for example by the Cologne Carthusian L. Surius (Sauer) (1522–78), read with enthusiasm by Charles Kingsley among others, and by the Belgian Jesuit I.G. Bolland and his collaborators (1615 onwards), are penetrated by the desire to purge out the old Epic leaven and to seek authorized and historically based accounts. In this country it was perhaps not until the Romantic movement of the late eighteenth and early nineteenth centuries, and its ecclesiastical echoes, that large numbers of people again began to be fascinated by the legends of saints. In the later nineteenth century Sabine Baring-Gould, following the eighteenth-century Alban Butler, issued a Lives of the Saints (1872), reprinted in 1898 in sixteen handily sized volumes; a lover of history as well as folklore, he was torn between the two, but included a special volume, an 'Epic' volume, on the Celtic saints.

Dean Bennett in the 1920s was riding still on the tide of a widespread fascination with the legends of the saints, which he fully shared. The Arts and Crafts contribution to church art and architecture was still continuing, and it had roots in the outlook of John Ruskin and the pre-Raphaelite group of artists, including Sir Edward Burne-Jones; Ruskin urged people to take the outlook of mediaeval art seriously, so largely a representation of saints, and Burne-Jones's stained glass is itself a new summit in this representation. Burne-Jones's grand-daughter recalled that in the 1890s he kept a set of Baring-Gould's Lives of the Saints on his bedroom mantelpiece, and that even an unassuming back window of his house was filled with wonderful stained glass illustrating the quest of the holy Grail.[9] At the same time William Morris magnificently republished Caxton's *Golden Legend* and *Morte Darthur*, and both were reproduced in cheap and handy but still artistic form in the series Temple Classics. In 1914 appeared an unassuming but repeatedly reprinted work, C.P.S. Clarke's *Every Man's Book of Saints*.

The scheme of the cloister windows was part of an at least threefold concern of Dean Bennett with the saints, manifest in the 1920s in the War Memorial outside the Cathedral, in the cloister windows, and in the revival of the cult of St Werburgh. The scheme of the windows arose against the background of the Dean's thoughts on the War Memorial, which is itself a great representation of appropriate saints, bringing together with national and local patrons (SS. George, David, and Werburgh) statues of two other soldier-saints, SS. Alban and Maurice, and their angel-patron St Michael, general of the heavenly host (Josh. 5:14–15, Dan. 12:1, Rev. 12:7).

The theme of the saints appeared in thought during the Great War of 1914–18 as well as the post-war years of its memorialization. A small but notable sign of this at the beginning of the war was Arthur Machen's September 1914 short story 'The Bowmen', about the brave and perilous retreat of the original British Expeditionary Force from Mons, under all but overwhelming enemy attack.[10] One soldier in the retreat remembers, in this story, how a vegetarian restaurant in London where he used to eat served food on plates with a representation of St George in blue, surrounded by the Latin motto 'May St George be a present help to the English'. (These plates may have been factory-made, but they were evidently in what we would now call the Arts and Crafts style.) As the soldier knew Latin and other useless things, says Machen, and as the field-grey-clad ranks of the enemy in large numbers were only about three hundred yards away, 'he uttered the pious vegetarian motto'. The roar of battle died down in his ears, and he seemed to hear a great voice and a shout as of thousands crying 'Array, array! St. George, Messire St George! Ha, St George, Ha, St George, a long bow and a strong bow!' The soldier next to him said in amazement, 'Those so and so's over there are going down, not in hundreds, but thousands.' And he himself seemed to see a long line of shapes, with a shining about them, like men that draw the bow, and a cloud of arrows flying towards the enemy hosts. And, the story concludes, that soldier who knew what a vegetarian diet was like knew also that St George had brought his Agincourt bowmen to help the English. The story was printed in the *London Evening News*, whether by accident or design, on Michaelmas Day 1914, the feast of St Michael and All Angels; and it is credited with having helped to give rise to the legend of the Angels of Mons, said to have been seen by soldiers in the retreating army.

The saints and angels then naturally reappear after the war on war memorials, by no means only in Chester; a striking example is the Scottish National War Memorial at Edinburgh (1917–27), which seeks restraint in deference to the Presbyterian aspect of Scottish tradition, but nonetheless has statues of St Michael and accompanying Angels, St Andrew, and St Margaret of Scotland, and also reliefs of animals and birds who served in the war – including elephants and oxen, horses and mules, dogs and canaries. Around the wall is inscribed, again strikingly in view of Presbyterian usage, the words from the book of Wisdom 'The souls of the righteous are in the hand of God' (Wisd. 3:1).[11]

Landmarks in literature concerning the saints over the same period include M.R. James's *The Apocryphal New Testament* (1924), making accessible the apocryphal Acts of the Apostles, and two books by Helen Waddell. Probably best known for her novel *Peter Abelard* and her collection and translation of *Mediaeval Latin Lyrics*, she was also a distinguished translator and interpreter of Latin saints' lives; her *Beasts and Saints* (1934) and *The Desert Fathers* (1936) went through many reprints. Bennett's scheme for the cloister windows fits, we have been seeing, closely into the early twentieth-century context of thought on saints and angels. Helen Waddell puts a finger on that in *The Desert Fathers* when, countering the secular view that the near-martyrdom of the desert ascetic discipline was a shameful waste of young lives, she compares the way in which, in years which in 1936 were recent, people have instinctively felt value in losses of young life in pursuit of art, as with Gauguin or van Gogh, or in the conquest of the air – or in the attempt to climb Everest.[12]

The cloister windows come now into a present-day context which is different again. A widespread empathy with the epic aspect of the lives of the saints, and of historical narrative more generally, marked the first part of the twentieth century, but it seemed to disappear in the changed climate of opinion of the 1960s and 1970s. But perhaps times may change again. The Protestant theologian Anne Marie Reijnen, writing in the year 2000 on angels under the title 'the obstinate angel', the angel declining to be cancelled, noted a continuing readiness to value what appeals to the imagination in the traditions concerning angels (closely linked, as we have seen, with those on the saints).[13]

If you asked me to identify the baby which goes out with the bathwater when you banish the epic dimension of tradition on the saints, I'd point to the hope for the redemption of the whole creation together which St Paul expressed. The wonders of God in his saints, their covenant, as the book of Job says, with the very stones of the field and the beasts of the field (Job 5:23), their representation of Christ in the desert with both beasts and angels (Mark 1:13): all these remind one of Romans 8 on the whole creation groaning together until now, waiting, Paul says, in a seeming echo of another passage in Job (14:14–15 'all the days of my service will I wait till my change come'), for the adoption, waiting for the revelation of the sons of God – the vision of angels and saints which we have been glimpsing, the sign of the redemption of all beings and things together (Rom. 8:19–23). One potential, at any rate, of the epic of the saints depicted in so many windows is to revive the pact in our religious thought and feeling between reason and imagination.

Endnotes

[1] This chapter is based on a Chester Cathedral Bible Talk, 3 March 2021.
[2] F.S.M. Bennett was Dean of Chester, 1920–37.
[3] S. Schechter, *Studies in Judaism* (London, 1896), 281.

[4] H. Delehaye, *Les passions des martyrs et les genres littéraires* (1921; 2nd edn, Brussels, 1966), discussed by T.D. Barnes, *Early Christian Hagiography and Roman History* (Tübingen, 2010), 361–2.

[5] Acts of Peter, ix–xii.

[6] P. Levi, *The Flutes of Autumn* (London 1983, repr. 1985), 137.

[7] *Navigation of St Brendan*, ed. C. Selmer, trans. J.F. Webb, *Lives of the Saints* [Brendan, Cuthbert, Wilfred] (Harmondsworth: Penguin, 1965), 55.

[8] Lines picked out for their charm by C.S. Lewis, *Poetry and Prose in the Sixteenth Century* (Oxford, 1954, repr. 1990), 122.

[9] Angela Thirkell, *Three Houses* (1931, repr. London, 2012), 188–9.

[10] A. Machen, *Tales of Horror and the Supernatural*, with an Introduction by Philip van Doren Stern (London, 1949), xiii (Introduction), 208–11.

[11] Ian Hay (John H. Beith), *Their Name Liveth: The Book of the Scottish War Memorial* (London, 1931), 123, 130–35, 147–8.

[12] H. Waddell, *The Desert Fathers* (London, 1936), 25.

[13] Anne Marie Reijnen, *L'ange obstiné. Ténacité de l'imaginaire spirituel* (Geneva, 2000).

11
ANOINTING IN ANCIENT ISRAEL
AND THE CHRISTIAN CHURCH

The tale I have to tell, the story of the oil of the olive-tree in the sacraments of the church, is in some ways a sad one.[1] In western Christianity, it is the story of the domestication and even the elimination of rites which could become just too significant. It is also, later on, the story of a decline in symbolic power. The oil of the olive was an almost infinitely fruitful symbol. It suggested cleansing and healing, beauty, light and life, and the touch of the divine spirit. Anointing, unction, was one of those rites of ancient Israel which Christians called sacraments of the old covenant. In Christianity, as administered to the sick it could betoken the whole range of healing, both spiritual and physical; in connection with baptism and confirmation, anointing could become almost *the* sacrament of the gift of the spirit. Inevitably, perhaps, it was disturbed; in Israel under Greek and Roman rule the high-priest seems no longer to have been anointed; in the Christian church anointing could become ancillary to other ceremonies, and in sixteenth-century reform it was judged to encourage superstition. Much of its symbolic power continues in eastern Christianity, but in the west this power is diminished by the dominance of an urban and technological way of life.

Rites of anointing are older than the biblical books, but this is also a biblical story. Sacred anointings are commanded, described and echoed in scripture, and in the penumbra of complementary narratives, later termed apocrypha, which grew up around the scriptural books in ancient times. Ritual developed in the communities which also formed and handed down biblical tradition, so that the rites of anointing can be said to interact with scripture, shaping it and being shaped by it. Biblical and apocryphal writing on this theme is one of the threads which unite the Hebrew scriptures and the New Testament.

In the west, perception of the symbolism of anointing now needs imagination. Yet the continuance of sacramental anointing in western usage, with its recovery among Anglicans, should not simply be put down to the power of authorized custom. Anointing has also been found to have 'some notable and special signification', to use the words of the first English Prayer-book on approved ceremonies.[2] In this belief I sketch some aspects of the story, from ancient Israel to the modern west. The tale takes on a pattern of repeated rise and fall, but it is touching experience not readily reduced to a pattern, that ever-varying apprehension of the sacramental and symbolic which is found both within and beyond the permeable boundaries of the church.

1.   From Ancient Israel to the Christian Sacraments

The promised land was to be, as Deuteronomy puts it (8:7–8), a land of streams of water, springs and depths, a land of wheat and barley, vines and figs and pomegranates, a land of oil-olives – the cultivated trees as opposed to the wild olive (Rom. 11:17) – and honey. In it God will bless 'your corn and your wine and your oil' (Deut. 7:13), the three staple products. The value of oil stands out in the stories of Elijah and Elisha (I Kings 17:8–16, II Kings 4:1–7). As Judaism developed after the Babylonian exile, a calendar arose in which, as seen from books found in the Qumran caves, some of the pious kept annual days of thanksgiving for the first-fruits of corn, wine and oil: for the new grain-offering and 'the bread of the first-fruits', the offering of two loaves (Lev. 23:20, 11Q19 xix 12), as part of Pentecost, the feast of Weeks; and then, at fifty-day intervals, the 'feast of wine' and the 'feast of oil' – the new wine and the fresh oil.[3] The importance of oil emerges in another way from the avoidance by many Jews of oil produced by gentiles, from before the beginning of Greek rule in Judaea down to Roman times.[4] Compare the Septuagint (LXX) Greek rendering of Ps. 141 (140):5, 'let not the oil of the sinner anoint my head'. So in retelling of scripture it was related that when Joseph first met his future wife Asenath, daughter of the priest of On in Egypt, he called her a gentile 'who anoints herself with the unction of destruction'.[5] Correspondingly, Judith brings with her into the Assyrian camp not only her own food, but her own oil (Judith 10:5). In the agriculture, liturgy and piety of Israel, therefore, we find the elements familiar in the Christian sacraments: the water of baptism, the eucharistic bread and wine, and the oil of anointing.

The olive was first choice for king of the trees in Jotham's fable (Judges 9:8–9). The symbolism of anointing arose from the practical functions of olive oil, of course in food preparation – the manna could taste like bread prepared with oil (Num. 11:8) – but especially in healing and care of the skin. The good Samaritan followed normal practice when he treated wounds with oil and wine (Luke 10:34); compare Isa. 1:6, where the prophet deplores wounds that 'have *not* been softened with oil'. Skin-care comes to the fore when the psalmist says, like a grateful guest, 'thou hast richly bathed my head with oil' (Ps. 23:5). As is often noted in discussion of baptism, anointing, with its aid towards cleansing and refreshing the skin, commonly accompanied washing or bathing (Ruth 3:3, Ezek. 16:9, Judith 10:3).

A little more than skin-care emerges when Judith goes to see Holofernes: 'she anointed her face with ointment … and her beauty took his soul prisoner' (Judith 16:7–8). As this passage hints, oil is also for fragrance, when mixed with balsam and other spices to form ointment, and above all for appearance: 'oil to make a cheerful countenance', as the psalmist says (Ps. 104:15) – compare Ps. 45:8 'the oil of gladness', Isa. 61:3 'the oil of joy' – oil signifying joy, and bringing out what is called the 'light of the countenance', a phrase familiar in connection with God (Ps. 4:6, cf. Num. 6:25–6) but also used of human beings ('the light of my countenance', Job 29:24). It is both for care and appearance that the runner is rubbed all over with oil, and becomes gleaming or luminous, a Greek practice also followed among Jews; in second-century BCE Jerusalem the young men of the priesthood flocked to a Greek-style gymnasium built by the high-priest, as noted indignantly in II Maccabees (4:9–15).

Further links between oil and light are the use of oil in lamps, from little clay hand-lamps (Matt. 5:15, John 5:35) to the temple candelabrum or menorah (Exod. 25:31, Lev. 24:4) and the perpetual sanctuary-lamp filled with 'pure beaten olive oil for light' (Exod. 27:20, Lev. 24:2) – the best oil, carefully beaten out rather than pressed – not to speak of the shimmering light of the olive-groves themselves. The olive-yards mentioned in Deuteronomy (6:11 LXX) are a symbol of light, says Philo (*Immut.* 94; 96), a Jewish contemporary of St Paul, in one of his countless associations of oil with light. These associations were Greek as well as Jewish; 'gleaming' is an epithet of Athens, the city of Athena, goddess of the olive-tree, as when Pindar wrote:

> O the gleaming and the violet-crowned and the sung in story, bulwark of Hellas, famous Athens, city divine –

'gleaming' perhaps not just from the temples on the acropolis but also from the olive-groves round about.[6] The cheerful light symbolized by the olive is also, however, one of the most universal symbols of divinity and beauty; in many religions, as Edwyn Bevan put it, 'the numinous is essentially the luminous'.[7]

Early Christians in due course, like their Jewish contemporaries, would be familiar with Hellenic and Roman uses of oil, functionally much the same as Jewish ones, but often contrasted. Against the background of function and symbolism apparent in ancient scripture it is unsurprising that among Jews at the time of Christ the ascetic Essenes abstained from olive oil on the skin, according to the first-century CE Jewish historian Josephus (*Jewish War* ii 123). This custom extended an abstention widely practised at times of mourning (II Sam. 14:1, Dan. 10:2–3) and fasting.[8] The symbolism of oil also appeared in its sacramental use, to represent and indeed effect divine choice. Thus the anointing of a prophet – Elisha – is commanded together with the anointing of the kings Hazael and

Jehu (I Kings 19:15–16); Jehu's anointing is described (II Kings 9:1–6), but Elisha is simply said to have been clothed, divinely, with Elijah's mantle (I Kings 19:19). 'The spirit of the Lord God is upon me, for he has anointed me' (Isa. 61:1) suggests, with prophetic as well as regal overtones, a divine anointing which conveys God's spirit. Anointing to the office of prophet reappears in Jewish retelling of scripture (Ps.-Philo, *Biblical Antiquities* 51.7, on Samuel) and gained a place in Christian thought. More central in Hebrew biblical literature, however, is the anointing of the high-priest and the king, the 'two sons of oil', as Zechariah calls them (Zech. 4:14).

Priestly and Royal Anointing
For both priest and king, anointing is seen as ordained by God. The context of the command is vision and revelation, vouchsafed to Moses on mount Sinai and in subsequent communion with God, and later to Samuel, the prophet Nathan and king David. This visionary context is of course highlighted in scripture as assurance that the command is God-given, but the biblical allusions to it also reflect a deep feeling that the ritual is numinous, a link with the sacred and divine.

For consecration to his dignity the high-priest is to be washed, and clothed with the holy garments. The importance of the ceremony of clothing (Exod. 28:1–3, 29:5; Lev. 8:7) is underlined when Moses strips the holy garments from the dying Aaron, and puts them upon Eleazar (Num. 20:27–8). Then the high-priest is to be anointed on his head (Exod. 29:7, Lev. 8:12, 21:10–12) with a divinely-ordained 'holy oil of anointing', as it is called in Exodus (29:7, 30:22–33) – the fragrant mixture of oil, balsam and other spices which took the name chrism, 'anointing oil', a transliteration of the Greek word *chrisma* used in the Septuagint translation of Exodus (LXX Exod. 29:7, 30:25, etc.). This mixed oil of priestly anointing is also called in the Septuagint (Exod. 30:25, Ps. 132 [133]:2) by the Greek name *myron*, 'sweet oil, unguent, perfume', a word found too in the four gospels in their accounts of the woman who anoints Christ. The chrism in the form of *myron* was used also for consecration of the tabernacle, its vessels and furniture (Exod. 30:25–30). Anointing signified divine choice, dedication to God, and purification for that purpose. Josephus wrote that Moses sanctified the priests and the tabernacle, 'accomplishing their purification (*katharsis*) in this way': he had the chrism made up, and 'having taken this, anointing both the priests and the tabernacle, he purified them' (*Antiquities* iii 197–8, summarizing Exod. 30:22–30). The chrism was prohibited for common use and for transmission to foreigners (Exod. 30:31–3); the high priest shall not defile himself, 'for the crown of the anointing oil of his God is upon him' (Lev. 21:12), a 'crown' in the sense of a covering for the head. Correspondingly, in the Qumran War Rule, priests accompanying troops in the war of the last days are not to come among the slain; 'they shall not defile the oil of the anointing of their priesthood with the blood of nations of vanity'.[9] This priestly chrism, in the words of Ps. 133:2, is

> the precious ointment upon the head, that ran down unto the beard: even unto Aaron's beard, and went down to the skirts of his clothing

– words later used to speak of the anointing received by Christ as head (Col. 1:18) overflowing upon the church, so that Christians who, like him, have loved righteousness and hated iniquity (Ps. 45:8, Heb. 1:9) can also be called 'christs', anointed ones (Origen, *Against Celsus* vi 79). In the Pentateuch this chrism is prescribed after Aaron's washing and clothing, and it helped accordingly to shape early Christian understanding of the chrism which accompanied the washing and clothing of baptism. Initially, however, the psalmist was describing a physical effect like that achieved in Ps. 45:8–9 by the king, anointed with the oil of gladness, all his garments smelling of myrrh, aloes and cassia, and in the Song of Songs by the bridegroom, whose very name was like fragrant oil poured out (Song of Sol. 1:3).

Priestly anointing was one part of a rite of institution, for those of priestly descent, to priestly functions. The whole week-long procedure, set forth at length in Exodus 29 and Leviticus 8, is briefly described as washing, clothing, anointing, filling of the hands and sanctifying (Exod. 28:41). In a later and still shorter summary, Moses, having clothed Aaron, 'filled his hands and anointed him with holy oil' (Eccl. 45:15). In the context of the rite of institution the expression 'filling of the hands', a general term for installation as priest (Judges 17:5, 12), also recalls the ordination sacrifices known in Hebrew as the offerings of *mill'uim*, 'filling': the 'ram of consecration (*millu'im*)' (Exod. 29:22, 26–7, 31; Lev. 8:22), and unleavened bread (Exod. 29:23, Lev. 8:26–7). Parts of the ram whose blood had been put upon the right ear, thumb and toe of the candidates were placed upon their hands, together with a loaf, cake and wafer of unleavened bread (Exod. 29:22–4, Lev. 8:27). This interpretation of 'filling the hands' appears in the Targums, the ancient Jewish Aramaic translations and paraphrases of scripture. Thus 'you shall fill their hand', at Exod. 28:41 (with similar wording at Exod. 29:9, 33 and 35), is rendered in Targum Onkelos as 'you shall offer their sacrifice'.

Through these rites the high-priesthood will pass from father to son – to 'the priest whom one shall anoint and whose hand one shall fill to minister as priest in the place of his father' (Lev. 16:32). Some passages on the anointing of Aaron's 'sons' could also be taken to refer to priests in general; Exod. 28:41, 30:30, and Num. 3:3 are examples. Anointing on the head, however, is mentioned only in the case of Aaron (Exod. 29:7, Lev. 8:12, 21:10, 12). For the 'sons', the oil seems simply to be sprinkled on them and their garments, with the blood of the same sacrificial ram, after the sprinkling of Aaron himself (Exod. 29:21, Lev. 8:30).

A different interpretation of the ordinance for 'filling the hands' became visible in liturgy when candidates for the Christian priesthood were anointed on their hands. The biblical accounts of institution to the priesthood interacted with the washing, clothing and anointing of early Christian initiation, as will be seen, and in time they also affected Christian ordination. The expression 'fill their hands' is often rendered in the Septuagint Greek as 'to perfect the hands' and in the Vulgate Latin as 'to consecrate the hands', although the literal 'fill the hands' does occasionally appear (as at Exod. 28:41 [LXX and Old Latin], Num. 3:3 [Vulgate 'filled and consecrated'], Ecclesiasticus 45:15 [LXX and Vulgate]). The Christian custom of anointing the hands in ordination to the priesthood – in the case of bishops, in addition to high-priestly anointing on the head – became general in the west. Already known in ninth-century Gaul, it was probably influenced by an understanding of 'to fill' in these passages as 'to consecrate', by 'filling the hands' with oil. This view could be suggested especially by Num. 3:3 in the Vulgate, which gives the double rendering 'filled and consecrated'.[10]

Yet the connection between the expression 'filling the hands' and the offerings of ram's-meat and bread placed on the hands was also remembered in the church. Thus in an adapted Jewish text, the Greek Testament of Levi, surviving as read by second-century Christians, Levi's hands are to be filled at his ordination with incense to offer (Testaments of the Twelve Patriarchs, Test. Levi 8:10); is the phrase 'incense of rams' in mind (Ps. 66:15, rendered in LXX 'incense *and* rams')? Then the Greek order for consecrating a bishop, in the fourth-century Apostolic Constitutions (viii 5, 9), echoes the Aaronic rite with the direction 'let one of the bishops offer the sacrifice' – now the eucharist – '*upon the hands* of the one who has been ordained'. Augustine comparably explained 'fill their hands' in an Old Latin (and LXX) rendering of Exod. 28:41 by reference to the sacrifices (*Questions on the Heptateuch,* ii [Exodus], no. 121, on Exod. 28:41 [37]). Perhaps with a similar thought, wafers and wine, as well as a chalice and paten, were given into the hands of candidates for the priesthood in the mediaeval and later ceremony of the 'tradition of instruments'. The much-consulted seventeenth-century Jesuit commentator Cornelius à Lapide came accordingly to combine the two interpretations of the biblical passages; the hands would have been filled both with sacrifices and with the oil of anointing.[11] This long-term influence of two different understandings of a difficult biblical expression, an influence seen not only in biblical commentary but also in ordination rites – the fourth-century Apostolic Constitutions and the ninth-century Gallic use – shows the impact of ancient scripture on Christian anointing.

A different rite of anointing is commanded in Leviticus 14 for a leper who has recovered. Like the anointing of priestly institution, it came to be associated with Christian baptism. The recovered leper undergoes a purification procedure ending with a bath. This is followed (Lev. 14:10–32) by the offering of a ram, whose blood is put upon the candidate's ear, thumb and toe as in priestly institution, and an offering of oil (not chrism), with which the candidate is anointed. Here anointing is again linked with purification, but it also suggests reinvigoration, for re-entry into Israelite common life. This rite was in use at the time of Christ, as the gospels suggest (Mark 1:44 and parallels). In early Christianity its sequence of washing and unction evoked baptismal interpretation. For Origen the leper's anointing represents not only purification, but also the gift of the Spirit whereby the repentant sinner can again live as a child of the Father (Origen, *Homilies on Leviticus*, 8.11 (end), on Lev. 14:14–18). Jerome specifically mentions Christian initiation. These things are written, he says, lest any who have lost their baptismal chrism – the seal of the Spirit conveyed by the chrism – should despair of recovering it (Jerome, *Commentary on Habakkuk*, book ii, on Hab. 3:13 LXX 'for the salvation of thy people, to save thine anointed ones'). Jerome's contemporary Ephrem the Syrian is probably close to basic teaching which both Origen and Jerome assume: the priest of old used to seal the cleansed leper with oil, and lead him to the water-spring; now 'the type has passed and the truth is come; with chrism have you been sealed, with baptism you are perfected'.[12] Ephrem's reference to oil before water, contrary to the order of events in Leviticus, reflects the early Syrian Christian custom of anointing before rather than after water-baptism.

To turn now to the royal anointing, it is described not in the commandments given through Moses concerning the king (Deut. 17:14–20), but in the histories and the psalms. It signified divine choice, strengthening, and guidance. Psalm 89 recalls the visionary prophetic figures of Samuel and Nathan, and also Nathan's oracle, imparted to David (II Samuel 7, I Chronicles 17). God spoke of old in an oracle to his saints, and said:

> I have found David my servant: with my holy oil have I anointed him;
> my hand shall hold him fast: and my arm shall strengthen him
> (Ps. 89:20–21)

David will receive the divine strength associated in other passages with God's spirit; 'the hand of the Lord was upon me, and he brought me out by the spirit of the Lord' (Ezek. 37:1). Anointing stands for this gift of the divine spirit, as in the prose account of David's anointing by Samuel (I Sam. 16:13–14). Anointing also remained the sign of the rightful king. The young Solomon is anointed in haste to foil a plot in favour of his half-brother Adonijah (I Kings 1:39), and the child-king Joash is anointed in secret, protected by Jehosheba and her husband the high-priest when queen Athaliah has slain other members of the royal house (II Kings 11:2, 12; II Chron. 22:11, 23:11).

David is anointed with 'my' – God's own – 'holy oil' (Ps. 89:20). With similar emphasis on this oil as belonging to God, in Leviticus Aaron and his sons have upon them 'the oil of the anointing of the Lord' (Lev. 10:7), and, in the case of Aaron alone, anointed on the head, 'the crown of the anointing oil of his God' upon him (Lev. 21:12). The divine aura of this anointing-oil is stressed again when Ps. 89:20 and Leviticus 10:7, 21:12 are echoed in the apocryphal Psalm 151, where David says: 'he [God] anointed me with the oil of his anointing' (Ps. 151:4 LXX); more simply, but similarly, the parallel Hebrew in the Qumran Psalms Scroll has 'the holy oil' or 'the oil of the sanctuary' (*shemen ha-qodesh*).[13]

In Psalm 151 here, in both Hebrew and Greek, the holy oil given by God through Moses is probably envisaged as kept in the sanctuary, as Zadok took the horn of oil to anoint Solomon from the tabernacle (I Kings 1:39), a view later found in both rabbinic and Christian literature. God's holy oil is revered as the sign, and perhaps also the medium, of the gift of the divine Spirit. The priest just anointed shall not loosen his hair (in mourning) or go out of the sanctuary, for the 'crown of anointing' is upon him, spread over his head (Lev. 10:6–7, 21:10–12); in the Septuagint rendering of these passages, he shall cover his head, keeping the 'crown' from profanation.

Rabbinic interpreters held that the kings whose anointing is described in scripture were anointed from the same holy oil of chrism which was ordained for Aaron; the horn of oil miraculously sufficed for kings as well as high-priests.[14] It was taken that, when the composition of the chrism was commanded, the future anointing of kings as well as high-priests was in view. Within scripture itself, the association of the two stands out when Psalm 133, on the anointing of Aaron, is placed in the Psalter immediately after the lines on the Davidic king as 'my anointed' which close Psalm 132. His 'crown' which is to blossom (Ps. 132:18) was then perhaps eventually understood not just as a royal diadem, but also as the divinely-bestowed 'crown of anointing', the holy oil which covered the head (Lev. 21:12); Hebrew *nezer*, 'crown', is used in both passages.

Association between the divinely-ordained priestly and royal anointings is implied here and in Ps. 151 and rabbinic comment on the chrism. This association is akin to the overlap in scripture between the figures of priest, king and prophet. Thus the high-priestly dignity is presented as royal, not simply sacerdotal. The linen mitre of the high-priest was encircled by a golden diadem supporting a plate or rosette inscribed with the divine Name: 'you shall engrave upon it, like the engraving of a signet, Holiness to the Lord' – 'Lord' rendering the sacred tetragram YHWH (Exod. 28:36, 39:30, LXX 'Holiness of the Lord'). The Revised English Bible notes on these verses that the Hebrew may be rendered 'engrave on it "YHWH" as on a seal in sacred characters'. The circlet around the mitre is 'the holy crown' (Lev. 8:9), 'the hallowed royal diadem (*basileion*) with the Name of God engraved in sacred letters on a rosette of gold', as it is described in Greek by an unknown Jewish author in the second-century BCE Letter of Aristeas (98).[15] Eleazar

212

the high-priest, under divine guidance, was to instruct Joshua when to lead the people to war (Num. 27:21). The regal character of the high-priest was again underlined by the rise of the Hasmonaean dynasty of high-priestly rulers in Israel after the Maccabaean revolt in the second century BCE. As appears in Jewish writings from the first century CE onwards, the high-priest could also have the gift of prophecy. Caiaphas in St John's Gospel (11:49–52) is one of a number in whom the gift was recognized.[16]

The king could likewise evince attributes of priesthood. Melchizedek is priest as well as king (Gen. 14:18–20, Ps. 110:4), Moses anoints Aaron, and intercedes in the divine presence (Exod. 32:11–15), and Solomon blesses the congregation and prays before the altar at the consecration of the temple (I Kings 8:12–66, II Chron. 6:1–7:7). Again, the figure of a prophet-king appears in biblical presentation of Moses and David. The unitive Jewish interpretation of priestly and royal anointing, and the biblical combination of priestly, royal and prophetic attributes, both influenced early Christian understanding of anointing in initiation.

Disuse and Hope for Restoration
The prestige of Aaron's institution to the priesthood, with anointing, gave rise, as has been seen, to the view that anointing must already have been received by his forefather Levi, the patriarch of the priestly tribe. In an Aramaic narrative probably current by the end of the third century BCE, Levi relates a dream in which he is told that he will receive the high-priestly anointing.[17] Yet Daniel was read in Jewish Greek translations as foretelling that one day 'the chrism shall be removed' (Dan. 9:26 LXX and Theodotion, both with *chrisma*). This rendering of prophecy may reflect disuse of anointing in the period of these translations, roughly from the second century BCE onwards. Disuse seems to be implied when the Mishnah, a Hebrew compilation of pronouncements and discussions on Jewish law and custom brought together at the end of the second century CE, deals with the position and obligations of high-priests who

had been instituted simply by clothing, without anointing.[18] The Qumran Temple Scroll probably reflects conditions in the second century BCE when it presents the laws of priestly institution; it follows the wording of Lev. 16:32 on filling the hands and clothing, but omits the statement that the priest shall have been anointed.[19] Viewed with the Mishnah and the Greek translations of Daniel, this passage helps to suggest a disuse of priestly anointing, going back to the second century before Christ, or earlier.

Reconstruction on these lines is encouraged by the fact that rabbinic tradition too envisages a lengthy lapse in anointing. According to a view current in Judaea by the early third century CE, the holy anointing-oil was hidden in the sanctuary at the same time as the ark.

> The jar of manna and the flask of anointing oil and Aaron's rod, with its buds and blossoms, and the coffer in which the Philistines returned an offering to the Lord God of Israel (I Sam. 6:8), all these were placed in the house of the Holy of Holies; after the ark had been hidden away, they were hidden with it.
>
> (Tosefta, Yoma 2.15 [3.7])

Talmudic tradition adds that this was done by king Josiah, who ordered the Levites to put the ark into the temple (II Chron. 35:3); for, through the finding of the book of the law in the temple (II Kings 22:8–12, II Chron. 34:18–21), he knew the prophecy of exile in Deut. 28:36.[20] Anointing was then not available at all in the second temple. In a saying attributed to the early fourth-century teacher Aha, from Lydda, five things lacking in the second temple, as opposed to the first, were 'the ark, the Urim and Thummim, the oil of anointing and the holy Spirit' (Jerusalem Talmud, Ta'anith ii 1, 65a). Here unction and the Spirit stand together, as in biblical tradition.

There was a sense, therefore, that priestly and royal anointing had been lost, and the Roman destruction of the temple would have deepened the feeling; but there was also a conviction that they would come back. According to Jewish interpretation of the early centuries CE, Elijah will restore the flask of anointing-oil to Israel.[21]

214

Moses is to anoint the tabernacle and the altar of burnt-offering (Exod. 40:9–10) because of the crown of the kingship of the house of Judah (Gen. 49:10) and the coming king messiah, and the crown of priesthood and Elijah, to return as high-priest (Targum Pseudo-Jonathan on Exod. 40:9–10). For these associations of the tabernacle and the altar with the messianic kingdom see Amos 9:11 'on that day will I raise up the tabernacle of David that is fallen', and Ps. 51:20–21 'O be favourable and gracious unto Zion … *then* shall they offer young bullocks upon thine altar'. The Christian philosopher Justin Martyr (*Dialogue with Trypho* 8.4), in the mid-second century CE, comparably depicts Trypho the Jew as maintaining that the messiah must be anointed by the returning Elijah.

Hope for restoration of the anointing-oil and the fully functioning priesthood and kingship which it signified was supported by related legend, focused on the oil of the temple menorah or candelabrum. The pure 'oil for the light' of the menorah is distinguished in Exodus from the compounded 'oil of anointing' – the chrism – but is listed together with it among the goods and furnishings of the tabernacle (Exod. 39:37–8). At the rededication of the temple under Judas Maccabaeus (165 BCE), remembered each winter at the feast of Hanukkah, 'Dedication' (John 10:22), 'they lighted the lamps that were upon the candelabrum, and they gave light in the temple' (I Macc. 4:50). Rabbinic legend relates that the priests found only one small flask of the consecrated 'oil for the light'; but (as with the flask of chrism which sufficed for kings as well as high-priests) it miraculously sufficed for all eight days of the dedication (Babylonian Talmud, Shabbath 21b). This narrative is remembered annually during the eight-day kindling of Hanukkah lights in houses; Josephus (*Ant.* xii 325) already says that the festival is generally named Lights. Prayers at the partly comparable later Christian feast of Candlemas, German *Lichtmesse*, have included remembrance of the commandment given through Moses, quoted already, 'that the purest olive oil should be prepared for lights to be set together continually before [God's] sight'.[22] Hanukkah has made the story of the small yet sufficient flask perhaps the best-known rabbinic legend of sacred oil, and a familiar instance of the association of oil with light; but it is notable too as one more sign of an atmosphere of lively hope, which also surrounded nascent Christianity.

The rabbinic traditions cited expect the priestly and royal anointings, from the one chrism revealed to Moses, to be restored in the last days. They also, like the terse name 'messiah' or 'Christ' – 'the anointed' – show the unbroken hold of sacred anointing on pious and patriotic imagination. Its place in future hope is bound up with expectation of a restored temple, high-priest and king, and with the biblical view of the whole people of Israel as a royal and priestly body. 'Ye shall be to me a kingdom of priests and a holy nation' (Exod. 19:6), or, as this divine promise to Moses was widely understood in the second century BCE and later, 'a kingdom, a priesthood, and a holy nation'.[23] With this understanding, it is said that, through the Maccabees, God restored 'the kingdom, and the priesthood, and the hallowing' (II Macc. 2:17), and Targum Onkelos renders Exod. 19:6 'ye shall be before me kings, priests, and a holy nation'.

Anointing in Christian Sacraments
Christians in the first and second centuries CE were aware of the linked priestly and royal anointings described in scripture and the gift of the Spirit linked with them, and shared in contemporary Jewish expectation connected with them. Elijah 'will restore all things' (Matt. 17:11). They shared too in the communal sense of a royal and priestly Israel, now focused for them in the royal and priestly figure of Jesus Christ. By the fifth century the ancient anointings were classified in the church, in a Latin phrase used by St Augustine which became standard, among the 'sacraments of the old covenant' (exemplified in Augustine, *Expositions on the Book of Psalms*, Ps. 73 [74].2). Given the use of Latin *sacramentum*, 'sacrament', to render the biblical Greek term *mysterion*, 'mystery',

this phrase could cover a range of signs of divine favour; but in later western discussion of sacraments in general, during the mediaeval and Reformation periods, the sacraments of the old covenant, as in the case of the new covenant, are often particularly the rites.

Among sacraments of the new covenant, anointing plays a part in no less than four out of the list of seven which became standard in the Middle Ages: Christian initiation – by mediaeval times divided into baptism and confirmation – ordination, mentioned already, and unction of the sick. The oil of the olive became a symbol of the remedial character attributed in earlier Christian thought to sacred anointing and to the sacraments in general; at least from Peter Lombard's twelfth-century compendium of patristic opinion onwards, a text used for expounding the sacraments in general was Luke 10:34, on the Samaritan 'pouring in oil and wine'.[24] A sixteenth-century trace of this remedial view of the sacraments appears in the opening address of the Prayer-book marriage service, on marriage as a remedy.

A list of seven sacraments might often begin with baptism and confirmation. In the early church, the gift of the Spirit, including what was later called confirmation, was held to be conferred by the chrism associated with baptism. In present-day eastern Christianity, holding to this early usage, infants as well as adults are baptized, anointed with chrism (previously consecrated by a bishop), and receive Holy Communion, all in an uninterrupted sequence. In the west, however, from the later Roman period onwards, the rite of confirmation was separated from baptism through the rule that it should be administered only by a bishop. In mediaeval times confirmation, by anointing with the sign of the cross and the imposition of the bishop's hand, was still usually received in infancy and early childhood, Holy Communion being also administered if age permitted. Anointing with chrism still continued, none the less, to be administered by a priest within the rite of baptism. Episcopal confirmation therefore duplicated the baptismal chrismation, and the special meaning of a strengthening and perfecting by the Spirit for the Christian life – 'confirmation' – frequently came to be attached to the second, episcopally administered chrismation. For biblical associations of the name, compare Ps. 51:14, in Latin 'confirm me (*confirma me*) with the governing (or, mighty) Spirit', and II Cor. 1:22 'he who confirms us (*qui ... confirmat nos*) with you into Christ and has anointed us is God, who has also sealed us and given the earnest of the Spirit in our hearts'.

The list of sacraments which began with baptism and confirmation would go on to include ordination, of which something has already been said, and might come to unction of the sick only at the end. In the mediaeval and later west this rite had indeed become the 'last' or 'extreme' unction for the dying. In modern Roman Catholicism, however, it is once more viewed as anointing of the sick in general, as in the Christian east.

The importance attached to the consecration of chrism and oil for use in these four sacramental rites appears from the late second century onwards, initially in connection with baptism. 'Bread and oil are sanctified by the power of the Name', according to Theodotus, a Christian who followed the Valentinian school of thought, as recorded at the end of the second century by Clement of Alexandria (*Excerpts from Theodotus*, 82). Clement's contemporary, Tertullian, writing on baptism, said similarly that waters acquire the sacred significance of sanctifying 'when God is invoked', and that 'we are anointed with the *blessed* unction' (*On Baptism*, 4.4, 7.1).

The association of Christian sacraments with the 'new covenant' recalls prophetic hope for a new covenant from God, as unfolded in II Corinthians 3 and Hebrews 8–10 with a sense of fulfilment which brings exaltation of the 'new' covenant over the 'old'. In the west a line runs from Augustine's epigram 'the sacraments of the new covenant *give* salvation; the sacraments of the old covenant *promised* a saviour' (*Expositions on the Book of Psalms*, Ps. 73. [74].2, quoted already) to the words of a eucharistic hymn by St Thomas Aquinas,

> Let us therefore, humbly bending,
> This great sacrament revere;

Types and shadows have their ending,
For the newer rite is here.[25]

Yet a counter-emphasis on the value of the ancient Jewish experience reflected in scripture is also found within the church. From early times there has been a Christian tendency to revere the rites of Jewish scripture, and to take them as models. Thus within the New Testament the affectionate and reverent picture of the temple and its piety drawn in the first two chapters of St Luke's Gospel contrasts with the equally reverent, yet also ultimately dismissive treatment of the same subject in Hebrews, where the sacrifices cannot take away sin (Heb. 10:1–18). By the beginning of the mediaeval period models in the ancient law shaped not only the baptismal and ordination anointings, but also the anointings used in the coronation of sovereigns and in the consecration of churches, altars, and sacred vessels. Already at the end of the second century Tertullian (*On Baptism* 7.1) wrote that the baptismal chrism comes 'from the ancient discipline' (*de pristina disciplina*) of anointing for priesthood with oil from a horn, as Aaron was anointed by Moses, so that the high-priest was called a christ (*christos*, Lev. 4:5 LXX); anointing gave this title to the Lord, who was anointed with the Spirit by God the Father.

Tension between the two types of Christian response to the ancient scriptures continued in the Middle Ages. Discussion of Christian sacraments recognized that they may correspond to rites of Israel described in scripture. Jewish scripture could be formative for the Christian rites, as seen already. Yet, in theological consideration of the sacraments, scripture might be viewed apart from apocryphal writings and in the light of doctrinal explanation of the new covenant. The earliest Christian rites of anointing commonly listed among the sacraments, the chrism of initiation and the unction of the sick, could both then seem new. 'In the old law', says St Thomas Aquinas, 'there was no sacrament which would correspond to confirmation' – a duplication of the post-baptismal chrism – 'and extreme unction'; confirmation gives the fulness of the Spirit for strength, extreme unction prepares for the reception of glory; neither function is within the limited scope of the old covenant (Aquinas, *Summa Theologiae*, iii 65, 1, Objection 4, with the Response).

The rites attested in Hebrew scripture were surrounded, however, by a broad tradition of thought, legends and hopes, which has been glimpsed already, and by related rites and customs, like the water-baptism of John the Baptist, which grew up around the scriptural rites in Jewish life. Thus the apocryphal Greek Life of Adam and Eve, a Jewish work probably from the first century BCE or CE, mentions not only penitential immersion in water (29.7) but also, separately from that, remedial anointing of the sick (9.3) and salvific anointing of the dead (13.1–5, 40.2). It is in this setting of thought and custom that the rise of the earliest Christian anointings can be envisaged.

2.   Anointing in the Early Church

The two principal and earliest Christian anointing rites are unction of the sick and the anointing of initiation. I begin with the oldest witness to them both, and then seek to illustrate the interpretation and the impetus of anointing, especially baptismal anointing, in the second and the third centuries. This approach permits a glimpse of sacramental anointing in the years, from the late second century onwards, when the church was not yet protected under Roman rule, but had taken the shape which is still familiar, with episcopal government and a body of Old and New Testament scriptures.

Beginnings
In St Mark's Gospel, when the Twelve go out after receiving a mission charge, they preach, cast out devils and anoint the sick (6:13). The clause on anointing is peculiar to Mark. Luke has a parallel but shorter account of the departure and preaching (9:6). In Matthew departure and preaching are not described; after Matt. 10:14–15, the point where the mission charge ends in Mark, in Matthew the charge continues. The anointing-clause might be a late addition

220

to Mark, but seems more likely to have been skipped in the brief Lucan account, which reads like a free summary of longer tradition. Mark here then probably reflects church custom, perhaps Judaean in origin, from the second half of the first century. In the Epistle of St James, perhaps from the early second century, the sick are anointed in the name of the Lord with prayer, by the elders (James 5:14).

The custom will have arisen in the setting of the Jewish anointing customs just mentioned, customs not ordained in scripture but related to the scriptures and their penumbra of fresh complementary narrative, such as the Life of Adam and Eve. The use of anointing for the sick, perhaps beginning in mainly Jewish church communities in Judaea, might well have encouraged its related use in initiation.

Christian initiation receives much reference in the New Testament, but the ceremonies most clearly mentioned are water-baptism and the laying-on of hands. Yet the name *Christos*, 'anointed', appears almost throughout, anointing of Christ by the Spirit is a theme of Luke-Acts (Luke 3:22, 4:18; Acts 4:26–7, 10:38), and his physical anointing by a woman with *myron* is prominent in the gospels, as already mentioned (Matthew 26:6–13, Mark 14:3–9; Luke 7:36–50; John 12:1–8). When initiation rites are documented more fully, from the late second century onwards, they are found to consist, with variations, of a series of ceremonies: water-baptism, anointing with chrism, clothing, the laying-on of hands and the eucharist.

In early Syrian and eastern baptismal usage, perhaps also found in Alexandria, there was a single anointing, immediately before rather than after the baptismal washing, as seen already from Ephrem the Syrian.[26] This perhaps followed a Jewish pattern for the admission of proselytes, in which circumcision – considered by Christians, like anointing, as a 'seal' (Rom. 4:11) – preceded a bath. A different early usage became widespread and has continued into modern times. As attested in the third-century Apostolic Tradition ascribed to Hippolytus, it provides for a pre-baptismal anointing with oil, forming a purification or exorcism at the end of the time of instruction as a catechumen; anointing with chrism through the laying-on of the bishop's hand filled with oil then follows the baptism. This washing, with unction beforehand and chrismation afterwards, recalls procedure in public baths in the ancient world; oiling aided removal of dirt before a bath, and perfumed ointment was applied after the bath.[27] Yet early Christians also saw a likeness, and a certain union, between their initiation rites, Christ's own baptism and reception of the Spirit, and the washing, anointing and clothing of the priests in ancient scripture. In the west that is evident, as seen already, in Tertullian at the end of the second century. The contemporary Jewish priesthood continued to enjoy high prestige within the Jewish community, to which Christians remained close.

The beginnings of anointing in Christian initiation will be earlier than the late second century CE, but the search for earlier traces is speculative. One probable trace, bringing an ancient vision to the fore and almost, so to say, dreaming it again, is a Christian adaptation of Levi's dream-vision of institution to the priesthood, mentioned already.[28] The officiants in his dream are seven men in white, probably archangels. The biblical institution rite begins with washing, clothing and anointing, in that order (Exod. 29:4-7, 40:12-13; Lev. 8:6-12); but now Levi, recounting his dream, alters this order, and speaks almost like someone describing Christian initiation: 'the first (man in white) anointed me with holy oil and gave me a staff, the second washed me with pure water, fed me by hand with bread and holy wine, and put on me a holy and glorious garment' (Testaments of the Twelve Patriarchs, Levi 8.4-5). This post-baptismal clothing, as it seems to be, then forms an item in the continuing account of the priestly investiture (verses 5-10). Anointing has come first, before washing, as in early Syrian usage for Christian initiation. In the Testament of Levi and elsewhere in the Testaments of the Twelve Patriarchs Christ is both high-priest and king (Test. Simeon 6.5-7.3, Test. Levi 18.2-14). Here, correspondingly, institution to the Israelite priesthood, including anointing, is one with Christian initiation.

It is possible that another early allusion to the chrism in initiation, again reflecting Syrian usage, may be found in the list of 'three who bear witness' in I John 5:7–8: 'the Spirit, the water and the blood'.[29] These three would signify the successive initiation ceremonies of chrismation, water-baptism and the eucharist. The writer puts 'Spirit' first, and reverses the order 'blood and water' found in John 19:34. Earlier in I John it has been claimed that 'we have an unction from the Holy One' (I John 2:27). This can be explained as a symbolic reference to the Spirit, but may also allude to physical anointing in initiation. It has been further suggested that initiatory anointing is reflected in St John's Gospel, when Christ mixes earth with his spittle and 'anoints' the blind man, telling him to wash in the pool of Siloam (John 9:6–7, 11).[30] If so, the Syrian order of chrismation and baptism would again be in view. In all three Johannine instances I think an allusion to physical anointing is likely, for the Johannine writings are probably close to Syrian and Judaean Christian and Jewish tradition; but the question remains debatable.

Outside the Johannine writings, the importance of the symbol of chrism for initiation, independently of any explicit association with water, stands out in II Cor. 1:21–2 'and the one who is strengthening us with you into Christ and has anointed (*chrisas*) us is God, who has also sealed us and given the earnest of the Spirit in our hearts'. The word-play, within a context looking back to Christian initiation, suggests that the thought of anointing is linked with understanding of the title *christos* as 'anointed', as happens again in early explanation of the initiatory chrism. Thus the high-priest 'is called a christ' (Lev. 4:5), says Tertullian, 'from chrism, which is anointing, and which also provided the Lord with his name' (*On Baptism*, 7.1). Once again, physical chrismation need not necessarily be implied here in II Corinthians, but the possibility should not be ruled out.[31]

223

Finally, thought conducive to the use of anointing in initiation can be perceived in some Christian writings ascribed to an earlier time than the late second century. Many Christians identified with the ancient self-awareness of Israel as a royal and priestly body, the 'royal priesthood' or 'kingdom and priesthood' of Exod. 19:6. The phrase from Exodus is applied to Christians in general in I Peter (2:9) and in Revelation – here (1:6, 5:10) with the Jewish interpretation 'a kingdom and priests' noted already, which is perhaps also assumed in I Peter. This self-awareness was heightened by the Christian sense that a new age had begun, marked by the appearance of the Lord's Anointed – regarded as both king and high-priest – and by the gift of the Spirit associated with anointing. Christ is termed 'high-priest' in a series of writings from the late first to the mid-second century, including Hebrews (2:17, etc.), I Clement (36.1, etc.), and Ignatius (*Philad.* 9.1, and perhaps also 17.1, on Christ as anointed on the head and imparting his fragrance, with implied reference to Ps. 133:2 as well as gospel tradition); also Polycarp (*Phil.* 12.2), and Justin Martyr (*Dialogue with Trypho* 115.4–116.1). Justin associates Joshua the high-priest (Zech. 3:1) with Christ, and (*Dialogue* 116.3) calls the Christians 'the true high-priestly race (*genos*) of God', bringing pure and acceptable sacrifices (Mal. 1:11).

Christ as high-priest was associated not only with the priesthood of Melchizedek (Gen. 14:18, Ps. 110:4), as in Hebrews (Heb. 2:17, 4:14, 6:20–8:6), but also, strikingly for the importance of anointing, with the Aaronic priesthood inherited from Levi. This is clearly seen in the perhaps mid-second century Christian adaptations of the Levi narrative noted already in the Testaments of the Twelve Patriarchs; the adaptations fit existing description of Levi in the Testaments (Test. Reuben 6.8) as 'until the fulfilment of the times *high-priest, anointed*' (Lev. 4:5) – words, highlighted by Tertullian as he explains the baptismal chrism, which could have been heard without need for change as referring not only to the levitical high-priest, but also to Christ. Association with Levi appears too in I Clement on Christ as 'the high-priest of our offerings' (36.1, cf. 61.3; 64.1). Against the background of the blessing of Jacob in Genesis 49, this epistle has already mentioned that 'from him come the priests and all the Levites who serve the altar of God, from him comes the Lord Jesus according to the flesh, from him come the kings and rulers in the tribe of Judah' (I Clement 32.1–2).

Here in I Clement it is perhaps also assumed that Christ is descended from Levi as well as Judah. This view complements, but is also in contrast with, the insistence of Hebrews on his descent from Judah, and his priesthood – greater than that of Levi – 'according to Melchisedek', to whom Levi had already paid tithes through Abraham (Gen. 14:20, Ps. 110:4; Heb. 7:4–10, 14–19). Christ's descent from Levi as well as Judah is regularly assumed in Christianized parts of the Testaments of the Twelve Patriarchs, where the one salvation or saving figure is to come from Levi and Judah jointly.[32] 'By thee and Judah shall the Lord be seen among mortals', as the angel of the Lord says to Levi (Test. Levi 2.11), with an echo of Baruch 3:37, understood, with early Christian tradition found also in Irenaeus (*Against Heresies*, iv 20 (34), 4) and the Vulgate, as 'afterwards [our God (Baruch 3:35)] was seen upon earth, and was conversant among mortals'. Towards the end of the second century this view of Christ's descent from Levi as well as Judah reappears: 'born according to the flesh as king and priest, from Levi and from Judah' (Irenaeus, fragment 17). The fourth-century Syriac writers Aphrahat and Ephrem Syrus probably reproduce earlier tradition when they associarte Christ's levitical descent with his priestly cousin John the Baptist, or with the aged Simeon in the temple (Luke 2:25–32).[33] Thus for Ephrem, Christ received the kingship through his birth from the house of David, but 'he received the priesthood of the house of Levi through a second birth, through baptism by the son of Aaron [John the Baptist]'.[34] Here Christ's baptism is at the same time institution to the Aaronic priesthood of the house of Levi, somewhat as the Aaronic rite in the Greek Testament of Levi is also Christian initiation.

These lines of thought, in the context of recognition of a new age, would have been consistent with ritual restoration of the ancient chrism, as in the Jewish expectations noted already, and consistent too with extension of the priestly chrism to the whole Christian people considered as 'a kingdom and priests', 'a high-priestly race'. The priesthood of Christians is linked with baptismal anointing in the third century by Origen (*Homilies on Leviticus*, 9.9, on Lev. 16:12): 'All who are anointed with the unguent of the holy chrism are made priests, as Peter says to the whole church, *But you are a chosen race, and a royal priesthood, a holy nation*' (I Peter 2:9). This connection passed into western as well as eastern baptismal interpretation. The ointment went down to Aaron's beard (Ps. 133:2) 'that you might become a chosen race, priestly and precious, for we are all anointed by spiritual grace to the kingdom of God and the priesthood' (Ambrose, *On the Mysteries* 6.30).[35] Not only the ancient functional link between washing and anointing, but also a sense of Christ as high-priest and his followers as a priesthood, would have encouraged association of the chrism, in its Aaronic setting of priestly institution, with Christian baptism.

This current of thought and feeling is probably Judaean and Syrian in origin, but spread to Asia Minor (represented by I Peter, Revelation, Ignatius, Polycarp, Irenaeus – in Gaul, but in touch with Asia Minor – and probably the Johannine writings) and the city of Rome (I Clement; Justin Martyr, from Flavia Neapolis (Nablus) in Palestine, and also probably in touch with Asia Minor). In both Asia Minor and Rome the church was open to influence from a numerous Jewish population, and from the Christianity of Syria and Judaea.

Conflict and Reinterpretation
These beginnings led to a baptismal rite which included both anointing and washing (water-baptism). By the later second century the two have stood together in the rite for some time, although their order varies. Tension between them, perhaps going back to the period of origins, is reflected in a source probably from the

late second century, the Gospel of Philip. The surviving text is in Codex II of the Nag Hammadi Coptic papyri, discovered in 1945.[36] Preserved in Coptic, but probably written in Greek, this gospel reflects the outlook of followers of Valentinus, who had taught in Rome from the 130s to the 150s; the widespread Valentinian school of thought, represented also by the Theodotus whose writing was excerpted by Clement of Alexandria, was criticized by Irenaeus, Hippolytus and Tertullian as well as Clement. Connections of the Gospel of Philip, or the teaching it represents, with Syria are suggested by the interest it shows (19; 47; 53) in Christian terms in the 'Syrian' language (Aramaic).[37]

Here unction clearly competes with water-baptism, although both appear to be needed and in use within the initiation rite. A group within the church none the less finds greater significance in the chrism. Thus 'there is water in water, there is fire in a chrism' (Gospel of Philip 25). The 'fire' of the oil, which lights the lamps, is also the fire signifying divinity; it mediates a 'real presence', and the gift of the Spirit. Again, with another argument, 'the chrism is superior to baptism, for from the chrism we are called Christians' (as in Tertullian), 'not because of the baptism; and Christ is so called because of the chrism. The Father anointed the Son, and the Son anointed the apostles, and the apostles anointed us. He who is anointed possesses the All. He possesses the resurrection, the light, the cross, the holy spirit' (95).

Valentinians towards the end of the second century were probably often found within the majority church, but some of their favoured rites could already be described as distinctive, and they eventually became a separated body.[38] The advocacy of anointing in the Gospel of Philip can be associated with the Valentinian view described by Irenaeus, according to which water-baptism only conveys forgiveness of sins, as with John's baptism, but perfect knowledge, spiritual perfection, is brought by a redemption given by Christ. Valentinian forms of initiation were sometimes water-baptism, but with added Aramaic invocations of the redeemer which recall the concern for Aramaic in the Gospel of Philip, and sometimes water-baptism with an anointing with ointment of balsam (chrism) which signified redemption; sometimes, however, without recourse to the baptismal waters, by anointing only, both with oil mixed with water and with the balsamic ointment – and sometimes through inner knowledge without any outward rites (Irenaeus, *Against Heresies* i 21, 3–4 [14, 2–3]).

Here anointing, and the chrism in particular, form the sign of a redemption which (many think) by water-baptism alone we cannot have. A position broadly of this kind was accepted more widely. When Tertullian describes initiation, he links the gift of the Spirit not with water-baptism but with the subsequent ceremony, the laying-on of hands with anointing: 'not that we receive the holy Spirit in the water, but that in the water, we, being made clean under the direction of the angel' (sent to make the waters spiritually cleansing), 'are made ready for the Holy Spirit' (*On Baptism*, 6.1). With close similarity, even when anointing came first, in the (?fourth-century) Syriac History of John the Apostle, after John's prayer over the oil and water of baptism, 'fire blazed forth over the oil', signifying divine presence, and angels' wings were spread over the water.[39] Emphasis on the anointing as opposed to the water continued in later ancient Christianity and the mediaeval west. In these interpretations of anointing it can be seen to have become a symbol which is also somehow the reality signified, both the medium and the presence of salvation – a symbol which can be called a sacrament.[40]

The Legend of the Oil of Anointing
Reverence for the consecrated chrism, with the conflict which this reverence evoked, can be seen again in Christian use of the biblically-based legend of anointing. Among Jews the holy anointing-oil which the high-priests and kings received was traced back to Levi, as seen already, and to the garden of Eden; it came from a tree in the garden, and Adam begged for it in his sickness, as the Greek Life

228

of Adam and Eve relates. Here we return to the subject-matter of vision, as in Enoch's vision of the mountain of God and its paradise of fragrant trees, including the tree of life (I Enoch 24–5, probably from the late third century BCE).

Among Christians the story is now complemented. In the late second century Celsus, a philosophical critic of Christianity, writes that a candidate for initiation, probably a sectary, responds after chrismation 'I have been anointed with white chrism from the tree of life' (Celsus in Origen, *Against Celsus* vi 27). 'White chrism' may indicate white oil, the purest and brightest oil, from beaten olives (Exod. 27:20, Lev. 24:2, cited already). The paradisal tree concerned is now the tree of life itself. In another Christian development of the legend it is in the end the Son of God, when he descends into Hades (I Peter 3:19, 4:6), who anoints Adam with the paradisal oil, that he may arise (Gospel of Nicodemus 3=Acts of Pilate 19, perhaps third or fourth century).

At the heart of the legend were biblical affirmations mentioned earlier: the chrism was given by God himself, 'the oil of the anointing of the Lord' (Lev. 10:7, 21:12), *his* 'holy oil' (Ps. 89:20). A claim to true 'Christian' anointing in this form is attributed to the group called by Hippolytus the Naassenes; they claim, he says, that 'out of all humankind we alone are Christians … anointed with unspeakable chrism from a horn, as David was (I Sam. 16:1), not an earthenware cruse, as Saul was (I Sam. 10:1)' (Hippolytus, *Refutation of all Heresies*, v 9, 22). Tertullian, quoted already, similarly derived baptismal anointing from the anointing of priests with oil from a horn (*On Baptism*, 7.1), used, as he noted elsewhere, for the kings, and kept in the temple (*Against the Jews*, xiii 6; cf. I Kings 1:39). Contemporary Jewish tradition will have influenced both Tertullian and the Naassenes, directly or indirectly (n.14, above). Both also follow the same church tradition, in which it is expressly taught that 'Christ' means 'anointed' (Tertullian, *On Baptism*, 7.1).

Comment on the legend as a whole survives in the Clementine Recognitions (i 44.6–48.5), within a section (i 44.4–52.6) which is viewed as a third-century insertion into a second-century sequence (i 27–71).[41] The apostle Peter is depicted as passing on to Clement what is perhaps one special form of more widespread instruction about 'the seal' of anointing. Conflict appears in a more negative treatment of Aaronic anointing. This reflects, once again, exaltation of Christ and his gift of the Spirit and immortality by contrast with the religion of Hebrew scripture, in implicit response to Jews, and also to any Christians like those who adapted the Testament of Levi, Christians for whom ancient scripture and the gospel, Jewish tradition and apostolic teaching, might seem to be esteemed alike. Here in the Clementine Recognitions, by contrast, the Christian anointing is firmly derived from Christ, and he is linked not with Aaron and the baptism of John but with Adam and paradise. Christ, says Peter, has his name as 'the *first* whom the Father anointed with the oil which had been taken from the tree of life' (i 45.4). The Father anointed the Son, as in the Gospel of Philip (95, quoted above).

This occurred, it seems (i 47), in the anointing of Adam, who is regarded as an initial manifestation of Christ; in the related Clementine Homilies (iii 20), Adam has 'the holy spirit of Christ'. Peter adds (45.5) that Christ anoints the pious with similar oil when they reach his kingdom, for refreshment from their labours, that their light may shine, and that, being filled with the holy Spirit, they may be granted immortality. Similarly, in the Gospel of Philip (92) Christ makes chrism from the oil of the paradisal olive-tree, for the resurrection of the dead, and in Ignatius (*Eph.* 17.1) 'for this reason did the Lord receive unguent (*myron*, as in Ps. 133 LXX and Matt. 26:7 and parallels) upon his head, that he might breathe incorruptibility upon the church'. This oil signifies the gift of the Spirit, which the Father had imparted to Christ by anointing him from the tree of life (*Clem. Rec.* i 45.4).

The chrism compounded for Aaron's anointing (*Clem. Rec.* i 46–7) was indeed powerful, for a time, to make kings, priests, and prophets; yet it was not from the tree of life. It was only a likeness of the unmixed and eternal anointing made by God (compare Heb.

8:5 on the tabernacle as 'a copy and shadow' of heavenly things, quoting Exod. 25:40). From Christ's appearance, accordingly (48.3–6), the Aaronic chrism ceased (Dan. 9:26 LXX, quoted already). The essentially Christian character and the heavenly and eternal virtue of the chrism are highlighted at the expense of its old and temporary manifestation in Israel – the mere shadow of the true anointing. The tension between the two types of Christian response to the ancient scriptures can be felt.

The Impetus of the Chrism in Early Christianity
These polemical comments on the legend bring out further aspects of the symbolism of the chrism used by Christians: it is connected not just with the olive, but with the tree of life, and not just with priesthood and healing, but, as in the Gospel of Nicodemus, with immortality. At the same time the impetus of the chrism is displayed. The chrism tended to become not just an esteemed element in the rites of initiation, but almost a separate sacrament. Thus the apologist Theophilus of Antioch, towards the end of the second century, points out that the name Christian is mocked at, but in fact means 'anointed', and everyone knows that oil is essential for use and beauty. Even the air is in some sense anointed by the oil of God, that is, light and spirit. 'And are you', he asks the pagan, 'unwilling to be anointed with the oil of God', as we Christians are? (Theophilus, *Autol.* i 12). The phrase 'oil of God' seems to echo the emphasis on the holy oil as God's own which has already been encountered in biblical texts underlying the legend of the oil – such passages as Lev. 10:7, 21:12; Ps. 89:20; and Ps. 151:4 LXX. No doubt partly because anointing was the first element in early Syrian Christian initiation, Theophilus seems also to think here of the chrismation in particular as the decisive moment of becoming Christian, and as a conferring of the divine light and spirit.

The impetus of chrism, the emphasis on Christ as its giver which marked the polemic of the Clementine Recognitions, and also some links of Christian anointing with general daily custom, can all be traced further in the third-century Acts of Thomas ('Judas Thomas'), preserved in Greek and Syriac. They begin with a glimpse of Christian and non-Christian self-anointing. The two are contrasted, as Jewish and non-Jewish anointing had already been.

The apostle Thomas, serving an Indian merchant as a carpenter and builder, is on the way to India with his master. They visit the city of Andrapolis, and go with the rest of the population to the wedding-feast of the king's daughter. After they have eaten and drunk (Thomas tastes nothing) unguents and garlands are brought. 'Some were anointing their faces, some their beards, and some other places; but Judas (Thomas) was praising God, and he moistened his nostrils with a little oil, and put some in his ears, and made the sign of the cross over his heart; and a garland of myrtle was put on his head, and he took a reed-branch in his hand.'[42]

The apostle's anointing falls in with custom, but takes a Christian form. Thus he also makes the sign of the cross with the oil, as stated in the Syriac text, showing that he is a Christian to those who understand; he moistens his nostrils with oil, as sometimes happened in baptism, and he wears the garland or crown of convention, but also takes a reed in his hand. For the Christian the two together may recall both the Passion of Christ (the crown of thorns and the reed, Matt. 27:29) and the contrasting signs of joy in baptismal practice; a garland and an olive-branch are bestowed in initiation in the Greek Testament of Levi (8.8–9). The description as a whole is a reminder of the Hellenic as well as Jewish customs of anointing, among which the Christians developed sometimes slightly adapted daily customs as well as their own sacramental usages.

Towards the end of the Acts the writer describes, with Syrian usage in view, the baptisms, often preceded by anointing and followed by the eucharist, which the apostle performed in India. His foe king Mazdai says: 'This sorcerer … bewitches with oil and water and bread (and wine)'.[43] The apostle's prayers over the oil disclose further symbolism and underline the claim of the consecrated oil to reverence. To give an example: 'Fair Fruit, that art worthy to be glowing with the word of holiness … yea, Lord, come, abide upon this oil, as thou didst abide upon the tree, and they who crucified thee were not able to bear thy word. Let thy gift come, which thou didst breathe upon thine enemies and they went backward and fell upon their faces, and let it abide upon this oil, over which we name thy name.'[44]

The 'word of holiness' is probably the divine Name associated with initiation, as suggested by Theodotus, quoted already, on oil as 'sanctified by the power of the Name' (Clement of Alexandria, *Excerpts from Theodotus*, 82). With 'holiness' compare the use of 'holiness' in connection with the divine Name in Exod. 28:36, 39:30, discussed already, on the Name to be engraved on the plate of the diadem encircling the high-priestly mitre. The Name is to make the oil glow like fire, in token of divine indwelling. Christ is to abide upon the oil – derived from a tree – just as he once abode upon the tree of Calvary. His 'gift', the divine Name which he received as his own (John 17:6, 12) and uttered or breathed out at his arrest (John 18:5-6, 'I am'), when his enemies fell down, is to abide upon the oil over which his name is named. Compare the summary of these points in another prayer: 'Glory to thee, beloved Fruit! Glory to thee, Name of the Messiah! Glory to thee, hidden power that dwellest in the Messiah!'[45] These references to the divine Name, identified with the name of Christ but also recalling that the high-priest bore the Name on the diadem of his mitre, form the main relic here of the old association of baptismal anointing with priestly initiation in the 'ancient discipline' of Moses and Aaron.

Oil in a luxurious form is not needed for Christian anointing. Longing for baptism and the eucharist, the lady Mygdonia says to her nurse '… bring a mingled draught in a cup, and one loaf, and a little oil, even if it be in a lamp'. The anointing of initiation is also an anointing for healing and pardon: 'holy oil, given to us for unction; hidden mystery of the cross, which is seen through it – thou straightener of crooked limbs, thou, our lord Jesus, life and health and remission of sins, let thy power come and abide on this oil, let thy holiness dwell in it'.[46] Water-baptism is used, but the anointing, in which Christ's holiness and power is present, signifies the fulness of 'life and health and remission of sins'.

The Acts also bring out, through the figure of Thomas, the importance of the human mediation of the divinely-given anointing rites. Through his prayer the oil receives consecration and brings deliverance, and he also seems like a conjurer with oil and water, able to work in a domestic setting with the most everyday material, 'a little oil, even if it be for a lamp'. This picture recalls the comparable importance of the figure of Moses in the consecration of Aaron.

In both the Gospel of Philip and the Acts of Thomas one sees the movement implicitly demanded in the Clementine Recognitions, a shift from emphasis on the Aaronic antecedents of baptismal anointing to association of the oil with Christ and the tree of life, identified in the Acts with the cross. The influence of the ancient priestly rites is still perceptible, however, in the importance of the Name, and is seen further in both east and west.

The association of divine presence and the gift of the spirit with anointing in particular continues for many centuries in east and west, alongside connection of the gift with the waters of baptism.[47] At the end of the ancient period it is summed up in a sixth- to eighth-century Latin hymn, still in use at the consecration of holy oil: *O redemptor sume carmen*, 'O redeemer, take the hymn'. 'When the brow is washed in the sacred font, accusations are put to flight; when the brow is anointed, holy spiritual gifts pour down.'[48] The font washes away sin, but it is anointing which conveys the holy spiritual gifts.

3. Mediaeval Custom and the English Prayer-books

Attempts were made to distinguish the meanings of the chrism administered by a priest after baptism, and the chrism conferred soon afterwards by a bishop in confirmation. Thus in the thirteenth century St Thomas Aquinas (*Summa Theologiae* iii 66, 10.2) urged that in baptism the matter, the necessary material element, is water;

the chrism is simply ancillary, to enhance the solemnity of the rite. The chrism had become, rather, the great token of confirmation; so for Aquinas (*Summa Theologiae* iii 72, 2) the matter of confirmation is chrism. In Italy, *cresima* remains the usual name for confirmation.

Yet much mediaeval feeling probably inclined rather towards the reverence for the baptismal chrism expressed by Aquinas's contemporary William Durandus. Anointing of the head with chrism is performed, he says, in order that the one so anointed may become a partaker of the heavenly kingdom. When bishops could no longer be at hand for everyone in confirmation, it was ordered, lest any should perish without the anointing of chrism, that priests should administer it after baptism.[49] Here the early association of water-baptism and chrism has been forgotten, but the salvific value set on the chrism in itself is clear. The opportunity to receive it immediately after baptism is precious. The salvific association of chrism was still brought out in the petition at anointing in the 1549 English baptism service, that God may 'anoint thee with the unction of his holy Spirit, and bring thee to the inheritance of everlasting life'.

Perhaps the most rapid and lasting change in the fortune of anointing was brought by western Christian movements for reformation in the sixteenth century. The sacraments were viewed with a narrower focus, with an emphasis, bound up with a new gospel-centred piety, on those instituted by Christ as recorded in the gospels. Thus only three sacraments – baptism, the eucharist and penance, with doubts whether the third is truly a sacrament – were recognized in Martin Luther's 1520 Latin tract on the Babylonian captivity of the church, answered by Henry VIII's reassertion of seven sacraments (n.1, above). Fresh concern with scripture kindled an abhorrence of any ceremony which seemed superstitious. In England under Edward VI an initial limitation of unction in the English services issued in 1549–50 was soon followed, when they were reissued in revised form in 1552, by its effective discontinuance apart from – an important exception – the royal anointing. Disuse has been countered by revivals. Nevertheless, the Anglican situation, in which the Prayer-book and *Common Worship* are marked by this history, contrasts with the continuity of anointing in Roman Catholicism, and in the eastern Christianity – Greek and Russian, Syrian and Indian, Coptic and Ethiopic – which has been increasingly represented in modern Britain.

To look more closely at the English changes, they were made while the young king Edward, ten years old at his accession in 1547, was governing through his Privy Council. Anointing was present, as seen already, in four of the seven sacramental rites which had continued in use under his father, Henry VIII: baptism, confirmation, ordination and extreme unction (now provided for as part of an order for the visitation of the sick). In the rites which were translated from Latin service-books, revised, and collected in the first Book of Common Prayer (1549) and its companion Ordinal (1550), anointing was dropped from confirmation and ordination – those two of the four sacraments concerned which were administered by bishops rather than parish priests. The Latin form of episcopal consecration of oils, used on Maundy Thursday, was not translated. In the second English Prayer-book (1552) anointing disappeared from baptism, and the provision for anointing was dropped from the order for the visitation of the sick. In these two contexts anointing had been readily accessible to parishioners, being administered by the parish clergy.

Anointing was not restored in the revised books issued under Elizabeth I in 1559, and Charles II in 1662 (still in use). It is still missing in the revision of 1928, approved by church authority but not by parliament, and widely drawn on in worship for fifty or more years.[50] To trace the initial changes which removed anointing, from 1549 to 1552, is also to glimpse the late-mediaeval custom which surrounded anointing with reverence.

In confirmation chrism was imparted in the late Middle Ages, as mentioned already, by a signing with the cross which was also an imposition of the hand by the bishop. In the 1549 book the signing was retained, but without chrism. A corrective remembrance of the

236

omitted chrism appeared at the beginning, in a prayer for spiritual anointing – confirmation and strengthening 'with the inward unction of thy Holy Ghost', a phrase from Gregory the Great (*On Job*, book xix 15 (24), on Job 29:6 'rivers of oil'). The bishop had formerly said to each candidate on whom he laid his hand, using an old formula, 'I sign thee with the sign of the holy cross, and confirm thee with the chrism of salvation' (*chrismate salutis*).[51] The phrase 'chrism of salvation' represented the salvific associations of the chrism. These were now lost. Emphasis fell simply on imposition of the hand, specifically mentioned in the new rubrics and the subsequent prayer. In Acts 8:16–17 the apostles lay hands on those already baptized, who now receive the Spirit. Although anointing is not mentioned, this apostolic act could be recognized in mediaeval thought as confirmation. When supporting the view that chrism is the necessary matter of confirmation, St Thomas Aquinas (*Summa Theologiae* iii 72, 2.1) envisages the objection that 'the apostles themselves conferred this sacrament by imposition of hands only, without unction', as is said in Acts 8. The Prayer-book retained from the missal the reading of this passage in Acts as the Epistle for the Tuesday in Whitsun Week, a great season for baptisms.

The omission of anointing in confirmation was naturally a sticking-point when proposed changes were discussed by bishops. The bishop of Chichester, George Day, refused to agree an initial set of proposals, first of all because in confirmation 'oil in the forehead' was left out.[52] The chrism had indeed retained high regard. That appears again, implicitly, in the initial rubric of the new 1549 confirmation service. Confirmation was usually conferred soon after baptism, as already mentioned. It was now further detached from baptism by a provision that 'none hereafter shall be confirmed, but such as can say' the creed, the Lord's Prayer and the Ten Commandments. The new rubric goes on, however, to stress that this deferment of confirmation does not imperil the salvation of children who have been baptized. In the background of this assurance is a public regard for confirmation which will often have fastened on the salvific character ascribed to the chrism. William Tyndale wrote bitterly, 'they think that if the bishop butter the child in the forehead that it is safe'.[53]

The anointing of hands in ordination to the priesthood has been mentioned already, in connection with priestly anointing in ancient Israel. This anointing too was now dropped. It had been revered, as seen in the custom of kissing the newly-consecrated hands; but the tradition of instruments also mentioned above, rather than the anointing, could be thought to impart the character of priesthood (so Aquinas, *Summa Theologiae* iii Suppl., 37, 5). In the new English Ordinal the instruments now comprised a bible as well as a chalice and bread; the bible alone was retained in 1552. In consecration of bishops, anointing of head and hands was also dropped in the 1550 ordinal.

Anointing as a rite thus remained in the first English Prayerbook simply in baptism and the visitation of the sick, the settings in which, with confirmation, it was probably most firmly rooted in general affection. The 1549 baptism service, however, as compared with that of the Sarum (Salisbury) liturgical use which formed the model for revision, now omitted the earlier pre-baptismal unction, with the oil 'of catechumens' or 'of exorcism' rather than chrism, which marked the purification of the candidates after the time of preparation and before baptism. Yet the importance of the chrism after baptism continued to stand out. Following existing usage the child was still given, but now just before chrismation instead of afterwards, a white vesture or coif, itself called a chrisom (Latin *chrismale*). The chrisom seems to be one more sign of the influence of the Aaronic institution rites; it safeguarded the 'crown of anointing', just as the anointed priest 'shall not uncover his head' because 'the crown of the anointing oil of his God is upon him' (Vulgate Lev. 10:6–7, 21:10–12, following the Septuagintal interpretation mentioned already). The chrisom covering the head was thus a token of the sanctity of the chrism. It was to be returned when the mother came back for her churching.[54] A chrisom had hitherto likewise been used at confirmations for the same reason; godparents might be enjoined by a priest to come with the children to church on the third day after confirmation, to restore the chrisom.[55] A chrisom was also worn by the sovereign after the coronation anointing.[56]

The oil for the sick and the two oils for baptism – oil of catechumens, and chrism – were treated with similar reverence. In mediaeval times the chrismatories in which these oils were kept and carried were to be provided in each parish and could be works of beauty and value. The reverence accorded to the consecrated chrism in particular appears in parochial use also of a ceremonial veil or sudary, cast round the shoulders – a humeral veil. The ends of the veil served to muffle the hands holding the chrismatory, when it was borne in procession to the font at baptism, much as a similar humeral veil has been used for holding eucharistic vessels without touching them.[57] In these provisions, notably the use of the sudary and the chrism, we meet once again a sense of 'real presence' associated with the chrism 'of salvation'. Anointing is treated as no less than a sacrament of the Holy Spirit, matching the eucharistic sacrament of Christ.

The anointings kept in the 1549 Prayer-book, in baptism and the visitation of the sick, were still disapproved in the reform movement. Further change followed swiftly. Cranmer had asked his

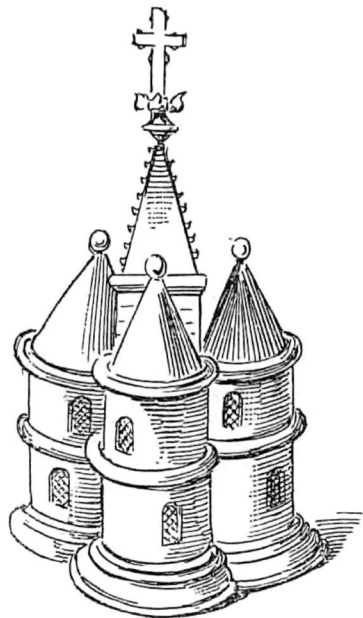

Figure 11.1: Chrismatory for the three oils, twelfth-century (S. Maria im Kapitol, Cologne), from D. Duret, *Mobilier: vases, objets et vêtements liturgiques. Étude historique* (Paris: Letouzey et Ané, 1932), fig. 238.

Biblical Voices and Echoes

friend Martin Bucer, the Strasbourg reformer who was now Regius
Professor of Divinity in Cambridge, to write a critique of the 1549
services. Bucer disapproved retention of anointing; extreme unction
was not ancient, he thought, but a wrong-headed imitation of an
apostolic deed, and anointing in general led to superstition.[58] Many
will have condemned as superstition the reverence accorded to
consecrated oil, and the treatment of chrism as a token of salvation
and sacred presence. The anointings surrounded by these customs
will now have been classed among the ceremonies of which the
1549 note 'Of Ceremonies' says: 'they were so far abused, partly by
the superstitious blindness of the rude and unlearned … , that the
abuses could not well be taken away, the thing remaining still'.

The chrism in baptism and the unction of the sick thus
disappeared in the revised Prayer-book of 1552. All four sacramental
anointings had now been dropped. They soon returned with the Latin
service-books under Mary I (1553–8), but again lost authorization
under Elizabeth I, whose Prayer-book (1559) took over 1552 with
a few significant revisions. Well on in Elizabeth's reign, however,
it was still thought possible that some of the parochial clergy were
administering baptismal oil and chrism, and perhaps also extreme
unction.[59]

Later on, one change in the 1662 revision of the Prayer-book
formed a new reminder of the biblical symbolism of unction. The
hymn *Veni Creator*, 'Come, Holy Ghost', which forms part of the
ordination services, has, both in Latin and in the English version
provided in 1550, just one reference to the Holy Ghost as 'Unction
spiritual'. In the 1662 Prayer-book the 1550 version was replaced
by a new rendering by John Cosin, bishop of Durham, which has
become classical. It makes anointing by the Spirit a central theme
of the hymn; unction soothes, enlightens, kindles and cheers (Ps.
104:15) with the sevenfold gifts promised to the anointed king (Isa.
11:1–2).

> Come, Holy Ghost, our souls inspire,
> And lighten with celestial fire;

Thou the anointing Spirit art
Who dost thy sevenfold gifts impart.

Thy blessed Unction from above
Is comfort, light and fire of love.
Enable with perpetual light
The dulness of our blinded sight.

Anoint and cheer our soilèd face
With the abundance of thy grace ...

In the early eighteenth century some of the non-jurors, who had refused the oath of allegiance to the crown since the accession of William III and Mary II, were again using chrism in confirmation, and were anointing the sick – not 'by way of extreme unction, but in order to recovery'.[60] Then from the 1830s onwards the Oxford Movement led by John Keble, J.H. Newman and E.B. Pusey helped to revive concern for the concept of the church, and church history and custom. The atmosphere became less unfavourable to a revival of unction. At Cambridge in 1839, J.M. Neale and Benjamin Webb founded the Camden Society, later named the Ecclesiological Society, and soon jointly translated the first book of William Durandus's *Rationale* (1843). Neale's *History of the Holy Eastern Church* (1850) discusses oil and chrism in Christian initiation, and 'the office of the prayer-oil' (*euchelaion*) for the sick. Expounding the Thirty-Nine Articles, A.P. Forbes, bishop of Brechin and a disciple of Pusey, urged in 1868 that – the Visitation of the Sick being a private office rather than a public servi– there is nothing to hinder the revival of 'the apostolic and Scriptural custom of anointing the sick', when a sick person desires it.[61] By the early years of the twentieth century the use of this custom was being encouraged in widely-read manuals like Vernon Staley's *The Catholic Religion* and Percy Dearmer's *Parson's Handbook*, and a printed 'Form for Unction' was available with the 1549 anointing prayer.[62]

This enthusiasm contrasts with the mingling of attraction and detachment with which sacramental anointing could be viewed at this period among those who lived, without accepting Christianity, in a mental atmosphere affected by it. Thus Émile Zola made the doomed love-affair in his novel *Rome*, set in Rome in the early 1890s, turn on two moments of anointing: Benedetta takes oil from a lamp burning before a revered Madonna to apply it to the wound of her beloved Dario when he has been stabbed; and on a later occasion, when he is dying of poison, he is given extreme unction in the vain hope that it might also serve as a God-given antidote.[63] Yet in the end unction, as it fails to fulfil the hopes of the devout, is for Zola a symbol not of light and the Spirit but of a whole ecclesiastical culture which is losing significance and dying. Then in 1916–17 it was simply with irony that E.H. Carr the historian, then a young man serving in the War Department of the Foreign Office and overseeing supplies sent to our Russian allies, noted that it had been necessary to ensure transit of a consignment of '660 tons of pure olive oil (for use in Russian churches)'.[64]

Still, against the ecclesiastical background just sketched the anointing of the sick was reappearing in Anglican use. It gained no mention in the 1928 Prayer-book, but the Scottish Prayer-book of 1929 provided for it, and in 1935 the Convocation of Canterbury approved a 'Form of Unction and the Laying on of Hands'.[65] During liturgical revision in England from the 1960s onwards unction of the sick held its place, and in new services gathered in *Common Worship* (2000) anointing was an option in baptism and confirmation and in ordination, as well as the visitation of the sick. Suggestions for a form for the episcopal consecration of oils were also now included.

Anointing and Sacramental Symbolism in Recent Times
Prayer-book development thus led in the Church of England to optional restoration of the anointings which were first limited and then discarded in the years 1549–52. This return will owe something to increased awareness of the value of ritual, and wider recognition of those links of anointing with scripture which were highlighted in Cosin's version of *Veni Creator*. From the 1940s onwards biblical

study had shown strong interest in symbolism and allegory, liturgy and the sacramental. In the church, during the 1940s and 1950s there was lively Anglican revival of the dispute whether the gift of the Spirit and full church membership should be associated with baptism or confirmation. This controversy was also a ghost of the old conflict between anointing and water-baptism; it included argument over the early or late appearance of a general use of the chrism in initiation, views represented by Gregory Dix and G.W.H. Lampe, respectively.[66] Irrespective of views held, the debate, together with the biblical study of the time, brought out the links of anointing with biblical teaching on the anointed king as representing the people, on Christ as the Anointed, on the Spirit as 'unction from the Holy One', and on the church as a royal priesthood. Other aspects of anointing which I have mentioned were also considered in biblical study: the importance of scriptural writings for reflection of early Christian worship and ritual, including anointing, and the related importance of visionary experience in the shaping of sacred rites and books. This biblical, doctrinal and historical discussion was echoed when initiation was reviewed during liturgical revision from the 1970s onwards.

Nevertheless, by the time of *Common Worship* in 2000 a certain retreat from anointing, at least in connection with baptism, was perceptible. For Roman Catholics, permission to omit not the chrism, but the pre-baptismal unction with the oil of catechumens, was available from 1984.[67] It is asked in modern France whether the post-baptismal chrism itself is appropriate – even though it is explained as a sign of the priesthood of all Christians – in view of the chrism which is to come in confirmation.[68] This line of thought will have been facilitated by the view of St Thomas Aquinas that baptismal anointings are ancillary. With its pastoral background, however, it suggests that for some who come to baptism or request it for their children sacred anointing may seem what the Prayer-book calls a 'dark' ceremony. This outlook would reflect a broader decline in sensitivity to biblical and Christian symbolism.

With this consideration, review of anointing meets secularization, in the sense of the modern change in the relation between European society and Christian elements of its past and present, a change impelled by urbanized life and the growth of new technical and scientific knowledge.[69] This change also affects the Jewish tradition, with which Christianity has always been intimately connected, and which has likewise been part of European life and history. Effects of the change could include a feeling of detachment from Christian or Jewish tradition, with a lack of interest in it and knowledge of it, as suggested by current pastoral concern over anointing in baptism. Such feeling can also be part of a more negative stance. Thus Zola, viewing Christianity from the outside, evinced both sympathy for the hopes of the pious, and a conviction that the time of the Christian church is rightly over.

In the mid-twentieth century the poet and artist David Jones correspondingly held that the mental atmosphere within which artists work and sacraments are received had decisively changed. There had been a break or 'lesion' in imaginative understanding, 'whether ephemeral or more enduring we do not know'. You could not any longer expect the signs and symbols of the artist or writer, or the signs and sacraments of the church, to be generally understood.[70] Jones was thinking in the first place of a practical difficulty encountered by the artist and poet. In their work the 'making of signs', symbolism and allusion is central; but since the break, modern imagination is deprived of much which makes signs and sacraments intelligible. Can the word 'wood', for instance, any longer evoke the wood of the cross? The same alienation obscures sacramental signs. Jones insisted on the character of sacraments as art-works – works manifesting what he regarded as the central activity of all art, the making of signs. Anointing would not then be the only sacramental sign to become 'dark', and sacramental rites would join the symbolism of art and poetry in a failure to meet understanding. Yet Jones as writer and artist persisted in the attempt to make signs, bound together and interpreted by a web of allusion.

For himself, he was able to start with his participation in the Mass, a context in which allusive recollection of a history through a sign does still occur.[71]

The change denoted by secularization has taken place. Sacramental symbols such as anointing can certainly become meaningless. Some sympathetic awareness of scripture and tradition is needed for the background of sacred anointing to be understood. Yet the situation remains ambiguous. The secularity associated with technological culture has come to coexist with a greater prominence of religion in general. In Europe, with its ongoing changes in population and education, there is increased awareness of the traditions of thought and ritual found in such great religions as Islam, Hinduism and Buddhism. The Christian religion as practised in the churches of the east has also become more widely noticed. The higher public profile of all these traditions may help to encourage reappropriation of Christian signs and sacraments.

Symbolic ritual plays a part likewise in movements of spirituality not involving commitment to Christianity, Judaism, or other major religions. There is interest, too, in a more private and individually-focused spirituality, considered simply as the sense of a connectedness with something greater, and expressed through rituals, which could include anointing, chosen by each person.[72] The advocacy of this form of spirituality itself attests detachment from the church and its symbolism. None the less, interest in ritual for the individual might help, among Christians, to rekindle imaginative understanding of anointing in the sacraments. The freedom and home-made character of the rituals recommended recall the Acts of Thomas, where the apostle prays in a domestic setting and using the materials available, 'a little oil, even if it be from a lamp'. Beside the advocacy of personal everyday ritual one can then perhaps place the affirmation, in a contemporary autobiographical sketch of Christian spirituality, that we can indeed 'recover the intrinsic power of sign, symbol and scripture' so that liturgy can 'speak to the heart in a language of sign and symbol'.[73]

It has been noted in reflection on Jones himself that art and poetry which engages with myth and the making of signs was indeed under a cloud after his death in 1974, but that it has since re-emerged, 'as in a Virgilian cycle of return'.[74] Without pressing this apt simile too hard, one may add that we should probably not expect the regularity associated with a cycle, or with the pattern of linear rise and fall which this tale of anointing in Israel and the church has taken on. Change which affects the understanding of anointing and other sacramental signs has indeed occurred, but we are also in an atmosphere which can permit movement towards, as well as away from, the symbolic and sacramental in literature and art, scripture and liturgy. Christian sacred anointing is precarious in its hold on present-day imagination, but – as the visionary aspect of its development suggests – it may still have a capacity for eliciting fresh response.

Endnotes

[1] This chapter is based on a Chester Cathedral Bible Talk in a series on 'The Sacraments', marking the quincentenary of Henry VIII's defence of the seven sacraments, *Assertio Septem Sacramentorum* (1521), a copy of which is in the Cathedral Library.

[2] 'Of Ceremonies', printed as an epilogue in the 1549 Prayer-book, but in the prefatory matter in the 1552, 1662 and 1928 revisions.

[3] Texts with translation in F. García Martínez & E.J.C. Tigchelaar, *The Dead Sea Scrolls: Study Edition* (2 vols., Leiden & Grand Rapids, Michigan, 1997–8), ii, 700–703 (4Q327, a calendrical fragment); 1238–45 (11Q19, the Temple Scroll, cols. 18.11–23.2).

[4] M.D. Goodman, 'Kosher Olive Oil in Antiquity', in P.R. Davies & R.T. White (edd.), *A Tribute to Geza Vermes: Essays on Jewish and Christian Literature and History* (Journal for the Study of the Old Testament: Supplement Series 100, Sheffield, 1990), 227–45.

[5] Joseph and Asenath 8.5, in J.H. Charlesworth (ed.), *The Old Testament Pseudepigrapha* (2 vols., London, 1983–5), ii, 212.

[6] Pindar (early fifth century BCE), fragment 64.

[7] Edwyn Bevan, *Symbolism and Belief* (London, 1938, repr. 1962), 115.

[8] II Sam. 12:20, Matt. 6:17; Mishnah, Yoma 8.1 'on the Day of Atonement, eating, drinking, washing, anointing, putting on sandals and marital intercourse are forbidden'.

[9] García Martínez & Tigchelaar, *The Dead Sea Scrolls: Study Edition*, i, 128–9 (1QM col. 9.7–9).

[10] Amalarius of Metz (ninth century), *On ecclesiastical offices* ii 13 'It is written in the book of Numbers [3:3]: *These are the names of the sons of Aaron who are anointed, the priests whose hand is filled by consecration, that they may perform the priest's office*. This custom is maintained by our bishops; they anoint the hands of the priests with oil.'

[11] Cornelius à Lapide (van den Steen), on Exod. 29:9 (giving the paraphrases 'you shall have filled with oil' and 'by anointing you shall consecrate'), Lev. 8:33, 16:32 (the high-priest anointed on head and hands) and also, now in combination with Augustine's view, on Num. 3:3 (the hands were filled both with sacrifices, and with the unction of oil) and Ecclesiasticus 45:15 (18), in C. à Lapide, *Commentaria in Scripturam Sacram*, ed. A. Crampon (24 vols., Paris, 1874–7), i, 701, ii, 49, 109 and 203, and x, 460.

[12] Ephrem Syrus, *Hymns for Epiphany* 3.17, transl. A.E. Johnston in P. Schaff & H. Wace (edd.), *A Select Library of Nicene and post-Nicene Fathers of the Christian Church*, Second Series, xiii.2 (New York & London, 1898), 270.

[13] García Martínez & Tigchelaar, *The Dead Sea Scrolls: Study Edition*, ii, 1178–9 (11Q5, col. 28.11).

[14] Babylonian Talmud, Horayoth 11b and Kerithoth 5a (foot)–5b, teaching attributed to R. Judah b. Ilai (second century).

[15] Charlesworth, *Old Testament Pseudepigrapha*, ii, 19.

[16] For other instances see Josephus, *Ant.* xi 327–8 (Jaddua, named in Neh. 12:11, 22), and *Jewish War* i 68–9, paralleled in *Ant.* xiii 299–300 (John Hyrcanus); Tosefta, Sotah 13.5–6 (John Hyrcanus and Simeon the Righteous), 13.8 (Simeon the Righteous).

[17] Aramaic Levi Document 4.11; the rite is summarized as clothing and filling of hands, Aramaic Levi 5:4, Jubilees 32:3. See J.C. Greenfield, M.E. Stone & Esther Eshel, *The Aramaic Levi Document: Edition, Translation, Commentary* (Leiden & Boston, 2004), 66–73, 141–52.

[18] Mishnah, Megillah 1.9; Makkoth 2.6; Horayoth 3.4, discussed by J.R. Porter, 'Oil in the Old Testament', in M. Dudley & G. Rowell (edd.), *The Oil of Gladness: Anointing in the Christian Tradition* (London, 1993, repr. 2008), 35–45 (36).

Biblical Voices and Echoes

[19] García Martínez & Tigchelaar, *The Dead Sea Scrolls: Study Edition*, ii, 1236–7 (11Q19, col. 15.15–17).

[20] Jerusalem Talmud, Shekalim vi 1, 49c; Babylonian Talmud, Horayoth 12a and Kerithoth 5b.

[21] Mekhilta of R. Ishmael, Wayassa', 6, on Exod. 16:33, in J.Z. Lauterbach (ed. & transl.), *Mekilta de-Rabbi Ishmael* (3 vols., Philadelphia, 1933, repr. 1976), ii, 126.

[22] Tridentine Roman Missal, Feast of the Purification of the Virgin (2 February), Blessing of Candles, fourth Collect.

[23] See II Macc. 2:17 'the kingdom, and the priesthood, and the hallowing'; Philo, *On Abraham* 56 'a kingdom and a priesthood and a holy nation'; Targum Onkelos on Exod. 19:6 'ye shall be before me kings, priests, and a holy nation'.

[24] Peter Lombard, *Sentences* iv 1, 1.1 (the Samaritan applied the bandagings of the sacraments, because God instituted the sacraments as remedies against the wounds of sin).

[25] From *Pange lingua gloriosi corporis mysterium*, translated as 'Now, my tongue, the mystery telling', *Hymns Ancient and Modern Revised* no. 383 and *Common Praise* no. 316, or 'Of the glorious body telling', *New English Hymnal* no. 268; Latin with prose translation in F. Brittain (ed.), *The Penguin Book of Latin Verse* (Harmondsworth, 1962), 255.

[26] S.P. Brock, 'The Transition to a Post-baptismal Anointing in the Antiochene Rite', in B.D. Spinks (ed.), *The Sacrifice of Praise. Studies ... in Honour of Arthur Hubert Couratin* (Rome, 1981), 215–25 (216–19); P.F. Bradshaw, 'Baptismal Practice in the Alexandrian Tradition, Eastern or Western?', in P.F. Bradshaw (ed.), *Essays in Early Eastern Initiation* (Alcuin/GROW Liturgical Study 8; Bramcote, Nottingham, 1988), 5–17.

[27] S.G. Hall, 'Institutions in the pre-Constantinian *ecclesia*', in Margaret M. Mitchell and Frances M. Young (edd.), *The Cambridge History of Christianity*, i, *Origins to Constantine* (Cambridge, 2006), 414–33 (423).

[28] T.W. Manson, 'Miscellanea Apocalyptica III. *Test. XII Patr.: Levi viii*', *Journal of Theological Studies* 48 (1947), 59–61, followed by J. Daniélou, *The Theology of Jewish Christianity* (translated and edited by J.A. Baker; London, 1964), 324–7.

[29] T.W. Manson, 'Entry into Membership of the Early Church', *Journal of Theological Studies* 48 (1947), 25–33 (arguing for the early priority of the gift

of the Spirit to baptism, he noted that physical anointing may be implied in I John 5:7, but left the question open).

[30] C.F.D. Moule, *The Birth of the New Testament* (3rd edn, London, 1982), 135, noted this with caution among other signs that John 9 looks like 'a narrative told with one eye on the circumstances of Christian baptism'.

[31] Among those who note it as possible is Wayne A. Meeks, 'Social and ecclesial life of the earliest Christians', in Mitchell & Young (edd.), *The Cambridge History of Christianity*, i, 145–73 (163).

[32] Testaments of the Twelve Patriarchs, Simeon 7.1–2, Levi 2.11, Dan 5.10, Gad 8.1, Joseph 19.11, Naphtali 8.2–3.

[33] R. Murray, *Symbols of Church and Kingdom* (Cambridge, 1975, repr. 1977), 178–80.

[34] Carmel McCarthy, *Saint Ephrem's Commentary on Tatian's Diatessaron* (1993, repr. with corrections Oxford, 2000), 85 (iv 3, on Matt. 3:15; preserved in Armenian translation).

[35] Further examples in G.W.H. Lampe, *The Seal of the Spirit* (London, 1951), 220.

[36] For the story of their discovery and publication see W.H.C. Frend, *The Archaeology of Early Christianity: A History* (London, 1996), 278–86.

[37] J. Frey, 'Texts about Jesus: Non-Canonical Gospels and Related Literature', in A. Gregory & C. Tuckett (edd.), *The Oxford Handbook of Early Christian Apocrypha* (Oxford, 2015), 13–47 (34–5); similarly, R. McL. Wilson, *The Gospel of Philip* (London, 1962), 3–5. Both scholars are indebted to the long-continued work of H.-M. Schenke on this gospel.

[38] I. Dunderberg, 'The School of Valentinus', in A. Marjanen & P. Luomanen (edd.), *A Companion to Second-Century Christian 'Heretics'* (Supplements to *Vigiliae Christianae*, 76; Leiden & Boston, 2005), 64–98 (64–5, 94–6).

[39] W. Wright, *Apocryphal Acts of the Apostles* (2 vols., London & Edinburgh, 1871), i, 59; ii, 54.

[40] On this understanding of symbol see G.B. Ladner, *God, Cosmos and Humankind: The World of Early Christian Symbolism* (English translation, Berkeley, California, 1995), Introduction.

[41] Translation with introduction in F. Stanley Jones, *An Ancient Jewish Christian Source on the History of Christianity: Pseudo-Clementine Recognitions 1.27–71* (Atlanta, Georgia, 1995), 74–80.

[42] Greek Acts of Thomas i 5; Syriac Acts of Thomas, ed. & transl. W. Wright, *Apocryphal Acts of the Apostles* (2 vols., London & Edinburgh, 1871), i, 150; ii, 175. Quotations follow Wright's translation of the Syriac.

[43] Greek Acts of Thomas xiii 152; Wright, *Apocryphal Acts of the Apostles*, i, 319; ii, 285.

[44] Greek Acts of Thomas xiii 157; Wright, *Apocryphal Acts of the Apostles*, i, 323; ii, 289.

[45] Greek Acts of Thomas x 132; Wright, *Apocryphal Acts of the Apostles*, i, 301; ii, 267.

[46] Greek Acts of Thomas x 121; Wright, *Apocryphal Acts of the Apostles*, i, 291; ii, 258.

[47] Lampe, *The Seal of the Spirit*, 215–19.

[48] Lota fronte sacro fonte aufugantur crimina; | Uncta fronte sacrosancta influunt charismata; text with prose translation in Brittain (ed.), *The Penguin Book of Latin Verse*, 116–18; metrical version 'Blest by the sun, the olive tree', *Common Praise* no. 131.

[49] William Durandus, *Rationale* i 8, 9–10, in Neale & Webb, *The Symbolism of Churches and Church Ornaments: A Translation of the First Book of the Rationale*, 169–70.

[50] For the Prayer-book I have used the texts in E.C.S. Gibson, *The First and Second Prayer Books of Edward VI* (Everyman's Library 448; London, 1910 and reprints), B. Cummings, *The Book of Common Prayer. The Texts of 1549, 1559 and 1662* (Oxford, 2011), and *The Book of Common Prayer with the Additions and Deviations approved in 1928* (Oxford, n.d.).

[51] Sarum use from fifteenth-century Pontifical, in W.G. Henderson, *Liber Pontificalis Chr. Bainbridge Archiepiscopi Eboracensis* (Surtees Society; Durham and London, 1875), 291.

[52] Report of Lords debate in December 1548 (the Lord Protector, Somerset, recalls Day's refusal), in F.A. Gasquet & E. Bishop, *Edward VI and the Book of Common Prayer* (3rd edn, London, 1899), 404 (Appendix V). The earlier meeting recalled was probably in September 1548; see D. MacCulloch, *Thomas Cranmer, A Life* (New Haven & London, 1996), 396–7.

[53] Tyndale, 'Obedience of a Christian Man', quoted by Lampe, *The Seal of the Spirit*, 310.

[54] Book of Common Prayer (1549), Order for the Purification of Women, final rubric: 'The woman that is purified, must offer her Chrisom and other accustomed offerings …'

[55] Direction in Sarum confirmation order in Henderson, *Liber Pontificalis Chr. Bainbridge*, 292.

[56] Direction in fourteenth-century *Liber Regalis*, translated in E.C. Ratcliff, *The Coronation Service of Queen Elizabeth II* (Cambridge and London, 1953), 74.
[57] Three examples of such veils from English parish churches in the late fifteenth and early sixteenth centuries, in one case (Great St Mary's, Cambridge, 1504) inventoried as 'for bearing the chrismatory to the font', are noted by J.T. Micklethwaite, *The Ornaments of the Rubric* (Alcuin Club Tract 1, 3rd edn, London, 1901), 36–7.
[58] M. Bucer, *Censura*, edited and translated by E.C. Whitaker, *Martin Bucer and the Book of Common Prayer* (Alcuin Club; Great Wakering, Essex, 1974), 86–9, 124–7.
[59] Articles 6 (are specified goods and ornaments of the church, including chrismatories, still found in the parish?) and 7 (are oil and chrism used at baptism?), in *Articles to be enquired of within the Province of Canterbury, in the Metropolitical Visitation of the most reverend father in God, Edmonde Archbishop of Canterburie* (London, 1576), repr. in W. Nicholson (ed.), *The Remains of Edmund Grindal* (Parker Society; Cambridge, 1843), 157–77 (159–60).
[60] G. Rowell, 'The Sacramental Use of Anointing in Anglicanism and the Churches of the Reformation', in Dudley & Rowell (ed.), *The Oil of Gladness*, 134–53.
[61] J.M. Neale, *A History of the Holy Eastern Church* (2 vols., London, 1850), ii, 965–71, 997–1009 ('The Mystery of the Holy Chrism'), 1035–8; Alexander Forbes, *An Explanation of the Thirty-Nine Articles* (Oxford, 1868), 474, quoted by D. Stone, *Outlines of Christian Dogma* (2nd edn, London, 1900), 207.
[62] Vernon Staley, *The Catholic Religion: A Manual of Instruction for members of the Anglican Church* ([1893] 17th edn, London, 1911), 300–302; P. Dearmer, *The Parson's Handbook* ([1899] 7th edn, London, 1909), 474–6, mentioning the printed 'Form' and the study by F.W. Puller, *The Anointing of the Sick in Scripture and Tradition* (London, 1904).
[63] E. Zola, transl. E.A. Vizetelly, *Rome* (London, repr. 1903), chapters 9 and 13.
[64] Jonathan Haslam, *The Vices of Integrity: E.H. Carr, 1892–1982* (London, 1999), 19.
[65] Considerations of liturgical history and health-care were set out by a mover for this result, C. Harris, 'Visitation of the Sick: Unction, Imposition of Hands, and Exorcism', in W.K. Lowther Clarke (ed.), with the assistance of C. Harris, *Liturgy and Worship: A Companion to the Prayer-books of the Anglican Communion* (London, 1932), 472–540.

66 Gregory Dix, *The Theology of Confirmation in Relation to Baptism* (Westminster, 1946), and elsewhere; Lampe, *The Seal of the Spirit*, vii–xiv (survey of debate), 127–31.

67 M. Dudley, 'Holy Joys in Store: Oils and Anointing in the Catholic Church', in Dudley & Rowell (edd.), *The Oil of Gladness*, 113–33 (124).

68 P. Hébert, *Le baptême, sacrement de la foi* (Paris, 2021), 58–9.

69 O. Chadwick, *The Secularization of the European Mind in the Nineteenth Century* (Oxford, 1975), 264.

70 David Jones, Preface to *The Anathemata* (London, 1952), 15–18, 22–5 (quotation from p. 18); further in 'Wales and the Crown' (1953), and 'Art and Sacrament. An Enquiry concerning the Arts of Man and the Christian Commitment to Sacrament in Relation to Technocracy' (1955), reprinted in David Jones, *Epoch and Artist: Selected Writings*, ed. H. Grisewood (London, 1959), 39–48 (see p. 40) and 143–79, respectively.

71 For the poetry of the *Anathemata*, set in the course of the Mass, as Jones's response to the problem outlined in his Preface, see Rowan Williams, *Grace and Necessity: Reflections on Art and Love* (London & Harrisburg, PA, 2005), 71–81.

72 Casper ter Kuile, *The Power of Ritual: Turning Everyday Activities into Soulful Practices* (London, 2020), 1–29, 153–5.

73 Frank T. Griswold, *Tracking Down the Holy Ghost* (Church Publishing: New York, 2017).

74 Paul Hills, in Ariane Bankes & Paul Hills, *The Art of David Jones: Vision and Memory* (Chichester & Farnham, 2015), 164.

12
THE ROYAL LAW:
SCRIPTURE AND CROWNING

The title recalls a well-known ceremony of modern coronations. A bible is presented to the sovereign – in 1953 and 2023, by the Moderator of the General Assembly of the Church of Scotland – with words ending: 'we present you with this book, the most valuable thing that this world affords. Here is Wisdom; This is the Royal Law; These are the lively Oracles of God'.

The Presentation of the Bible arrived on the scene only in 1689, late in the long history of coronations in Britain.[1] Still, it makes a good starting-point, for it is akin through scripture to the three older ceremonies which are central in the coronation, after the sovereign has been presented to the people for the initial Recognition. These three are the Promise and oath, the Anointing, and the Crowning. In the Middle Ages and until the late seventeenth century they were performed in a single sequence before the beginning of the eucharist. In 1689 they were placed within the eucharist, after the sermon which followed the gospel and Creed and before the Offertory. The new placing was not without some early mediaeval precedent, but may have been influenced, rather, by the Prayer-book placing of the Consecration of Bishops at this point in the eucharist. At the coronation of George VI in 1937 the Promise was moved back to the beginning of the service, before the collect for purity at the start of the eucharist, so as to follow the Recognition once again.[2] The Anointing and the Crowning still come later in the eucharist, after the gospel. The acclamation and anthem after the Crowning are followed by the offertory hymn and the rest of the eucharist.

Like the Presentation of the Bible, the older ceremonies of the Promise, Anointing and Crowning are rooted in scripture. Their roots spread through the laws and the histories, through prophecy, psalmody, and wisdom literature, to the gospels and the apostolic writings. In the landscape of the coronation these ceremonies stand out like ancient trees. I want to bring them into clearer view, together with their largely unseen biblical root-system. I hope to bring out two points. First, the extensive biblical roots form a single system. They represent different historical situations and outlooks. With due care, however, one can speak of a biblical teaching on sovereignty and governance which the ceremonies express. Then, secondly, the coronation proceeds by sign and symbol. Approached through scripture, it forms a lively symbol, and should be understood as sacramental, indeed as a sacrament.

The Presentation of the Bible
The coronation of 1689 was unusual. From James II's accession in 1685 his daughter Mary, married to William of Orange, had been heir presumptive to the throne. In 1688, however, a son, who now became the heir to the throne, was born to James and his second wife, the Italian princess Mary of Modena. The revolution of 1688 led to the flight of James to France, and brought in his son-in-law William and his daughter Mary to reign as joint sovereigns.

For the 1689 coronation of William and Mary this new ceremony of presenting a bible was devised by Henry Compton, bishop of London. He was one of those leading personages who, risking their lives, had initiated the revolution of 1688 by signing a written invitation to William of Orange. Earlier, he had been tutor to the two princesses, Mary and Anne, daughters of James by his first wife, Anne Hyde; they would now successively become queens of England. At the 1689 coronation Compton replaced the likewise courageous archbishop of Canterbury, William Sancroft, who had led the seven bishops imprisoned in the Tower of London by James in 1688, but now conscientiously refused the oath of allegiance to the new sovereigns, for James II was still alive.

Compton had the task of revising the whole service. In 1685 James II had asked for the eucharist to be omitted. It was now restored, the Promise, Anointing and Crowning were placed within it, and the new Presentation of the Bible was added immediately after the Crowning. This new ceremony took up the biblical link between sovereignty in Israel and the holy scriptures. It affirmed the loyalty of the sovereign to scripture, and by implication to a scriptural and lawful constitution in church and state. To the Anglican church and Protestant dissenters from it alike, that had seemed in danger from James's sedulous appointment of Roman Catholics to positions of authority. A sense of peril was sharpened from the year of his accession onwards by the flight of French Protestants – the Huguenots – to Britain, Brandenburg and Holland, after their protection by the French crown was revoked by Louis XIV in 1685. In the context of the coronation, however, the new ceremony remained close in theme to the Crowning, which it originally followed, and to the Promise, with which it has been placed more recently.

Thus the declaration 'Here is Wisdom; This is the Royal Law; These are the lively Oracles of God' alludes successively to biblical texts from Proverbs, the Epistle of James and the Acts of the Apostles. It begins by recalling the biblical view that the divine wisdom depicted in scripture is the guide of sovereigns: 'by me kings reign', says the figure of Wisdom in Prov. 8:15. Then, 'the royal law' is a phrase from James 2:8, on the law of love to be followed without respect of persons, in the manner expected of royal justice; but it also recalls the 'law of the king' in Deut. 17:14–20, part of the 'lively oracles' given to Moses – this phrase being quoted from St Stephen's speech in Acts 7:38. In words which were widely understood among Jews and Christians as mandatory rather than permissive, Deuteronomy prescribes (Deut. 17:15) that 'you shall make a king over you', who shall write out (or have written) a copy of the law of Moses, to be always with him (Deut. 17:18–19) – indeed the 'royal law', kept with him that he may follow it and meditate upon it day and night, as Joshua, a model for kings, was exhorted to do (Jos. 1:7–8).

The giving of the bible itself was modelled on the perilous coronation in Jerusalem of the boy-king Joash (II Kings 11:12). This event itself might have seemed in part to prefigure the 1689 situation, but it was also regularly understood to display the close link between crown and scripture. The child Joash, son of Ahaziah king of Judah, had been kept in hiding in the temple. He was the last hope of the house of David. After his father's death he had been saved by his aunt, Ahaziah's sister the princess Jehosheba, who was married to Jehoiada the high-priest, when Joash's grandmother the queen-mother Athaliah massacred his brother-princes and ruled alone. Some years later his secret coronation and anointing, arranged by Jehoiada, was swiftly followed by the execution of Athaliah by armed priests and Levites. The occasion stood for the providential vindication of true religion and the true royal line; Athaliah, daughter of Jezebel, was not only a usurper of the throne of David, but also a devotee of Baal. Yet it also stood for the sovereign's commitment to scripture and law.

'They put on him' (Joash), says II Kings (11:12), 'the crown and the testimony, and made him king'. In the parallel passage in Chronicles (II Chron. 23:11), the Latin Vulgate translation gives the free explanatory rendering 'they put on him the diadem, and they gave him the law to be kept in his hand, and made him king'. The 'testimony' was understood by Compton, following the old Jewish and Christian interpretation seen already in the Vulgate rendering of II Chronicles, to be the book of the law which the king was to read and keep by him, according to Deuteronomy 17. Bestowal of the crown and this 'testimony' together would then represent the ruler's commitment to the law of God, which was also the ancient law of the Israelite people. The 1689 ceremony followed this model, bringing the crown and the book together.

The emphasis thereby laid on the king's loyalty to the law of God was new in the coronation in this particular form, but it was not alien to the coronation. A royal commitment to law, justice and mercy, in the name of God, was indeed embodied in the older coronation ceremony of the sovereign's Promise and oath, sworn on the gospels. Moreover, the biblical words 'Be strong … keep the commandments' (I Kings 2:2–3), which were sung in the Middle Ages as the sovereign was invested with the regalia, and have survived in modern coronations, make explicit the royal commitment to scriptural law which is implied in the Promise.

The divinely-blessed revolution which brought Joash to the throne of David was of course carefully studied in the sixteenth and seventeenth centuries, ages of personal royal rule. The biblical lesson of royal commitment to divine and human law seemed equally appropriate on either side of the Reformation divide. In early 1689 in France, while Compton was working the biblical model into the April 11 coronation service for William and Mary, the great poet Jean Racine had just begun to make the same narrative of Joash the basis of his tragedy *Athalie*. The composition took over eighteen months, and after various difficulties and delays the play was eventually performed before Louis XIV and the Dauphin on 5 January 1691. On 22 February it was performed again, in the presence of the exiled James II and Mary of Modena.

Racine dramatizes the coronation of Joash in a form closely similar to the model envisaged by Compton. Once again the 'testimony' is the book of the ancient law, as in the Vulgate of II Chronicles, the book which is to be always with the king, according to Deuteronomy 17. This book is at the heart of the proceedings (Act IV, scene iii). To begin with, it is brought in and laid on a table together with the diadem, the hereditary crown of David, and also – in view of what is to come – a sword. The high-priest asks Joash, alluding to II Kings 11:12 and II Chron. 23:11, if he remembers what laws a king worthy of the crown must impose on himself. The young king answers, alluding to Deuteronomy 17, that a wise king must fear God and keep his precepts always before him. The priests and Levites then swear loyalty to Joash 'upon this reverend book'. Jehoiada, like a second Samuel, now warns him against 'the intoxication of absolute power'. The king in turn promises 'upon this book' to keep what the law ordains. At this point the scene recalls not only the biblical link between the crown and the book, but also the royal Promise which formed part of the French as well as the English coronation. Joash is then taken to be anointed, as in the biblical narratives.

Racine and Compton may even have used some of the same biblical scholarship. Racine in his published Notes concerning *Athalie* cites the work of two seventeenth-century English scholars whose writings were available to him in Latin, John Lightfoot – 'Lichfot', as Racine smoothed out the barbarous name – and Matthew Poole or Pole.[3] He mentions Pole's *Synopsis of Critical and other Interpreters and Commentators on Holy Scripture* (Plate 17) in connection not with the crowning, but with the equivocation in which Jehoiada is involved, thought to be paralleled in Exodus; but Racine will probably also have noted that on II Kings 11:12 Pole gives the identification of the 'testimony' put upon Joash as the book of the law a prominent place among the interpretations presented.

Compton, on this biblical model, joined the presentation to the crowning. Its introduction has facilitated a procedure in the English coronation like that envisaged in Racine's drama, where king Joash promises upon the book associated with his Crowning. The English sovereign's Promise and oath had been taken upon the gospels. It could be taken on the gospels in the complete bible which would soon be presented. This still happened in 1953, when the Presentation of the Bible was moved from the Crowning to a place at the beginning of the service, but just after the Promise. In 2023 the Presentation preceded the Promise, and the book presented was then immediately used as the book on which the oath sealing the Promise was taken.

The Promise
The sovereign's Promise goes back in this country at least to the tenth century, and is probably older. It is first attested in England in the year 973, when king Edgar was crowned by St Dunstan at

Bath. His acknowledgement as sovereign and overlord is linked with Chester by his famous short voyage on the Dee from Edgar's Field to St John's church, where he would receive the homage of the group of neighbouring kings who rowed the boat (see Plate 18). 'Three things I promise in Christ's name', he is said to have declared before his anointing:

> First that the Church of God and the whole Christian people shall have true peace at all times by our judgment; Second, that I will forbid extortion and all kinds of wrong-doing to all orders of men; Third, that I will enjoin equity and mercy in all judgments, that God, who is kind and merciful, may vouchsafe his mercy to me and to you.

This promise was still taken by William the Conqueror and his successors, but then it felt the wind of change. Edward II in 1307 now bound himself to 'grant to be held and observed the just laws and customs that the community of the realm shall determine'. In another 200 years the initiative accorded here to 'the community of the realm' was at odds with the larger view of royal power which characterized sixteenth-century sovereignty. For the young Edward VI in 1547 the oath was changed to show that the initiative in legislation lay with the king. This form in turn lasted until the pendulum swung back again in 1689, when the oath was defined by Act of Parliament as one to maintain the statutes, laws and customs of the realm. So in 1953 and 2023 the sovereigns have promised to govern their peoples 'according to their respective laws and customs'.

This all sounds constitutional rather than biblical, but the bible has its constitutional aspect, seen clearly but not only in the Deuteronomic 'law of the king'. The royal promise to uphold law, justice and mercy is implicit in this law, and explicit elsewhere, notably in the psalms. A great instance is Psalm 72, which begins

Give the king thy judgments, O God,
And thy righteousness unto the king's son;

Then shall he judge thy people according unto right,
And defend the poor –

without respect of persons, as stressed in the Epistle of James. The link between the royal commitment to justice and mercy, signified in the Promise, and the subsequent ceremony of Anointing (which originally followed the Promise more closely), stands out in another royal psalm. In Psalm 45:7 the sovereign is addressed as follows – in words applied to Christ in the Epistle to the Hebrews (1:8–9) –

Thou hast loved righteousness and hated iniquity;
Therefore God, even thy God, hath anointed thee
with the oil of gladness above thy fellows.

The Anointing and Crowning
The anointing of course recalls the Israelite anointing of high-priests and kings. Christian royal anointing is first clearly attested at the end of the ancient period, from the seventh century onwards. In the Anglo-Saxon kingdoms in this country Offa, king of Mercia, Offa of Offa's Dyke, had his son Ecgfrith anointed as his successor in the year 787, probably following continental practice; Offa was in touch with Charlemagne in Gaul, and entertained the papal legate in England. The anointing of a designated successor, as in the case of Ecgfrith, may be inspired by the biblical model of the anointing of Solomon in particular. This had taken place while king David was still alive, and his eldest surviving son Adonijah was being put forward as the heir and successor (I Kings 1:5–53).

Royal anointing first comes into view in the same period when anointing in Christian ordination begins to be attested. Ecclesiastical and royal authority share the same symbol. Their common participation in what is regarded as a God-given anointing is an inheritance, through a fresh consideration of biblical models, from scripture and from ancient Jewish and early Christian tradition.

Within early Christianity, the Israelite pattern of priestly and royal anointing had quickly been adopted in Christian initiation (see the preceding chapter). The church as a whole could be called a royal priesthood, as in I Peter (2:9), and its members kings and priests, as in Revelation (1:6). In both cases the writers take up words from Exodus (19:6) on the vocation of Israel: Ye shall be unto me a kingdom of priests, and a holy nation – with their prophetic analogue in Isaiah: But ye shall be named the priests of the Lord (Isa. 61:6).

Now, later on in church history, Christian priestly and lay rulers were being anointed through renewed recourse to the same scriptural pattern. Like the high-priests and kings of old in Israel, bishops and kings were anointed on their heads with chrism, the unguent composed of oil and spices which was prescribed for the anointing of Aaron (Exod. 30:22–31) and used further, as it was held, for the anointing of David, Solomon and the kings. A tradition was current among ancient Jews, and shared by their Christian contemporaries, to the effect that the one horn of holy oil or chrism, the precious ointment (Ps. 133:2) with which Aaron and his sons were anointed, sufficed also for David and Solomon and the kings (pp. 211–12, 229, above). It had been kept in the holy place, as suggested by I Kings (1:39), where 'Zadok the priest took the horn of oil out of the tabernacle, and anointed Solomon'. Jews were followed by Christians in thinking that prophets too might be anointed, as Elijah was commanded to anoint Elisha (I Kings 19:16).

The holy chrism is treated in scripture as God-given:

I have found David my servant:
with my holy oil have I anointed him (Ps. 89:20)

Accordingly, it is the sign and medium of the gift of God's spirit. So it is written of David: 'Then Samuel took the horn of oil, and anointed him in the midst of his brethren: and the Spirit of the Lord came mightily upon David from that day forward' (I Sam. 16:13). Compare the beginning of the poem called 'the last words of David' (II Sam. 23:1–2):

The word of David, son of Jesse,
The word of the man whom the High God raised up,

Biblical Voices and Echoes

The Anointed of the God of Jacob,
and the sweet psalmist of Israel:
The Spirit of the Lord spoke by me,
and his word was upon my tongue.

Compare too the words in the book of Isaiah (61:1) which gospel tradition envisages as read out by Christ in the synagogue at Nazareth:

The Spirit of the Lord is upon me,
because he has anointed me to preach the gospel to the poor.

Correspondingly, the anointing of the sovereign is preceded by the hymn *Veni Creator Spiritus* – Come, Holy Ghost, our souls inspire – and by prayer which in modern times has taken this form:

O Lord and heavenly Father, who by anointing with Oil didst make and consecrate kings, priests and prophets, to teach and govern thy people Israel: Bless and sanctify thy chosen servant, who by our office and ministry is now to be anointed with this Oil, and consecrated King: Strengthen him, O Lord, with the Holy Ghost the Comforter; Confirm and stablish him with thy free and princely Spirit: the Spirit of wisdom and government, the Spirit of counsel and ghostly strength, the Spirit of knowledge and true godliness; and fill him, O Lord, with the Spirit of thy holy fear, now and for ever.

The phrase 'free and princely spirit' echoes Psalm 51, regarded in Israelite tradition (Ps. 51:1) as a petition uttered by king David. The anointing prayer here combines two alternative translations of Ps. 51:12: Stablish me with thy free spirit – or, thy governing spirit.

In 2023 there was some recurrence towards a more ancient form, still surviving at James I's coronation, in which this prayer began with thanksgiving, following the style of a eucharistic preface ('it is very meet, right and our bounden duty, that we should at all times and in all places give thanks unto thee … because …'). In the 2023 order the archbishop now prayed as follows:

Blessed art thou, Sovereign God, upholding with thy grace all who are called to thy service. Thy prophets of old anointed priests and kings

> to serve in thy name, and in the fulness of time thine only Son was anointed by the Holy Spirit to be the Christ, the Saviour and Servant of all. By the power of the same Spirit, grant that this holy oil may be for thy servant Charles a sign of joy and gladness ...

The new form strengthens our recollection of 'the oil of gladness' associated with the Israelite king (Ps. 45:7); but it also takes away that biblical emphasis on anointing as the divine consecration of the kings of old which was kept in the prayer previously used – 'O Lord ... who by anointing with Oil didst make and consecrate kings, priests and prophets'. Still, in 2023 the anointing itself was accompanied, as before, by the prayer:

> Be your head anointed with holy oil, as kings, priests, and prophets were anointed. And as Solomon was anointed king by Zadok the priest and Nathan the prophet, so may you be anointed, blessed and consecrated King over the peoples, whom the Lord your God has given you to rule and govern.

This prayer was followed, still as before, by the blessing beginning 'Our Lord Jesus Christ, the Son of God, who by his Father was anointed with the oil of gladness above his fellows, by his holy anointing pour down upon your head and heart the blessing of the Holy Spirit ...'. The screen provided for the 2023 anointing, without the canopy formerly used, kept the sense of the sanctity of the moment. The canopy had, however, formed a reminder of the mediaeval custom of honouring not only the sovereign, but also the consecrated oil being poured out (Ps. 133:2), by the bearing of a canopy over the head during the anointing.

This anointing was accompanied, already in king Edgar's coronation, by the anthem 'Zadok the priest and Nathan the prophet anointed Solomon king ...' (I Kings 1:38-9, 45), words for which, 800 years later, Handel would compose new music.

The anointing, in which the God-given authority of the new sovereign is affirmed, is naturally followed by the handing-over of the garb and instruments of authority, including the orb and the ring, the sceptre and the rod, and finally the crown itself. The Crowning is hailed by the acclamation, followed by the enthroning and homage. The words of the anthem sung in 2023 are from the encouragement given by king David to Solomon, with exhortation to follow the law of Moses: 'Be strong … keep the commandments of the Lord thy God …' (I Kings 2:2–3). Words from these verses have been sung or said at this point in the rite since the Middle Ages. In emphasis on royal commitment to biblical law this passage from I Kings is close to the exhortation of Moses to Joshua, 'Be strong and of a good courage …' (Jos. 1:7–8), mentioned in connection with the Presentation of the Bible and read as a lesson for Accession Day. As seen already, the Presentation took up a theme which was explicit as well as implicit in the existing coronation service.

Scripture and Sacrament
The various scriptures at the roots of the Promise, the Anointing and the Crowning combine to declare that God bestows on rulers their power, as the Anointing suggests, but also judges their use of it, as the Promise suggests. The office of a sovereign may be corrupted, both by the abuse of power and by the people's instinctive longing for a leader, as shown when the people insistently demand a king to succeed the aged Samuel, and he utters a denunciation of royal tyranny (I Sam. 8:4–22), Racine's 'intoxication of absolute power'. Nevertheless, for the general good we should obey 'the powers that be' (Rom. 13:1), as biblical writers teach with regard to rulers from Nebuchadnezzar to Nero – rendering to Caesar what is Caesar's due, as in the saying of Jesus (Matt. 22:21 and parallels), without neglecting the claims of the kingdom of God – for earthly sovereignty is given to whomsoever *God* wills (Dan. 4:32). Rulers are officers or ministers of God's kingdom, as the book of Wisdom puts it (Wisd. 6:4), agents entrusted with a particular task by God, as St Paul writes (Rom. 13:4–6).

Yet again, kings as well as subjects should remember this. 'Be wise now, therefore, O ye kings; be instructed, ye that are judges of the earth. Serve the Lord with fear' (Ps. 2:10–11). 'Love righteousness, ye that are judges of the earth' (Wisd. 1:1, echoing Ps. 45:7 as well as Ps. 2:10). Indeed all this state of things, for biblical hope, is provisional. St Paul says that in the end Christ shall deliver up the kingdom to God, 'that God may be all in all' (I Cor. 15:24–8); in his capacity as messianic king, Christ remains an officer of *God's* kingdom.

Against the background of these primary convictions, scripture gives constitutional hints and models, outlined in the Old Testament and reflected again in the foreshadowings of a messianic kingdom in the New. Representing historical friction and change as well as continuity, but with a measure of overall coherence, these bring the associations of a personal and dynastic kingship together with arrangements more typical of a constitutional monarchy, notably co-operation with the high-priest (Num. 27:18–23), another power in the land; in Zechariah the two likewise appear to rule together (Zech. 4:11–14, 6:9–13). So great was the high-priest's prestige after the exile, notably but not only when the Maccabaean high-priests were also kings, that in the first century CE Josephus the Jewish historian, himself a priest, could teach (*Antiquities* iv 223–4, xiv 41; *Against Apion* ii 185) that the Jews are traditionally ruled by a high-priest, with whom a king may be associated – 'you shall make a king over you' (Deut. 17:15) being understood as permissive. Others held that the Deuteronomic law was indeed a command to have a king, as the prophecies of kings to be descended from the patriarchs and matriarchs might also suggest (Gen. 17:6 and 16 [Abraham and Sarah], 35:11 [Jacob], 49:10 [Judah]); this opinion survives in rabbinic literature.[4] In either case, the old personal monarchy is seen, when the biblical books are viewed together, as a monarchy which has become constitutional. As the differences of interpretation show, the Old and New Testament books hardly lay down a constitution; but their hints point in the direction of constitutional monarchy, under the monarchy of God. They illuminate the mutual obligations and high aspirations inherent for sovereigns and peoples in a polity of that kind.

Thus personal and constitutional aspects of sovereignty come together in the Deuteronomic 'law of the king'. At his accession, 'when he sits upon the throne of his kingdom', he shall make a copy of the scriptures for his own personal use and constant study; 'he shall read therein all the days of his life' (Deut. 17:18–20). Here the king of Israel becomes a counterpart of the Greek philosopher-king. In later times, therefore, the student-king of Deuteronomy suited the Renaissance model of education through 'good literature'.

In this spirit the old reforming bishop Hugh Latimer expounded Deuteronomy in a sermon before the young king Edward VI, on 22 March 1549, quoting 17:18:

> *And when the king is set in the seat of his kingdom* – what shall he do? Shall he dance and dally; banquet, hawk, and hunt? No, forsooth, sir. … What must he do then? He must be a student, he must write God's book himself; not thinking, because he is a king, he hath licence to do what he will. … And yet a king may take his pastime in hawking and hunting, or such like pleasures. But he must use them for recreation, when he is weary of weighty affairs, that he may return to them the more lusty … He shall *read* in [God's book] not once a year, for a time or for his recreation when he is weary of hawking and hunting, but … *all the days of his life.*[5]

This biblical view of royal responsibility has been alive in the religion of contemporary as well as earlier sovereigns in Britain. Yet it is also constitutionally momentous. In Deuteronomy, it is an aspect of royal cooperation with priestly authority. The king's copy of scripture is to be made from the copy kept by the levitical priests, 'from that which is before the priests the Levites' (Deut. 17:18). Still more significantly, the Deuteronomic law embodies the constitutional expectation that the sovereign shall respect the law of God and the law of the land.

Further biblical traces of constitutional thought in some ways recall the present British arrangement, whereby sovereignty is exercised within a smaller Privy Council and the great council of the nation in Parliament. Thus the Israelite king might also co-operate with a council, formed by the twelve princes of the tribes (Num. 1:4–16), or a larger body of seventy or seventy-two elders (Num. 11:16–17, 24–30). These hints are taken up in further Jewish thought, which also shows signs of the political tensions between king and people, priesthood and laity suggested by the biblical arrangements themselves.

Thus among the Dead Sea Scrolls, the Temple Scroll, interpreting Deuteronomy 17 in the third or second century BCE, gives the king a council comprising twelve princes, twelve priests and twelve Levites (11Q19, cols. 56–9). When Josephus paraphrases the biblical narrative in the first century CE he tends to downgrade the twelve princes in favour of the larger council and the high-priest; summarizing Deuteronomy 17 he adds, with marked resemblance to the Temple Scroll, that the king shall do nothing without the advice of the high-priest and the council (*Ant.* iv 223–4). In Judaea in the second century CE, the revolt leader Bar Kokhba appears to have ruled his realm together with a high-priestly figure, named on coins as 'Eleazar the Priest'. Among these developments may be set the New Testament interpretation of Christ as both king and high-priest, and the gospel association of Christ as messianic king both with the Twelve, to sit on twelve thrones judging the twelve tribes (Matt. 19:28, Luke 22:30), and with the seventy or seventy-two disciples in Luke (Luke 10:1–20).

To come back now to the coronation service, the primary biblical teachings on sovereignty outlined to begin with are symbolized especially in the Anointing and Crowning, signifying divine support and the gift of Spirit to a sovereign who shall love righteousness and hate iniquity. The new monarch accepts this responsibility and prays for divine help. Then two aspects of the biblical and biblically-inspired sketches of kingship are particularly important for understanding the coronation rites. From the ethos of personal kingship comes the thought of the sovereign as focus of the life of the nation: the very breath of our nostrils, to quote Lamentations (4:20), or the lamp of Israel, as David was called (II

Sam. 21:17). The personal relationship of sovereign and people is at the heart of national unity. The coronation Promise expresses a living relationship as well as a constitutional arrangement. Then, from the more clearly constitutional passages of scripture, I would pick out the picture of the king in Deuteronomy and Joshua, studying his own copy of the scriptures. The Presentation and the Promise together presuppose it and illustrate it. Once again it unites the personal – the sovereign's relationship with God – with the constitutional – the sovereign's loyalty to law. The picture of the monarch studying the 'royal law' of holy scripture, with its high claims and aspirations, is one which can be appreciated beyond the bounds of specifically Christian tradition.

I have been considering the coronation rites and ceremonies as signs, with a signification disclosed by the scriptures from which they derive. Inevitably this treatment can suggest that the rites are symbols only in a weak sense; they convey a biblical meaning which in principle could be found without the signs. Sometimes, however, still with the biblical writers, I have verged on something more: the moment when the sign somehow becomes the thing signified, and those who see the sign seem to be brought close to sacred presence and divine creativity. The consecrated oil is then indeed 'my' – God's – 'holy oil'; in the humility of the anointing it may be sensed that a sovereign is being divinely 'made and consecrated' by the Holy Spirit, and that the sovereign is becoming in turn a living sign of common life and unity. In the coronation the poet David Jones likewise understood the sovereign to be made a sign, sacramentally, of monarchy as historically received in Britain, linking us all not only with the Anglo-Saxon kingdoms of Offa or Edgar, but also, through the early Welsh kings at the end of the fourth century, with the Christian rulers and peoples of the later Roman empire.[6]

In Christian symbolism, weaker and stronger interpretations of ritual signs are not mutually exclusive, but come together, especially through scripture. This applies also to the signs called sacraments. Before the number of seven Christian sacraments became conventional, the anointing of a sovereign had occasionally been counted among the sacraments of the new covenant as well as the old. Yet whether coronation is called a sacrament or not, we may glimpse in the anointing the effective operation of the Holy Ghost, 'making and consecrating' a new ruler, very much as a Christian is made and renewed in baptism and confirmation. We may also glimpse, as Jones suggested, a setting-apart of the new sovereign in which the ruler becomes a sign of common life, summing up monarchy as historically received among the peoples of Britain. If the term sacrament may be used for a symbol in which the thing signified becomes, under God, somehow present and effective, we are, in the rare solemnity of a coronation, indeed encountering a sacrament.

Endnotes

[1] On the modern coronation and its antecedents see E.C. Ratcliff, *The Coronation Service of Her Majesty Queen Elizabeth II, with a short Historical Introduction, Explanatory Notes and an Appendix* (London & Cambridge, 1953).

[2] J.G. Lockhart, *Cosmo Gordon Lang* (London, 1949), 411, quoting archbishop Lang's written account of his changes in the coronation service.

[3] For Racine's Notes and the details given here see the edition of *Athalie* by G. Forestier in J. Racine, *Oeuvres complètes*, i (Bibliothèque de la Pléiade; Paris, 1999), 1009–1089.

[4] Second-century CE interpretation is probably reflected in sayings to this effect in the name of R. Judah ben Ilai, for example in Tosefta, Sanhedrin 4.5 (to make a king is one of three commandments laid upon Israel when they would enter the land).

[5] G.E. Corrie (ed.), *Sermons by Hugh Latimer* (Parker Society; Cambridge, 1844), 119–21.

[6] David Jones, 'Wales and the Crown', in David Jones, *Epoch and Artist: Selected Writings*, ed. Harman Grisewood (London, 1959), 39–48.

APPENDIX

PAUL AND VIRGIL

TO VIRGIL

WRITTEN AT THE REQUEST OF THE MANTUANS
FOR THE NINETEENTH CENTENARY
OF VIRGIL'S DEATH

Roman Virgil, thou that singest
    Ilion's lofty temples robed in fire
Ilion falling, Rome arising,
    wars, and filial faith, and Dido's pyre;

Landscape-lover, lord of language,
    more than he that sang the Works and Days,
All the chosen coin of fancy
    flashing out from many a golden phrase;

Thou that singest wheat and woodland,
    tilth and vineyard, hive and horse and herd;
All the charm of all the Muses
    often flowering in a lonely word;

Poet of the happy Tityrus
    piping underneath his beechen bowers;
Poet of the poet-satyr
    whom the laughing shepherd bound with flowers.

Chanter of the Pollio, glorying
    in the blissful years again to be,
Summers of the snakeless meadow,
    unlaborious earth and oarless sea;

Appendix

Thou that seëst Universal
    Nature moved by Universal Mind;
 Thou majestic in thy sadness
    at the doubtful doom of human kind;

Light among the vanish'd ages;
    star that gildest yet this phantom shore;
Golden branch amid the shadows,
    kings and realms that pass to rise no more;

Now thy Forum roars no longer,
    fallen every purple Caesar's dome –
Tho' thine ocean-roll of rhythm
    sound for ever of Imperial Rome –

Now the Rome of slaves hath perish'd,
    and the Rome of freemen holds her place,
I, from out the Northern Island
    sunder'd once from all the human race,

I salute thee, Mantovano,
    I that lov'd thee since my day began,
Wielder of the stateliest measure
    ever moulded by the lips of man.
              ALFRED, LORD TENNYSON (1881)

THE LAST ODE
(*Nov.* 27, B.C. 8)
[the day of Horace's death]

HORACE, Ode 31, Bk. V.

As watchers couched beneath a Bantine oak,
    Hearing the dawn-wind stir,
Know that the present strength of night is broke
    Though no dawn threaten her
Till dawn's appointed hour – so Virgil died,
    Aware of change at hand, and prophesied

Change upon all the Eternal Gods had made
    And on the Gods alike –
Fated as dawn but, as the dawn, delayed
    Till the just hour should strike –

A Star new-risen above the living and dead;
    And the lost shades that were our loves restored
As lovers, and for ever. So he said;
    Having received the word ...

Maecenas waits me on the Esquiline:
    Thither to-night go I. ...
And shall this dawn restore us, Virgil mine,
    To dawn? Beneath what sky?
                    RUDYARD KIPLING (*c.*1925)

This poem, entirely a composition by Kipling, is presented as a translation of an imaginary Ode of Horace, envisaged as coming at the end of a Book V of Horace's Odes. Four books of Horace's Odes, only, are known. Kipling had taken part with a group of scholars and writers, including Ronald Knox, in the publication of an imaginary Book V, with newly-composed Latin texts and English

Appendix

translations: *Q. Horati Flacci Carminum librum quintum* ..., ed. A.D. Godley (Oxford: Basil Blackwell, 1920). This poem did not appear there, but was issued, at the end of Kipling's story 'The Eye of Allah', in Rudyard Kipling, *Debits and Credits* (London: Macmillan, 1926, repr. 1949), 395.

Bantia (line 1) was a small upland town set among wooded rocky hills and dales used for pasture (see Horace, Odes iii 4, 15), close to Horace's birthplace, Venusia; the watchers are probably shepherds, as in Virgil (*Ecl.* viii 14–17, Damon before dawn).

Maecenas (line 15) had died shortly before, sending a farewell message to Horace, and was interred on the Esquiline Hill in Rome, where Horace also wished his ashes to lie.